Japanese
for
Busy
People I

Japanese for Busy People I

Revised 4th Edition

Kana Version

Association for
Japanese-Language Teaching

AjALT

This icon () means that there is free audio available. To download these contents, search for "Japanese for Busy People" at kodansha.us.

The Association for Japanese-Language Teaching (AJALT) was recognized as a nonprofit organization by the Ministry of Education in 1977. It was established to meet the practical needs of people who are not necessarily specialists on Japan but who wish to communicate effectively in Japanese. In 1992 AJALT was awarded the Japan Foundation Special Prize. In 2010 it became a public interest incorporated association. AJALT maintains a website at www.ajalt.org.

Published by Kodansha USA Publishing, LLC, 451 Park Avenue South, New York, NY 10016

Distributed in the United Kingdom and continental Europe by Kodansha Europe Ltd.

First published in Japan in 1984 by Kodansha International
Fourth edition 2022 published by Kodansha USA, an imprint of Kodansha USA Publishing

Printed in Italy
25 24 23 22   5 4 3 2 1

ISBN: 978-1-56836-620-3

Editorial supervision by Kodansha Editorial, Ltd.
Editing and DTP by Guild, Inc.
Illustrations by Shinsaku Sumi and Kaori Ikeda
Cover design by Masumi Akiyama

Audio narration by Yoko Ibe, Fumiaki Kimura, Shogo Nakamura, Asahi Sasagawa, Yuji Suzuki, Ai Tanaka, and Hiroaki Tanaka
Audio recording and editing by the English Language Education Council, Inc.

Photo credits: © kou/PIXTA, 19, 171. © cowardlion/Shutterstock.com, 49, 189. © iStock.com/Xavier Arnau, 1. © さるとびサスケ /PIXTA, 73. © レイコ /PIXTA, 95. © iStock.com/Yongyuan Dai, 141. © a-clip, 217.

Library of Congress Control Number: 2021950845

www.kodansha.us

KODANSHA

CONTENTS

UNIT **1**   AT THE OFFICE   1

LESSON **1**   **Meeting: Nice to Meet You**   2

- noun 1は   noun 2です。
- noun 1は   noun 2ですか。
- companyの   person
- Omission of the topic

・スミスさんは　アメリカじんです。
・スミスさんは　アメリカじんですか。
・こちらは　のぞみデパートの　たなかさんです。
・（わたしは）　スミスです。

CAN-DO
- Introduce yourself and others, at your workplace or at a party
- Talk about nationalities
- Give your name at the reception desk of a place you visit and give the name of the person you want to meet

WORD POWER
- Countries and nationalities
- Work affiliation

LESSON **2**   **Possession: Whose Pen Is This?**   9

- これは   nounです。
- これは   nounじゃありません。
- personの   noun

・これは　とけいです。
・これは　とけいじゃありません。
・これは　スミスさんの　とけいです。

CAN-DO
- Talk about a nearby object and its owner
- Ask for telephone numbers
- Ask for words to be repeated when you do not understand

WORD POWER
- Numbers
- Business vocabulary
- Personal belongings

UNIT **2**   SHOPPING   19

LESSON **3**   **Asking the Time: What Time Is It?**   20

- （いま）   timeです。
- nounは   time 1から   time 2までです。
- time 1の   time 2

・いま　3じです。
・しごとは　9じから　5じまでです。
・かいぎは　あしたの　4じからです。

CAN-DO
- Talk about opening times and closing times
- Talk about the present time and time in cities overseas

WORD POWER
- Services and activities
- Numbers
- Times
- Time expressions

LESSON **4**   **Shopping (1): How Much Is This?**   28

- これ／それ／あれ
- nounも
- nounを　ください。／
  nounを　おねがいします。
- noun 1と   noun 2

・それは　スマホです。あれは　タブレットです。
・これは　3,000えんです。あれも　3,000えんです。
・これを　ください。
・カレーと　サラダを　おねがいします。

CAN-DO
- Point to something and ask what it is
- Ask the prices of items in a store and make a purchase
- Place an order at a restaurant

WORD POWER
- Home appliances
- Food and drink
- Numbers

PREFACE TO THE REVISED 4TH EDITION

Japanese for Busy People is composed of three levels: Book I (romanized version and kana version), Book II, and Book III. The first edition of *Japanese for Busy People I* was compiled on the basis of teaching materials developed over more than ten years by AJALT teachers involved in teaching Japanese language at various levels and published in 1984. It was designed for efficient mastery of Japanese by busy people and was used in many countries.

In 1994, when the textbooks were first revised, Book II was divided into two parts, Book II and Book III, and only minimal revisions were made to Book I. For the third edition published in 2006, a variety of changes were made, including grouping the lessons into units, adding the new features such as Culture Notes, Word Power, and Active Communication, and expanding the Exercises. These changes were made to clarify the situations for practical use of Japanese based on the latest results of research in Japanese-language education and to help learners feel confident in their communication skills.

This fourth edition carries on the editorial policy of the third edition, updating the vocabulary and dialogues and adding further explanation in Grammar and Notes in order to help learners studying independently. New pages introducing casual-style speech are also added.

We hope that *Japanese for Busy People* will help learners seeking to master Japanese amid busy lives get off to a pleasant start.

In the compilation of this revised edition, we would like to express our gratitude to Mio Urata of Kodansha Editorial and Makiko Ohashi of Guild, Inc. for their cooperation.

Acknowledgments for *Japanese for Busy People I* (1st edition, 1984)
Compilation of this textbook has been a cooperative endeavor, and we deeply appreciate the collective efforts and individual contributions of Sachiko Adachi, Nori Ando, Haruko Matsui, Shigeko Miyazaki, Sachiko Okaniwa, Terumi Sawada, and Yuriko Yobuko.
For English translations and editorial assistance, we wish to thank Dorothy Britton.

Acknowledgments for *Japanese for Busy People I, Revised Edition* (1994)
We would like to express our gratitude to the following people: Haruko Matsui, Junko Shinada, Keiko Ito, Mikiko Ochiai, and Satoko Mizoguchi.

Acknowledgments for the *Kana Version of Japanese for Busy People I, Revised Edition* (1995)
We would like to express our gratitude to the following people: Haruko Matsui, Junko Shinada, Mikiko Ochiai, and Satoko Mizoguchi.

Acknowledgments for *Japanese for Busy People I, Revised 3rd Edition* (2006)
We would like to express our gratitude to the following people: Yoko Hattori, Sakae Tanabe, Izumi Sawa, Motoko Iwamoto, Shigeyo Tsutsui, and Takako Kobayashi.

Acknowledgments for *Japanese for Busy People I, Revised 4th Edition*
Ten AJALT teachers have contributed to the writing of this textbook. They are Reiko Sawane, Hisako Aramaki, Eiko Ishida, Soko Onishi, Yuka Tanino, Yuko Hashimoto, Yumiko Matsuda, Yasuko Yako, Tomoko Waga, and Shinobu Aoki. They were assisted by Yuko Harada, Misuzu Imuta, and Yuko Takami. Preparation for this textbook was assisted by a grant from the Shoyu Club.

INTRODUCTION

Aims

This first volume of *Japanese for Busy People, Revised 4th Edition* has been developed to meet the needs of busy beginning learners seeking an effective method of acquiring a natural command of spoken Japanese in a limited amount of time. The book is suitable for both those studying with a teacher and those studying on their own. In order to minimize the burden on busy learners, the vocabulary and grammar items presented have been narrowed down to about a third of those introduced in a typical first-year course. However, the textbook is set up so that learners can use the material they have learned right away in conversations with speakers of Japanese. In other words, *Japanese for Busy People I* is a textbook for learning "survival Japanese."

Despite this, *Japanese for Busy People I* does not present simple, childish Japanese. That is, we do not focus on mere grammatical correctness. Instead, we place our emphasis on actual conversational patterns. Thus, by studying with this book, learners will acquire the most essential language patterns for everyday life, and be able to express their intentions in uncomplicated adult-level Japanese. They will also start to build a basis for favorable relations with the people around them by talking about themselves and their surroundings and circumstances, and asking about those of others.

This book is intended for beginners, but it can also provide a firm foundation for more advanced study. Learners can acquire a general idea of the nature of the Japanese language as they study the Target Dialogues, Speaking Practice, and Notes. For this reason, *Japanese for Busy People I* is also suitable as a review text for those who already know a certain amount of Japanese but want to confirm that they are using the language correctly.

Major Features of *Japanese for Busy People I, Revised 4th Edition*

Japanese for Busy People I, Revised 4th Edition, incorporates a number of features designed to make beginning study of Japanese enjoyable and effective.

FREQUENTLY USED EXPRESSIONS

The book begins with a list of expressions frequently used in daily life. Illustrations are provided to give a better idea of the situations where these expressions can be used. By repeated listening to the audio versions of these expressions, learners can accustom themselves to the sound of the Japanese language.

UNIT STRUCTURE

The book is divided into 10 units, each unit consisting of two or three lessons linked by a common theme. Studying these units with their interrelated social and cultural information, language information, and communications strategies is important to gaining a natural and appropriate mastery of Japanese.

CULTURE NOTES

Each unit begins with Culture Notes that describe Japanese customs and events as well as other aspects of life in Japan. Learners who can better understand people's lives and customs are sure to gain a greater desire to learn the language and deepen their understanding of it. We hope the social and cultural information presented in these notes will heighten learners' awareness of cultural diversity and give them specific mental images of the themes introduced in the units.

LESSONS

Each lesson is composed of the parts described below. Newly introduced vocabulary is given with English translations in the shaded sections at the bottom of the pages.

Target Dialogue

The first feature of each lesson is the Target Dialogue, which provides a specific example of the kind of dialogue the learner will be able to engage in after studying the lesson. The dialogues contain practical expressions and grammatical points necessary for daily conversation. Notes to explain particularly difficult expressions are provided.

Key Sentences
These are simple sentences incorporating the key points of study in each lesson. The Grammar section immediately below gives concise grammatical explanations of the sentences given in the Key Sentences that are easily accessible for self-study. Points under Key Sentences and Grammar that "are not used in normal speech but added for better understanding" are enclosed in parentheses. The explanations given here are provided as much as possible without requiring more advanced knowledge or information than is available in the grammatical notes provided in the current lesson.

Word Power
Basic vocabulary to be mastered before moving on to the Exercises is introduced here. The vocabulary is presented in clusters of related words so as to help the learner remember them efficiently. Most of the words given in this section are introduced in the illustrations and charts.

Exercises
In order to allow the learner to move smoothly from the basic expressions to more advanced applications, the exercises are presented in stages (I, II, III, etc.). The Exercises are composed of five types:
(1) Exercises for repeating vocabulary and conjugating verbs and adjectives.
(2) Standard sentence patterns for grasping Japanese sentence structures and learning their meanings.
(3) Substitution drills and dialogue-style drills linked to conversation practice.
(4) Conversation exercises geared to practical occasions and situations in which Japanese is used.
(5) Listening practice with questions to be answered after listening to the audio.
The goals of the exercise ("can-dos") to be mastered are set in italics so as to focus attention not just on doing the exercises but on the goal to be achieved through the exercises.

Speaking Practice
These relatively short conversations present useful expressions and various patterns of exchange. As with the Target Dialogue, cautions regarding use of the specific phrases and expressions are provided in the Notes below.

Active Communication
The last section of each lesson presents one or two tasks that can be used in actual situations or for communication activities in the classroom.

CASUAL STYLE
To respond to increased interest among students of Japanese in attaining comprehension of the informal language used in animation films, television dramas, or among the people around them, pages are set aside in two places to present the casual style.

OTHER FEATURES
Audio recordings may be downloaded for Frequently Used Expressions, Target Dialogue, Word Power, Listening Exercises, Speaking Practice, as well as the Sample Dialogues for the Casual Style pages. A Quiz is provided after every two units so as to help learners check their understanding and progress. The answers for Exercises and Quizzes are available on download for the convenience of those studying independently. The answers are based on the content learned in this textbook.

Using *Japanese for Busy People I*

Progress through this textbook should be flexible in accordance with the circumstances of the learners, but in general *Japanese for Busy People I* can be completed in about 60 hours. Each lesson will take about two to two-and-a-half hours to complete.

Whether using the textbook with a teacher's guidance or when studying from it independently, we recommend proceeding as follows:

Frequently Used Expressions	First, listen to the audio recording while looking at the illustrations. Next, the expressions should be practiced by either repeating after the recording or shadowing until they can be spoken fluently.
▼	
Contents	The items to be learned and goals of the lesson ("can-dos") are briefly outlined. Scan the contents to grasp the targets of the lesson.
▼	
Culture Notes	This section is aimed at expanding learners' awareness by providing social and cultural background to the topics treated in each unit.
▼	
Lesson	Each unit is made up of two or three lessons. Please proceed through each lesson following the instructions on the following page.
▼	
Quiz	A quiz is provided after every two units. First fill in the answers without looking anything up, and then check yourself using the answer sheet. To remedy mistakes or confirm understanding of the expressions, review the lesson for study of that item.
▼	
Casual Style	Pages introducing casual style are included after Unit 7 and Unit 10. Study of Casual Style (1) can be done after completing Unit 7 or both Casual Style (1) and (2) can be done after completing Unit 10. Intonation is very important in use of casual style, so please listen carefully to the audio.

Japanese for Busy People I : The Workbook for the Revised 4th Edition

The *Workbook* coordinated with *Japanese for Busy People I, Revised 4th edition* is available for sale. The effectiveness of studying with this textbook can be greatly enhanced by use of the *Workbook*.

How to Proceed through Each Lesson

Target Dialogue	This section presents the kind of dialogue one can engage in after completing the lesson. Listen to the audio and read the dialogue text alongside the English translation. At this point it is not necessary to spend too much time studying the dialogue. The lesson returns to this dialogue after the Exercises (see below). At this stage, you may skip over the Target Dialogue and keep going.
↓	
Key Sentences and Grammar	This section provides an explanation for the grammar points of this lesson. After grasping the grammar, listen to the audio and repeat the key sentences over several times so as to memorize them.
↓	
Word Power	The words used in the Exercises are collected here. Listen to the audio and practice saying them to commit the sound to memory.
↓	
Exercises	This section begins with repetition of vocabulary and practice with conjugation, practice creating sentences and exchanges, and proceeds toward re-creation of a full-fledged conversation. The listening practice at the end allows one to check listening and comprehension of conversations and sentences.
↓	
Speaking Practice	The conversations in this section include useful expressions to be learned in the lesson. Practice speaking thoroughly while listening to the audio. Once you can enunciate the words naturally, they will become useful for all kinds of situations.
↓	
Target Dialogue	The Target Dialogue is the summation of what is learned in the lesson. After completing the Exercises and Speaking Practice, listen to the Target Dialogue audio and read the script again. By now the conversation that seemed to be difficult when first read should now be more easily grasped. After reading the Notes in order to understand the details, listen to the audio and repeat consecutively or by shadowing.
↓	
Active Communication	The tasks here can be put into practice by the learner in person when circumstances allow. In the absence of a conversation partner, try imagining what one will say in each case.

The Kana Version

This textbook is for learners who want to learn hiragana and katakana at an early stage. It is designed for students who are either already able to read both hiragana and katakana or who are about to complete a kana study textbook. Learners who lack confidence in their kana reading ability should use *Japanese for Busy People I, Romanized Version*.

Introducing the Characters

The following fictitious characters bring this textbook to life. Their names come up frequently in this book, so here we introduce their names, faces, and how they are related. Some of the characters are called by their first names and this is because in this fictional setting they prefer to be called that way.

スミス

Mike Smith is American. He is a member of the Product Development Department of the ABC Foods Tokyo branch.

エマ

Emma Robert is French. She is a member of the Product Development Department of the ABC Foods Tokyo branch.

すずき

Daisuke Suzuki is Japanese. He is a member of the Product Development Department of the ABC Foods Tokyo branch.

なかむら

Mayumi Nakamura is Japanese. She is a member of the Product Development Department of the ABC Foods Tokyo branch.

かとう

Akira Kato is Japanese. He is section chief of the Product Development Department of the ABC Foods Tokyo branch.

ささき

Keiko Sasaki is Japanese. She is head of the Product Development Department of the ABC Foods Tokyo branch.

グリーン

Frank Green is American. He is president of the Tokyo branch of ABC Foods.

チャン

Mei Chan is from Hong Kong. She works at the Osaka branch of ABC Foods.

たなか

Shingo Tanaka is Japanese. He works at Nozomi Department Store, which is a client of ABC Foods.

ラジャ

Naresh Raja is Indian. He is a student at the University of Tokyo.

ポール

Paul Hudson is American. He is Mike Smith's cousin.

リサ

Lisa Smith is American. She is Mike Smith's younger sister.

CHARACTERISTICS OF JAPANESE GRAMMAR

The grammar presented in this textbook is not interpreted in accordance with grammatical constructions of Western languages but following the natural analysis of the Japanese language. Specialized terms are used selectively in order to assure a smooth transition from the basic level to more advanced learning.

The following are the basic characteristics of Japanese grammar. This list highlights in particular the differences between Japanese and English grammar.

1. Japanese nouns do not have gender or number. Some nouns express number by attachment of a suffix.

2. The verb (or copula です) comes at the end of a clause or sentence.
   e.g. わたしは　にほんじん<u>です</u>。　　"I am Japanese."
   わたしは　きょうとに　<u>いきます</u>。　"I go (or will go) to Kyoto."

3. In general, the gender, number, or person (first, second, or third) of the subject does not affect other parts of the sentence, but some sentences cannot be used depending on the person.

4. There are only two tenses of verbs: present and past. Whether "present form" refers to a customary action or refers to the future, and whether "past form" is equivalent to the past, present perfect, or past perfect must usually be judged according to the context.

5. Japanese adjectives are different from English adjectives in that they are inflected for present, past, positive, and negative forms.

6. The grammatical function of a noun is shown by the particle following it. The role of particles is similar to that of prepositions in English. As they always come after the word, they are sometimes called postpositions.
   e.g. とうきょう<u>で</u>, "in Tokyo"
   にちようび<u>に</u>, "on Sunday"

7. Politeness is expressed in various ways in Japanese, but the sentences used in this textbook adopt a style of courtesy that can be used when speaking to anyone.

NOTE: The following abbreviations are used in this book.

e.g.	example
aff.	affirmative
neg.	negative
い-adj.	い-adjective (see L10, GRAMMAR 1, p. 97)
な-adj.	な-adjective (see L10, GRAMMAR 1, p. 97)
R2	Regular 2 verb (see L15, GRAMMAR 2, p. 143)

*Regular 2 verbs are marked R2 in the Vocabulary sections for Lesson 15 and onward and the Glossary, but are not listed in the Vocabulary sections for Lesson 1 to 14.

FREQUENTLY USED EXPRESSIONS

① おはようございます。
Good morning.

② こんにちは。
Hello./Good afternoon.
(A rather informal greeting
used from about 10:00 A.M.
until sundown.)

③ こんばんは。
Good evening.

④ じゃ、また。
See you.

⑤ さようなら。
Good-bye.

⑥ しつれいします。
(Said when entering another person's room.)

⑦ しつれいします。
Good-bye. (Said on formal occasions.)

⑧ A：おさきに　しつれいします。
Good-bye. (Said when leaving the office before other people.)

B：おつかれさま（でした）。
Good-bye. (Said when your colleague leaves the office before you.)

⑨ A：どうぞ。
Please.

B：ありがとうございます。
Thank you.

C：いいえ。
Not at all.

⑩ いただきます。
(Said before eating a meal.)

⑪ ごちそうさま（でした）。
(Said after eating a meal.)

⑫ すみません。
Excuse me.

⑬ すみません。
I'm sorry.

⑭ ちょっと　まってください。
Wait just a moment, please.

⑮ もう　いちど　おねがいします。
Once more, please.

Audio, Script and Answers Download

The audio, script, and answers for this book can be downloaded to your smartphone, tablet, or PC, free of charge.

To download these contents, search for "Japanese for Busy People" at kodansha.us.

The audio files are in MP3 format and include Frequently Used Expressions, Target Dialogue, Key Sentences, Word Power, a part of the Exercises, Speaking Practice, and the Sample Dialogues for the Casual Style pages.

AT THE OFFICE

In Japan, people bow to each other on many occasions. They bow when meeting people, formally expressing gratitude, and apologizing for something. The typical way of bowing is to stand with the feet drawn together and bend the body at a 15 to 45 degree angle. Men tend to hold their hands at their sides while women hold their arms in front, elbows slightly bent, and hands folded. The eyes remain open during the bow, and the bowing person's line of sight moves with his or her torso rather than staying fixed on the other person. Generally, the deeper and slower the bow, the politer it is. Bowing properly is essential to making a good first impression.

Meeting: Nice to Meet You

TARGET DIALOGUE 🔊 016

Smith meets Tanaka for the first time. Tanaka is visiting ABC Foods.

スミス：すみません。のぞみデパートの　たなかさんですか。

たなか：はい、そうです。

スミス：はじめまして。ABC フーズの　スミスです。

　　　　よろしく　おねがいします。

　　　　(*Hands over business card.*)

たなか：はじめまして。たなかです。

　　　　(*Hands over business card.*)

　　　　こちらこそ、よろしく　おねがいします。

Smith:　Excuse me, are you Tanaka-san of the Nozomi Department Store?
Tanaka: Yes, I am.
Smith:　Nice to meet you. I am Smith of ABC Foods. I look forward to working with you.
Tanaka: Nice to meet you, too. I am Tanaka.
　　　　I look forward to working with you as well.

VOCABULARY

すみません。	Excuse me.	はい	yes
のぞみデパート	Nozomi Department Store (fictitious company name)	そうです	that's right
		はじめまして。	Nice to meet you.
デパート	department store	ABC フーズ	ABC Foods (fictitious company name)
の	(particle; see GRAMMAR 3, p. 4)	よろしく　おねがいします。	I look forward to working with you.
～さん	Mr., Mrs., Ms., Miss		
～です	be	こちらこそ	same here
か	(particle; see GRAMMAR 2, p. 3)		

NOTES

1. たなかさん

   さん is a title of respect added to a person's name, so it cannot be used after one's own name. さん is used regardless of gender and can be used with both the last name and the given name. In business situations, "last name + さん" is the most common, but "first name + さん" is also used.

2. はい、そうです。

   When replying to "noun ですか," そう can be used instead of repeating the noun. When replying in the negative, say いいえ、ちがいます.

3. よろしく　おねがいします。

   A phrase used when being introduced, よろしく　おねがいします is usually combined with はじめまして. It is also used when taking one's leave after having asked a favor. よろしく means "well" and is used as a request for the other person's favorable consideration in the future.

4. Exchanging business cards

   In business situations, people usually exchange business cards when meeting for the first time.

KEY SENTENCES

 017

1. スミスさんは　アメリカじんです。
2. スミスさんは　アメリカじんですか。
3. こちらは　のぞみデパートの　たなかさんです。
4. （わたしは）　スミスです。

1. Smith-san is an American.
2. Is Smith-san an American?
3. This is Tanaka-san of the Nozomi Department Store.
4. [I am] Smith.

GRAMMAR

1. noun 1は　noun 2です。   (KEY SENTENCES 1, hereafter abbreviated as KS1)

The particle は is the topic marker. It is used in the same sense as "as for" in English but is used much more frequently. The particle は follows noun 1, singling it out as the "topic" of the sentence. Noun 2 is then identified, and the phrase is concluded with です. The topic is the person or thing that the sentence is about. The topic is often the same as the subject but not necessarily.

2. noun 1は　noun 2ですか。   (KS2)

It is easy to make questions in Japanese. Simply place the particle か at the end of the sentence. No change in word order is required even when the question contains interrogatives like "who," "what," "when," etc.
Intonation normally rises on か, i.e., …ですか.↗
はい is virtually the same as "yes," and いいえ is virtually the same as "no."

e.g. スミスさんは　アメリカじんですか。　　Is Smith-san American?
　　 はい、アメリカじんです。　　　　　　Yes, (he is) American.
　　 いいえ、イギリスじんです。　　　　　No, (he is) British.

VOCABULARY

| は | (particle; see GRAMMAR 1, above) | こちら | this one (polite for "this person") |
| アメリカじん | American (person) | わたし | I |

3. company の　person
(KS3)

The particle の expresses belonging or affiliation. Here it shows that a person belongs to, in a sense that he works for, a company. Japanese customarily give their company name when being introduced in a business situation.

4. Omission of the topic
(KS4)

When the topic is clear to the other person, it is generally omitted. For example, たなかさんですか means "Are you Tanaka-san?" and since it is clear who the topic is, it is omitted. The same is true of the answer to the question; the topic is often omitted. (see GRAMMAR 2, p. 3)

WORD POWER

Ⅰ Countries and nationalities
 018

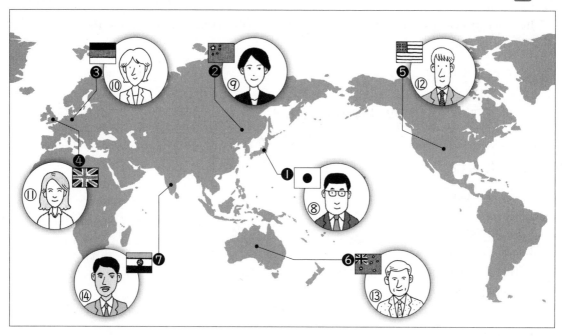

❶にほん	❹イギリス	❼インド	⑩ドイツじん	⑬オーストラリアじん
❷ちゅうごく	❺アメリカ	⑧にほんじん	⑪イギリスじん	⑭インドじん
❸ドイツ	❻オーストラリア	⑨ちゅうごくじん	⑫アメリカじん	

Ⅱ Work affiliation
 019

 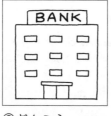 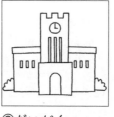 

①デパート	②ぎんこう	③だいがく	④たいしかん

VOCABULARY

にほん	Japan	アメリカ	United States	ぎんこう	bank
ちゅうごく	China	オーストラリア	Australia	だいがく	university, college
ドイツ	Germany	インド	India	たいしかん	embassy
イギリス	United Kingdom	～じん	-ese, -ian (person from)		

EXERCISES

I *State someone's nationality.* Make up sentences following the pattern of the example. Substitute the underlined parts with the alternatives given.

スミスさん   ホフマンさん   ブラウンさん   チャンさん   たなかさん

e.g. <u>スミスさん</u>は　<u>アメリカじん</u>です。

1. .... （ホフマンさん、ドイツじん）

2. .... （ブラウンさん、イギリスじん）

3. .... （チャンさん、ちゅうごくじん）

4. .... （たなかさん、にほんじん）

II Make up dialogues following the patterns of the examples. Substitute the underlined parts with the alternatives given.

A. *Ask and answer what someone's nationality is.*

e.g. A：<u>スミスさん</u>は　<u>アメリカじん</u>ですか。
　　　B：はい、<u>アメリカじん</u>です。

1. A：... （ホフマンさん、ドイツじん）

　 B：... （ドイツじん）

2. A：... （ブラウンさん、イギリスじん）

　 B：... （イギリスじん）

3. A：... （チャンさん、ちゅうごくじん）

　 B：... （ちゅうごくじん）

4. A：... （たなかさん、にほんじん）

　 B：... （にほんじん）

VOCABULARY

| ホフマン | Hoffman (surname) |
| ブラウン | Brown (surname) |

B. *Ask and answer what someone's nationality is.*

e.g. A：<u>スミスさんは</u>　イギリスじんですか。

　　 B：いいえ、<u>アメリカじん</u>です。

1. A：..（ホフマンさん）

　 B：..（ドイツじん）

2. A：..（チャンさん）

　 B：..（ちゅうごくじん）

Ⅲ *Confirm the identity of someone you are meeting for the first time.* Make up dialogues following the pattern of the example and based on the information provided.

e.g. 	1. 	2. 	3. 	4. 
ＡＢＣフーズ スミスさん	ベルリンモーターズ ホフマンさん	ロンドンぎんこう ブラウンさん	とうきょうだいがく ラジャさん	オーストラリア たいしかん ハリスさん

e.g. あなた：すみません。<u>ＡＢＣフーズの　スミスさん</u>ですか。

　　 スミス：はい、そうです。

1. あなた　：..

　 ホフマン：..

2. あなた　：..

　 ブラウン：..

3. あなた：..

　 ラジャ：..

4. あなた：..

　 ハリス：..

いいえ	no	とうきょうだいがく	University of Tokyo
ベルリンモーターズ	Berlin Motors (fictitious company name)	とうきょう	Tokyo
ベルリン	Berlin	ハリス	Harris (surname)
ロンドンぎんこう	Bank of London (fictitious bank name)	あなた	you
ロンドン	London		

Ⅳ *Introduce yourself.* Make up dialogues following the pattern of the example. Substitute the underlined parts with the alternatives given.

e.g. スミス　：はじめまして。ＡＢＣフーズの　スミスです。
　　　　　　よろしく　おねがいします。

　　ホフマン：はじめまして。ベルリンモーターズの　ホフマンです。
　　　　　　よろしく　おねがいします。

1. ブラウン：...

　　　　　　　　　　　　　　　（ロンドンぎんこう、ブラウン）

2. ラジャ　：...

　　　　　　　　　　　　　　　（とうきょうだいがく、ラジャ）

3. ハリス　：...

　　　　　　　　　　　　　　　（オーストラリアたいしかん、ハリス）

Ⅴ *Introduce people.* Referring to the illustration, introduce A and B to each other.

e.g. A：ベルリンモーターズ
　　　　ホフマンさん
B：ＡＢＣフーズ
　　　　スミスさん

1. A：ロンドンぎんこう
　　　　ブラウンさん
B：とうきょうだいがく
　　　　ラジャさん

2. A：のぞみデパート
　　　　たなかさん
B：オーストラリアたいしかん
　　　　ハリスさん

e.g. あなた：こちらは　ベルリンモーターズの　ホフマンさんです。
　　　　　　こちらは　ＡＢＣフーズの　スミスさんです。

1. あなた：...

　　　　　...

2. あなた：...

　　　　　...

Ⅵ Listen to the audio and fill in the blanks based on the information you hear. 🔊020-022

1. スミスさんは　.............................です。

2. ラジャさんは　.............................です。

3. チャンさんは　.............................です。

SPEAKING PRACTICE

1. Tanaka and Smith, who have just met for the first time, are talking.　🔊 023

たなか：スミスさん、おくには　どちらですか。

スミス：アメリカです。

Tanaka:　Smith-san, what country are you from?
Smith:　　I'm from the United States.

2. Sasaki introduces Brown to Tanaka.　🔊 024

ささき　　：たなかさん、こちらは　ロンドンぎんこうの　ブラウンさんです。

ブラウン：はじめまして。ブラウンです。よろしく　おねがいします。

たなか　　：はじめまして。のぞみデパートの　たなかです。

　　　　　　よろしく　おねがいします。

Sasaki:　Tanaka-san, this is Brown-san of the Bank of London.
Brown:　Nice to meet you. I am Brown. I look forward to working with you.
Tanaka:　Nice to meet you. I am Tanaka of the Nozomi Department Store. I look forward to
　　　　　working with you.

3. Smith is visiting the Nozomi Department Store.　🔊 025

スミス　　：ABC フーズの　スミスです。たなかさんを　おねがいします。

うけつけ：はい。

Smith:　　　　I am Smith of ABC Foods. I would like to see Tanaka-san.
Receptionist: Yes [, just a moment].

NOTES

1. おくには　どちらですか。
The prefix お is added to the word くに to specify the country or birthplace of the person you are talking to.
The basic word for "where" is どこ, but どちら is more polite.

2. たなかさんを　おねがいします。
Use "personを　おねがいします" when asking a receptionist to summon somebody you want to see.
おねがいします is a very convenient phrase often used in making polite requests.

Active
Communication

1. Introduce yourself to a classmate. Then introduce two classmates to
   each other.

2. Try introducing yourself when you meet a Japanese person.

VOCABULARY

おくに	your country	〜を　おねがいします	please (get me …)(see NOTES 2, above)
お〜	(honorific prefix)		
くに	country	うけつけ	reception desk, receptionist
どちら	where (polite word for どこ)		

LESSON 2

Possession: Whose Pen Is This?

TARGET DIALOGUE

🔊 026

A meeting has just ended. Nakamura finds a pen on the floor.

なかむら：これは　だれの　ペンですか。

すずき　：さあ、わかりません。

(*Turning toward Smith.*)

スミスさんのですか。

スミス　：いいえ、わたしのじゃありません。

Nakamura runs after Tanaka, who left the meeting room earlier.

なかむら：たなかさん、これは　たなかさんの　ペンですか。

たなか　：はい、わたしのです。ありがとうございます。

Nakamura:	Whose pen is this?
Suzuki:	I don't know. Is it yours, Smith-san?
Smith:	No, it isn't mine.

Nakamura:	Tanaka-san, is this your pen?
Tanaka:	Yes, it is. Thank you.

VOCABULARY

これ	this one	ペン	pen	スミスさんの	Smith-san's
だれの	whose	さあ、わかりません。	(See NOTES 1, p. 10)	わたしの	my, mine
だれ	who			～じゃありません	is/are not
の	(particle; see GRAMMAR 3, p. 10)	わかりません	I don't know	ありがとうございます。	Thank you.

9

NOTES

1. さあ、わかりません。

The さあ here expresses the speaker's hesitation about immediately answering, "I don't know."

2. スミスさんのですか。

In Japanese, the word あなた is the equivalent of "you," but here Suzuki doesn't say あなたのですか. In Japanese conversation, the word あなた is little used other than for members of one's family and other close associates. あなた is never used with people of higher status. Instead of あなた they are addressed by their "surname/first name+さん" or by their job title.

3. ありがとうございます。

This is the frequently used way of expressing thanks. Saying どうも　ありがとうございます gives greater weight or formality to an expression of thanks. The casual form is either ありがとう or どうも　ありがとう.

KEY SENTENCES 027

1. これは　とけいです。
2. これは　とけいじゃありません。
3. これは　スミスさんの　とけいです。

1. This is a watch.
2. This is not a watch.
3. This is Smith-san's watch.

GRAMMAR

1. これは　nounです。 (KS1)

これ is a pronoun that indicates something near to the speaker (see L4, GRAMMAR 1, p. 29).

2. これは　nounじゃありません。 (KS2)

～じゃありません or ～ではありません is the negative form of ～です. じゃ is more informal than では, but commonly used; otherwise they are the same. The chart below summarizes the forms of ～です.

Present form		Past form	
aff.	neg.	aff.	neg.
～です	～じゃありません ～ではありません	～でした	～じゃありませんでした ～ではありませんでした
is	is not	was	was not

3. personの　noun (KS3)

The particle の connects two nouns, and the noun-の combination modifies the word that comes after it. Particle の has various functions and here it expresses possession (see L1, GRAMMAR 3, p. 4). In cases when the noun is obvious from the situation, the noun may be omitted.

e.g. これは　わたしの　ペンです。　This is my pen.
これは　わたしのです。　This is mine.

VOCABULARY

| とけい | watch, clock

WORD POWER

I Numbers 🔊 028

0	1	2	3	4	5	6	7	8	9
ゼロ／	いち	に	さん	よん／し	ご	ろく	なな／	はち	きゅう／
れい							しち		く

II Business vocabulary 🔊 029

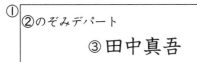

① ② のぞみデパート
③ 田中真吾
④ 東京都港区虎ノ門 3–25–2
⑤ (03)3459-9620*
(090)8765-4321
⑥ s.tanaka@nozomidpt.com

Nozomi Department Store
Shingo Tanaka
3–25–2 Toranomon, Minato-ku, Tokyo
(03) 3459-9620
(090)8765-4321
E-MAIL: s.tanaka@nozomidpt.com

①めいし   ③なまえ   ⑤でんわばんごう
②かいしゃの　なまえ   ④じゅうしょ   ⑥メールアドレス

*The area code for Tokyo is 03. When saying a phone number aloud, put の between the area code (e.g., 03) and the exchange, and between the exchange and the last four numbers. The phone number here is pronounced ゼロ　さんの　さん　よん　ご　きゅうの　きゅう　ろく　に　ゼロ.

NOTE: The 0 used in telephone numbers is usually pronounced ゼロ.

III Personal belongings 🔊 030

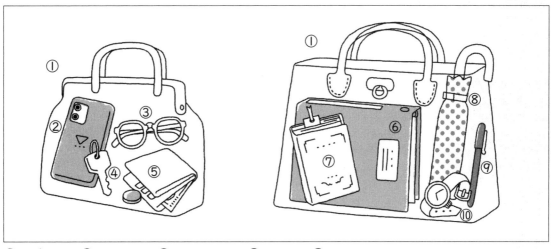

①かばん   ③めがね   ⑤さいふ   ⑦ほん   ⑨ペン
②スマホ   ④かぎ   ⑥ファイル ⑧かさ   ⑩とけい

めいし	business card	でんわばんごう	telephone number	めがね	glasses
かいしゃの　なまえ		でんわ	telephone	かぎ	key
	company name	ばんごう	number	さいふ	wallet
かいしゃ	company	メールアドレス	mail address	ファイル	file
なまえ	name	かばん	bag	ほん	book
じゅうしょ	address	スマホ	smart phone	かさ	umbrella

EXERCISES

I Make up sentences following the patterns of the examples. Substitute the underlined part with the alternatives given.

A. *State what an object is.*

e.g. これは　ほんです。

1. ....（かぎ）

2. ....（とけい）

B. *State what an object is not.*

e.g. これは　ほんじゃありません。

1. ....（かぎ）

2. ....（とけい）

II Make up dialogues following the patterns of the examples and based on the information provided.

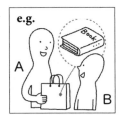 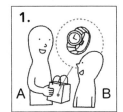 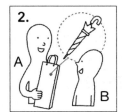 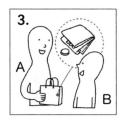

A. *Ask and answer whether or not an object is what it appears to be.*

e.g. A：これは　ほんですか。

B：はい、ほんです。

1. A： ....

　　B： ....

2. A： ....

　　B： ....

3. A： ....

　　B： ....

B. *Answer whether or not an object is what it appears to be.*

e.g. A：これは　かさですか。

B：いいえ、<u>かさ</u>じゃありません。

1. A：これは　さいふですか。

B：...

2. A：これは　とけいですか。

B：...

3. A：これは　ほんですか。

B：...

Ⅲ *Ask and answer what an object is.* Make up dialogues following the pattern of the example and based on the information provided.

  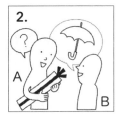 

e.g. A：これは　なんですか。

B：<u>ほん</u>です。

1. A：...

B：...

2. A：...

B：...

3. A：...

B：...

なん　　　　what

IV *State who the owner of an object is.* Make up sentences following the pattern of the example and based on the information provided.

  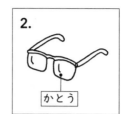 

e.g. これは　スミスさんの　ほんです。

1. ....

2. ....

3. ....

V Make up dialogues following the patterns of the examples and based on the information provided.

  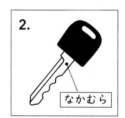 

A. *Ask and answer whether or not an object belongs to someone.*

e.g. A：これは　ささきさんの　めがねですか。

B：はい、ささきさんのです。

1. A：..

　　B：..

2. A：..

　　B：..

3. A：..

　　B：..

B. *Answer whether or not an object belongs to someone.*

e.g. A：これは　なかむらさんの　めがねですか。

B：いいえ、<u>なかむらさんの</u>じゃありません。

1. A：これは　ささきさんの　スマホですか。

B：

2. A：これは　エマさんの　かぎですか。

B：

3. A：これは　スミスさんの　さいふですか。

B：

C. *Ask and answer who an object's owner is.*

e.g. A：これは　<u>だれの</u>　<u>めがね</u>ですか。

B：<u>ささきさんの</u>です。

1. A：

B：

2. A：

B：

3. A：

B：

VI Make up sentences or dialogues following the patterns of the examples based on the information in the table.

	Name	Telephone number		Name	Telephone number
e.g.	スミス	080-1234-5678	4.	ぎんこう	03-5690-3111
1.	ささき	080-5642-2963	5.	のぞみデパート	03-3459-9620
2.	たなか	090-8765-4321	6.	たいしかん	03-3225-1116
3.	すずき	030-6435-2187			

A. *State someone's phone number.*

e.g. スミスさんの　でんわばんごうは　ゼロ　はち　ゼロの　いち　に　さん　よんの　ご　ろく　なな　はちです。

1.

2.

3.

B. *Ask for and provide someone's phone number.*

e.g. A：スミスさんの　でんわばんごうを　おしえてください。
B：ゼロ　はち　ゼロの　いち　に　さん　よんの　ご　ろく　なな　はち　です。

4. A：

B：

5. A：

B：

6. A：

B：

～を　おしえてください　　please tell me

Ⅶ *Talk about who an object's owner is.* Make up dialogues following the pattern of the example and based on the information provided.

e.g. スミス　　：これは　なかむらさんの　ペンですか。

　　　なかむら：(*looking at the pen*) いいえ、わたしのじゃありません。

　　　スミス　　：だれの　ですか。

　　　なかむら：エマさんのです。

1. スミス　　：
　　なかむら：
　　スミス　　：
　　なかむら：

2. スミス　　：
　　なかむら：
　　スミス　　：
　　なかむら：

3. スミス　　：
　　なかむら：
　　スミス　　：
　　なかむら：

Ⅷ Listen to the audio and fill in the blanks based on the information you hear. 🔊 031, 032

1. スミスさんの　でんわばんごうは
　　　　　　　　　　　　　　　　　　　です。

2. かばんは　　　　　　　　　　　　　のです。

SPEAKING PRACTICE

1. Smith finds something in the break room.　　🔊 033

　　スミス　　：これは　なんですか。

　　なかむら：にほんの　おかしです。どうぞ。

　　スミス　　：ありがとうございます。

Smith:　　　What are these?
Nakamura:　They are Japanese sweets. Please help yourself.
Smith:　　　Thank you!

2. Smith and Nakamura are working at the office.　　🔊 034

　　スミス　　：のぞみデパートの　でんわばんごうを　おしえてください。

　　なかむら：03-3459-9620 です。

　　スミス　　：すみません。もう　いちど　おねがいします。

Smith:　　　Please tell me the telephone number of the Nozomi Department Store.
Nakamura:　It is 03-3459-9620.
Smith:　　　Excuse me. Could you say that again?

NOTES

1. どうぞ。

どうぞ is used when handing something to someone. It is also used when asking a visitor to enter a room or office.

Active Communication　If you're in Japan, ask an employee of a restaurant or store what the establishment's phone number is.

VOCABULARY

にほんの　おかし	Japanese sweets		もう　いちど　おねがいします。		いちど	one time
おかし	sweets			One more time,	おねがいします	
お〜	(polite prefix)			please.		please (lit. "I request you")
かし	sweets		もう　いちど	one more time		
どうぞ。	Please (have one).		もう	more		

SHOPPING

Japan is a paradise for shoppers. There are many kinds of stores, from grand department stores and luxury brand goods shops to small shops in local town street malls, 100-yen shops, and more, so there are many ways to enjoy shopping. Large-scale shopping centers that have numerous shops, restaurants, and movie theaters are always crowded with families and young people. Shopkeepers are courteous and kind. People who enter a store, are almost always greeted with the word, "Irasshaimase!"

Asking the Time: What Time Is It?

TARGET DIALOGUE
🔊 035

Smith is calling the "Sushiyoshi" sushi shop.

みせの　ひと：すしよしです。

スミス　　　　：すみません。ランチタイムは　なんじからですか。

みせの　ひと：１１じはんからです。

スミス　　　　：なんじまでですか。

みせの　ひと：２じはんまでです。

スミス　　　　：ラストオーダーは　なんじですか。

みせの　ひと：２じです。

スミス　　　　：ありがとうございます。

■ランチタイムは　１１じはんから　２じはんまでです。

Restaurant employee:	This is Sushiyoshi.
Smith:	Excuse me. What time does lunchtime start?
Restaurant employee:	From 11:30.
Smith:	What time does lunchtime end?
Restaurant employee:	It goes until 2:30.
Smith:	What time is the last order?
Restaurant employee:	2:00.
Smith:	Thank you.

■Lunchtime is from 11:30 to 2:30.

VOCABULARY

みせの　ひと	restaurant employee	なんじ	what time	まで	until (particle; see
みせ	restaurant, shop	から	from (particle; see		GRAMMAR 2, p. 21)
ひと	person, employee		GRAMMAR 2, p. 21)	２じはん	2:30, two-thirty, half
すしよし	Sushiyoshi (fictitious	１１じはん	11:30, eleven-thirty, half		past two
	restaurant name)		past eleven	ラストオーダー	last order
ランチタイム	lunchtime	～はん	…thirty, half past (hour)	２じ	2:00, two o'clock

KEY SENTENCES

 036

1. いま　３じです。
2. しごとは　９じから　５じまでです。
3. かいぎは　あしたの　４じからです。

1. It is 3:00 now.
2. Work is from 9:00 to 5:00.
3. The meeting is tomorrow, from 4:00.

GRAMMAR

1.（いま）　time です。 (KS1)

When stating the present time, no subject is given. Sometimes いま may be added adverbially. When speaking of the present time in a specified place, the geographical name will be made the topic and accompanied by は.

2. noun は　time 1 から　time 2 までです。 (KS2)

The particle から attached to a time indicates a starting time and the particle まで indicates ending time. These particles are used when stating business hours.

3. time 1 の　time 2 (KS3)

When more than one expression of time is used, the series begins with the larger unit, followed by the smaller unit(s) linked together with the particle の. Sometimes の is omitted. When asking "When is the event?" the expression "event は　いつですか" is used.

WORD POWER

① Services and activities

 037

①スーパー

②レストラン

③ジム

④しごと

⑤かいぎ

⑥ひるやすみ

⑦パーティー

VOCABULARY

いま	now	かいぎ	meeting	ジム	gym
３じ	3:00, three o'clock	あした	tomorrow	ひるやすみ	lunch break
しごと	work	４じ（よじ）	4:00, four o'clock	ひる	noon
９じ（くじ）	9:00, nine o'clock	スーパー	supermarket	やすみ	break, time off
５じ	5:00, five o'clock	レストラン	restaurant	パーティー	party

Ⅱ Numbers
038

10	じゅう	20	にじゅう	30	さんじゅう
11	じゅういち	21	にじゅういち	40	よんじゅう
12	じゅうに	22	にじゅうに	50	ごじゅう
13	じゅうさん	23	にじゅうさん	60	ろくじゅう
14	じゅうよん／じゅうし	24	にじゅうよん／にじゅうし	70	ななじゅう
				80	はちじゅう
15	じゅうご	25	にじゅうご	90	きゅうじゅう
16	じゅうろく	26	にじゅうろく		
17	じゅうなな／じゅうしち	27	にじゅうなな／にじゅうしち		
18	じゅうはち	28	にじゅうはち	100	ひゃく
19	じゅうきゅう／じゅうく	29	にじゅうきゅう／にじゅうく		

Ⅲ Times
039

1:00	いちじ	3:05	さんじ ごふん	3:10	さんじ じゅっぷん
2:00	にじ	3:15	さんじ じゅうごふん	3:20	さんじ にじゅっぷん
3:00	さんじ	3:25	さんじ にじゅうごふん	3:30	さんじ さんじゅっぷん／はん
4:00	よじ	3:35	さんじ さんじゅうごふん		
5:00	ごじ	3:45	さんじ よんじゅうごふん	3:40	さんじ よんじゅっぷん
6:00	ろくじ	3:55	さんじ ごじゅうごふん	3:50	さんじ ごじゅっぷん
7:00	しちじ				
8:00	はちじ			4:00 A.M.	ごぜん よじ
9:00	くじ			9:00 P.M.	ごご くじ
10:00	じゅうじ				
11:00	じゅういちじ				
12:00	じゅうにじ				

NOTE: Hours and minutes are written in hiragana here, but throughout the rest of the book they are written with numerals, e.g., 1じ for "1:00," 10じ20ぷん for "10:20," etc.

Ⅳ Time expressions
040

①きょう　　②あした

～じ	...o'clock	きょう	today
～ふん／ぷん	...minute(s)		
ごぜん	A.M., in the morning		
ごご	P.M., in the afternoon		

EXERCISES

I *State the time.* Practice telling the times indicated below.

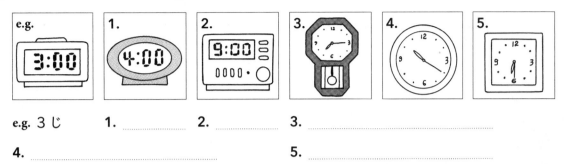

e.g. 3 じ   **1.** ....   **2.** ....   **3.** ....

4. ....   **5.** ....

II *Ask and give the time.* Make up dialogues following the pattern of the example. Substitute the underlined part with the times indicated in EXERCISES I.

e.g. A：いま　なんじですか。

B：<u>3 じ</u>です。

1. A：...

B：...

2. A：...

B：...

3. A：...

B：...

4. A：...

B：...

5. A：...

B：...

III Make up sentences following the patterns of the examples. Substitute the underlined part(s) with the alternatives given.

A. *State the opening time.*

e.g. スーパーは　9じからです。

1. .... (8:00)

2. .... (10:00)

B. *State the closing time.*

e.g. デパートは　8じまでです。

1. .... (7:00)

2. .... (9:00)

C. *State the opening and closing times.*

e.g. しごとは　9じから　5じまでです。

1. .... (9:30、5:30)

2. .... (10:00、6:00)

IV Make up dialogues following the patterns of the examples. Substitute the underlined parts with the alternatives given.

A. *Ask and answer what the opening time is.*

e.g. A：デパートは　なんじからですか。
    B：10じからです。

1. A：... (レストラン)

   B：... (11:30)

2. A：... (ぎんこう)

   B：... (9:00)

B. *Ask and answer what the closing time is.*

    e.g. A：<u>レストラン</u>は　なんじまでですか。

        B：<u>ごご　１１じ</u>までです。

    1. A： .... （かいぎ）

        B： .... （4:30）

    2. A： .... （ジム）

        B： .... （ごご　9:00）

C. *Ask and answer what the opening and closing times are.*

    e.g. A：<u>かいぎ</u>は　なんじから　なんじまでですか。

        B：<u>１じ</u>から　<u>３じ</u>までです。

    1. A： .... （ひるやすみ）

        B： .... （12:30、1:30）

    2. A： .... （ハッピーアワー）

        B： .... （4:00、7:00）

Ⓥ *Ask and answer when events are held.* Make up dialogues following the pattern of the example. Substitute the underlined parts with the alternatives given.

    e.g. A：<u>かいぎ</u>は　いつですか。

        B：<u>あしたの　９じ</u>からです。

    1. A： .... （プレゼン）

        B： .... （きょうの　３じ）

    2. A： .... （パーティー）

        B： .... （あしたの　５じ）

    3. A： .... （コンサート）

        B： .... （きょうの　６じ）

VOCABULARY

ハッピーアワー	happy hour
いつ	when
プレゼン	presentation
コンサート	concert

VI *Talk about the opening time.* Make up dialogues following the pattern of the example. Substitute the underlined parts with the alternatives given.

Smith is staying at a hotel. He asks about the hotel services.

e.g. スミス　：すみません。<u>あさごはん</u>は　なんじからですか。

フロント：<u>7じ</u>からです。

スミス　：ありがとうございます。

1. スミス　：＿＿＿＿＿＿＿＿＿＿＿＿＿＿＿＿＿（ばんごはん）

フロント：＿＿＿＿＿＿＿＿＿＿＿＿＿＿＿＿＿（6:00）

スミス　：＿＿＿＿＿＿＿＿＿＿＿＿＿＿＿＿＿

2. スミス　：＿＿＿＿＿＿＿＿＿＿＿＿＿＿＿＿＿（プール）

フロント：＿＿＿＿＿＿＿＿＿＿＿＿＿＿＿（8:00 A.M.）

スミス　：＿＿＿＿＿＿＿＿＿＿＿＿＿＿＿＿＿

3. スミス　：＿＿＿＿＿＿＿＿＿＿＿＿＿＿＿＿＿（ジム）

フロント：＿＿＿＿＿＿＿＿＿＿＿＿＿＿＿（9:00 A.M.）

スミス　：＿＿＿＿＿＿＿＿＿＿＿＿＿＿＿＿＿

VII Listen to the audio and fill in the blanks based on the information you hear.　🔊 041, 042

1. ジムは＿＿＿＿＿＿＿から＿＿＿＿＿＿＿までです。

2. あさごはんは＿＿＿＿＿＿＿から＿＿＿＿＿＿＿までです。

VOCABULARY			
あさごはん	breakfast	ばんごはん	evening meal, dinner, supper
あさ	morning		
ごはん	meal, cooked rice	ばん	evening
フロント	reception desk	プール	swimming pool

SPEAKING PRACTICE

1. Sasaki wants to call the London branch of her company. 🔊 043

ささき　　：なかむらさん、いま　なんじですか。

なかむら：４じはんです。

ささき　　：ロンドンは　いま　なんじですか。

なかむら：ごぜん　８じはんです。

ささき　　：そうですか。どうも　ありがとう。

Sasaki: Nakamura-san, what time is it now?
Nakamura: It's 4:30.
Sasaki: What time is it in London now?
Nakamura: It's 8:30 in the morning.
Sasaki: I see. Thank you.

NOTES

1. そうですか。
This expression, meaning "I see." or "Is that so?" is used as a comment on what someone else has said. It is spoken with falling intonation.

1. Ask someone for the time.

2. If you're in Japan, try asking for the business hours of a restaurant or other facilities you are interested in.

VOCABULARY

そうですか。　　　　　I see. (see NOTES 1, above)
どうも　ありがとう。 Thank you.

Shopping (1): How Much Is This?

TARGET DIALOGUE

🔊 044

Smith is shopping.

みせの　ひと：いらっしゃいませ。

スミス　　　：(*Pointing.*) それを　みせてください。

みせの　ひと：はい、どうぞ。

スミス　　　：ありがとう。これは　いくらですか。

みせの　ひと：3,000 えんです。

スミス　　　：(*Pointing.*) あれは　いくらですか。

みせの　ひと：あれも　3,000 えんです。

スミス　　　：じゃ、これを　ください。

みせの　ひと：はい、ありがとうございます。

Salesperson: May I help you?
Smith: Please show me that item.
Salesperson: Here you go.
Smith: Thank you. How much is this?
Salesperson: It is 3,000 yen.
Smith: How much is that one over there?
Salesperson: That one over there is also 3,000 yen.
Smith: All right. I'll take this one.
Salesperson: Fine. Thank you.

VOCABULARY

いらっしゃいませ。	May I help you?, Welcome.		～えん	...yen
それ	that one		あれ	that one over there
みせてください	please show me		も	also, too, either (particle; see GRAMMAR 2, p. 29)
いくら	how much		じゃ	well then
3,000 えん（さんぜんえん）3,000 yen			ください	please give me

1.　いらっしゃいませ。

This phrase is used in shops etc. to welcome customers. Literally it means "Please come in."

2.　それを　みせてください。

When you want to take a closer look at an item in a store, use "thingを　みせてください" ("please show me …").

3.　じゃ、これを　ください。

じゃ and では correspond to "well" or "well then," interjections that express conclusion or resignation.

KEY SENTENCES

 045

1.　それは　スマホです。あれは　タブレットです。
2.　これは　3,000えんです。あれも　3,000えんです。
3.　これを　ください。
4.　カレーと　サラダを　おねがいします。

1. That is a smart phone. That one over there is a tablet.
2. This one is 3,000 yen. That one over there is also 3,000 yen.
3. I would like this one, please.
4. I would like curry and salad, please.

GRAMMAR

1. これ／それ／あれ

(KS1, 2, 3)

Whereas English has only "this" and "that," Japanese has three separate demonstrative pronouns: これ, それ, and あれ. これ (see ① right) indicates something near the speaker, それ (see ② right) something near the listener, and あれ (see ③ right) something distant from either person.

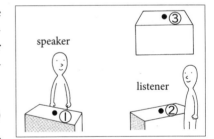

2. nounも

(KS2)

The particle も means "too," "also," "either," etc. It is used in both affirmative and negative sentences.

　　e.g. これは　わたしの　かさじゃありません。それも　わたしのじゃありません。

　　　This is not my umbrella. That is not mine either.

も is always used with a noun.

3. nounを　ください。／nounを　おねがいします。

(KS3, 4)

"nounを　ください" means "please give me," and can be used when shopping or placing an order in a restaurant. "nounを　おねがいします" can be used not only for making purchases or placing a restaurant order but for asking someone to do something or for requesting a service.

タブレット	tablet
カレー	curry
と	and (particle; see GRAMMAR 4, p. 30)
サラダ	salad

4. noun 1 と　noun 2

(KS4)

The particle と ("and") is used to connect two or more nouns. It is used only to connect nouns. It cannot be used to connect verbs, adjectives or clauses.

WORD POWER

Ⅰ Home appliances

 046

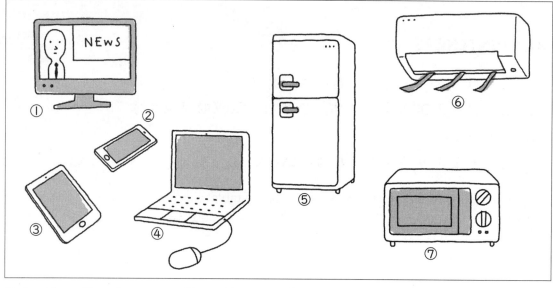

①テレビ　　③タブレット　　⑤れいぞうこ　　⑦でんしレンジ
②スマホ　　④パソコン　　　⑥エアコン

Ⅱ Food and drink

 047

①コーヒー　　②こうちゃ　　③ジュース　　④サンドイッチ　　⑤カレー　　⑥サラダ

VOCABULARY

テレビ	television	でんしレンジ	microwave oven	サンドイッチ	sandwich
パソコン	(personal) computer	コーヒー	coffee		
れいぞうこ	refrigerator	こうちゃ	(black) tea		
エアコン	air conditioner	ジュース	juice		

Ⅲ Numbers

 048

100	ひゃく	1,000	せん	10,000	いちまん
200	にひゃく	2,000	にせん	20,000	にまん
300	さんびゃく	3,000	さんぜん	30,000	さんまん
400	よんひゃく	4,000	よんせん	40,000	よんまん
500	ごひゃく	5,000	ごせん	50,000	ごまん
600	ろっぴゃく	6,000	ろくせん	60,000	ろくまん
700	ななひゃく	7,000	ななせん	70,000	ななまん
800	はっぴゃく	8,000	はっせん	80,000	はちまん
900	きゅうひゃく	9,000	きゅうせん	90,000	きゅうまん

Intermediate numbers are made by combining the numbers composing them.

e.g. 135　ひゃくさんじゅうご　　　1,829　せんはっぴゃくにじゅうきゅう

NOTE: Large numbers are written in hiragana here, but throughout the rest of the book, numerals are used to write them, e.g., 3,000えん for "3,000 yen."

PLUS ONE

The system of counting large numbers is different in Japanese and English. The chart below shows how to count from a thousand to a trillion.

1,000	せん
10,000	いちまん
100,000	じゅうまん
1,000,000	ひゃくまん
10,000,000	せんまん
100,000,000	いちおく
1,000,000,000	じゅうおく
10,000,000,000	ひゃくおく
100,000,000,000	せんおく
1,000,000,000,000	いっちょう

ちょう　おく　まん

2,222,222,222,222
にちょう　にせんにひゃくにじゅうにおく　にせんにひゃくにじゅうにまん
にせんにひゃくにじゅうに

Decimals (The word for "decimal point" is てん.)

0.7	れいてんなな
0.29	れいてんにきゅう
0.538	れいてんごさんはち

Fractions (ぶん means "part.")

1/2	にぶんの　いち	2/3	さんぶんの　に
1/4	よんぶんの　いち		

31

EXERCISES

Ⅰ *State an item's price.* Look at the illustrations and state the price of each item.

e.g. ¥90	1. ¥100	2. ¥120	3. ¥300	4. ¥400
5. ¥860	6. ¥1,200	7. ¥3,000	8. ¥6,800	9. ¥79,000

e.g. きゅうじゅうえん

1. _____   4. _____   7. _____

2. _____   5. _____   8. _____

3. _____   6. _____   9. _____

Ⅱ *Ask and answer an item's price.* Make up dialogues following the pattern of the example and based on the information provided.

e.g. A : これは　いくらですか。

B : 500 えんです。

1. A : ....

   B : ....

2. A : ....

   B : ....

3. A : ....

   B : ....

Ⅲ *Ask and give an item's price.* Make appropriate questions for each of the answers given and based on the information provided.

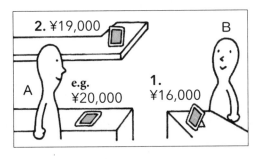 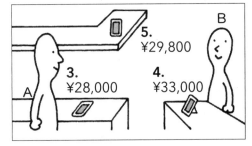

e.g. A : <u>これは</u>　いくらですか。

　　 B : 20,000 えんです。

1. A : ....

   B : 16,000 えんです。

2. A : ....

   B : 19,000 えんです。

3. A : ....

   B : 28,000 えんです。

4. A : ....

   B : 33,000 えんです。

5. A : ....

   B : 29,800 えんです。

IV *Give two things and state what they have in common.* Make up sentences following the pattern of the example. Substitute the underlined parts with the alternatives given.

e.g. <u>これ</u>は　<u>90,000 えん</u>です。<u>それ</u>も　<u>90,000 えん</u>です。

1. ....（これ、50,000 えん、それ）

2. ....（これ、とけい、それ）

3. ....

　　（たなかさん、にほんじん、ささきさん）

4. ....

　　（とうきょう、ごぜん　10 じ、ソウル）

V *Ask the price of more than one item.* Make up dialogues following the patterns of the examples. Substitute the underlined parts with the alternatives given.

A. e.g. スミス　　　：これは　いくらですか。

　　みせの　ひと：<u>8,000 えん</u>です。

　　スミス　　　：あれも　<u>8,000 えん</u>ですか。

　　みせの　ひと：はい、あれも　<u>8,000 えん</u>です。

1. スミス　　　：...

　　みせの　ひと：...（7,000 えん）

　　スミス　　　：...（7,000 えん）

　　みせの　ひと：...（7,000 えん）

2. スミス　　　：...

　　みせの　ひと：...（9,000 えん）

　　スミス　　　：...（9,000 えん）

　　みせの　ひと：...（9,000 えん）

B. e.g. スミス　　　　：これは　いくらですか。

みせの　ひと：<u>5,000 えん</u>です。

スミス　　　　：あれも　<u>5,000 えん</u>ですか。

みせの　ひと：いいえ、あれは　<u>5,000 えん</u>じゃありません。

<u>4,000 えん</u>です。

1. スミス　　　　：..

みせの　ひと：...（3,000 えん）

スミス　　　　：...（3,000 えん）

みせの　ひと：...（3,000 えん）

....

2. スミス　　　　：..

みせの　ひと：...（4,500 えん）

スミス　　　　：...（4,500 えん）

みせの　ひと：...（4,500 えん）

....

Ⅵ *Place your order at a restaurant.* Make up sentences following the pattern of the example and based on the information provided.

 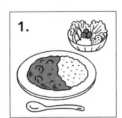  

e.g. <u>サンドイッチ</u>と　<u>コーヒー</u>を　おねがいします。

1. ....

2. ....

3. ....

VOCABULARY

オレンジジュース　orange juice
チョコレートケーキ　chocolate cake

Ⅶ *Talk about some item, ask its price, and say what you want to buy.* Make up dialogues following the pattern of the example. Substitute the underlined parts with the alternatives given.

e.g. スミス　　　　　：すみません。あれは　<u>パソコン</u>ですか。

　　みせの　ひと：いいえ、<u>タブレット</u>です。

　　スミス　　　　　：それは　<u>パソコン</u>ですか。

　　みせの　ひと：はい、そうです。

　　スミス　　　　　：いくらですか。

　　みせの　ひと：<u>50,000 えん</u>です。

　　スミス　　　　　：じゃ、それを　ください。

1. スミス　　　　　：..（ボールペン）

　　みせの　ひと：..（シャーペン）

　　スミス　　　　　：..（ボールペン）

　　みせの　ひと：..

　　スミス　　　　　：..

　　みせの　ひと：..（170 えん）

　　スミス　　　　　：..

2. スミス　　　　　：..（でんしレンジ）

　　みせの　ひと：..（トースター）

　　スミス　　　　　：..（でんしレンジ）

　　みせの　ひと：..

　　スミス　　　　　：..

　　みせの　ひと：..（13,000 えん）

　　スミス　　　　　：..

Ⅷ Listen to the audio and fill in the blanks based on the information you hear. 🔊 049-051

1. でんしレンジは　....................................です。

2. タブレットは　....................................です。

3. れいぞうこは　....................................です。

ボールペン	ballpoint pen
シャーペン	mechanical pencil
	(colloquial shortening of シャープペンシル)
トースター	toaster

SPEAKING PRACTICE

1. Smith is placing his order at a coffee shop.   🔊 052

    スミス　　　　：すみません。サンドイッチと　コーヒーを　おねがいします。

    みせの　ひと：はい。

    Smith: Excuse me. I would like a sandwich and coffee, please.
    Server: Thank you.

2. Smith is shopping in a store.   🔊 053

    スミス　　　　：これを　ください。

    みせの　ひと：8,300 えんです。

    スミス　　　　：カードで　おねがいします。

    みせの　ひと：はい。

    Smith: I would like this, please.
    Shopkeeper: That will be 8,300 yen.
    Smith: I would like to pay by credit card.
    Shopkeeper: Yes [, that will be fine].

NOTES

1. カードで　おねがいします。
    When stating a means or method of payment, the particle で is used.

> **Active Communication**
>
> If you're in Japan, try asking the prices of items at vendors where prices are not listed or are written in *kanji*.

VOCABULARY

カード	credit card
で	by means of (particle; see NOTES 1, above)

Shopping (2): Two Bottles of That Wine, Please

TARGET DIALOGUE 🔊 054

Smith is at the information desk in a shopping mall.

スミス　　　　　　　　　：すみません。ワインショップは　どこですか。

インフォメーションの　ひと：ちか　１かいです。

スミス　　　　　　　　　：どうも　ありがとう。

(*In the liquor store.*)

スミス　　　　：すみません。その　ワインは　どこのですか。

みせの　ひと：フランスのです。

スミス　　　　：いくらですか。

みせの　ひと：2,600 えんです。

スミス　　　　：じゃ、それを　２ほん　ください。

　　　　　　　　ふくろも　２まい　ください。

Smith:	Excuse me. Where is the wine shop?
Information desk staff:	It is in the first-floor basement.
Smith:	Thank you.

Smith:	Excuse me. Where is that wine from?
Salesperson:	It is from France.
Smith:	How much is it?
Salesperson:	It is 2,600 yen.
Smith:	I see. Then I would like to have two bottles. Please let me have two bags as well.

ワインショップ	wine shop		その	that
どこ	where		ワイン	wine
インフォメーション	information desk		フランス	France
ちか　１かい　（いっかい）	first-floor basement		２ほん	two (long objects)
ちか	basement		ふくろ	bag
１かい	first floor		２まい	two (flat objects)

1. それを　2ほん　ください。

~ほん (ぼん／ぽん) is a unit for counting long, slender objects like pencils and bottles. Japanese has two numerical systems: the ひとつ, ふたつ, みっつ system and the abstract いち, に, さん system. Counting things can be done in two ways: (1) using the ひとつ, ふたつ, みっつ system independently (see WORD POWER II, p. 40), or (2) using the いち, に, さん system combined with a counter such as ~ほん (ぼん／ぽん) or ~まい, the latter for thin, flat objects like shirts and pieces of paper.

　　The ひとつ, ふたつ, みっつ system, however, only goes as far as とお (10), after which the いち, に, さん system is used: じゅういち, じゅうに, じゅうさん, etc.

KEY SENTENCES

 055

1. レストランは　5かいです。
2. この　Tシャツは　2,000えんです。
3. あの　あおい　Tシャツは　3,000えんです。
4. これは　フランスの　ワインです。
5. その　ワインを　2ほん　ください。

1. The restaurant is on the 5th floor.
2. This T-shirt is 2,000 yen.
3. That blue T-shirt over there is 3,000 yen.
4. This is a wine from France. / This is a French wine.
5. I would like two bottles of that wine, please.

GRAMMAR

1. noun は　place です。 (KS1)

This is the expression used when stating the location or place of a thing or person. When asking the location of the thing or person, say "noun は　どこですか."

2. この／その／あの　noun (KS2, 3, 5)

この, その, and あの have similar meanings to これ, それ, あれ, but they modify nouns.

3. adjective ＋ noun (KS3)

When the adjective modifies a noun, it is placed before the noun.

4. place の　noun (KS4)

The place which comes before the noun indicates the place of production or manufacture of the thing or product that follows.

5. noun を　number　ください。 (KS5)

When purchasing or ordering multiple items, the number comes after "noun を." There is no particle after the number.

5かい	fifth floor	あの	that (over there)
この	this	あおい	blue
Tシャツ	T-shirt		

WORD POWER

Ⅰ Items for sale

🔊 056

①Tシャツ   ④くろい   ⑦ワイン   ⑩りんご
②あかい   ⑤しろい   ⑧(お)さら   ⑪おおきい
③あおい   ⑥ビール   ⑨コップ   ⑫ちいさい

Ⅱ Numbers and counters

🔊 057

	〜 👕 etc.	🍾 ☂ etc.	🍎 🍔 etc.
1	いちまい（1まい）	いっぽん（1ぽん）	ひとつ（1つ）
2	にまい（2まい）	にほん（2ほん）	ふたつ（2つ）
3	さんまい（3まい）	さんぼん（3ぼん）	みっつ（3つ）
4	よんまい（4まい）	よんほん（4ほん）	よっつ（4つ）
5	ごまい（5まい）	ごほん（5ほん）	いつつ（5つ）
6	ろくまい（6まい）	ろっぽん（6ぽん）	むっつ（6つ）
7	ななまい（7まい）	ななほん（7ほん）	ななつ（7つ）
8	はちまい（8まい）	はっぽん（8ぽん）	やっつ（8つ）
9	きゅうまい（9まい）	きゅうほん（9ほん）	ここのつ（9つ）
10	じゅうまい（10まい）	じゅっぽん（10ぽん）	とお（10）

Ⅲ Floors

🔊 058

①いっかい（1かい）   ④よんかい（4かい）   ⑦ちか　いっかい（1かい）
②にかい（2かい）   ⑤ごかい（5かい）
③さんがい（3がい）   ⑥ろっかい（6かい）

VOCABULARY

あかい	red	りんご	apple	〜ほん／ぼん／ぽん	(counter for long, slender objects)	〜かい／がい	…floor
くろい	black	おおきい	big, large				
しろい	white	ちいさい	small	にかい（2かい）	second floor		
ビール	beer	〜まい	(counter for flat objects)	さんがい（3がい）	third floor		
(お)さら	dish, plate			よんかい（4かい）	fourth floor		
コップ	glass			ろっかい（6かい）	sixth floor		

EXERCISES

I *Ask for the location of a shop or where certain goods are sold.* Make up dialogues following the pattern of the example. Substitute the underlined parts with the alternatives given.

> e.g. A：<u>ワインショップ</u>は　どこですか。
>
> B：<u>１かい</u>です。

1. A： .... （レストラン）

    B： .... （6 かい）

2. A： .... （そうじき）

    B： .... （3 がい）

3. A： .... （パソコン）

    B： .... （ちか　１かい）

II *Single out a specific item and state its price.* Make up sentences following the pattern of the example and based on the information provided.

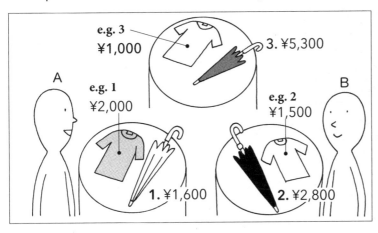

> e.g. 1　A：<u>この</u>　Ｔシャツは　<u>2,000</u> えんです。
>
> e.g. 2　A：<u>その</u>　Ｔシャツは　<u>1,500</u> えんです。
>
> e.g. 3　A：<u>あの</u>　Ｔシャツは　<u>1,000</u> えんです。

1. A： ....

2. A： ....

3. A： ....

VOCABULARY

| そうじき　vacuum cleaner

III *Ask and give a specific item's price.* Make up dialogues following the pattern of the example and based on the information provided.

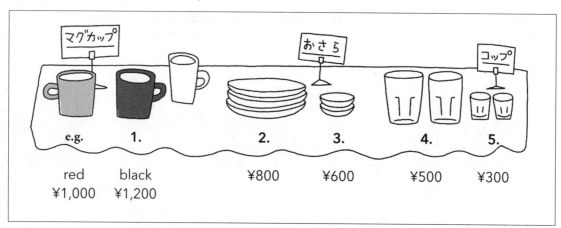

red   black
¥1,000   ¥1,200   ¥800   ¥600   ¥500   ¥300

e.g. A : <u>あかい　マグカップ</u>は　いくらですか。

   B : <u>1,000 えん</u>です。

1. A : ....

   B : ....

2. A : ....

   B : ....

3. A : ....

   B : ....

4. A : ....

   B : ....

5. A : ....

   B : ....

IV Make up dialogues following the patterns of the examples and based on the information provided.

A. *Ask and answer whether an item is from a given country.*

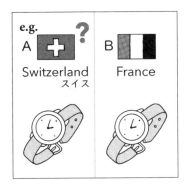 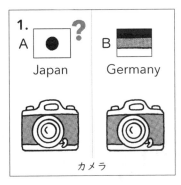 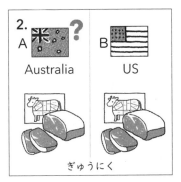

e.g. A：これは　スイスの　とけいですか。

B：いいえ、スイスのじゃありません。フランスのです。

1. A： ....

B： ....

2. A： ....

B： ....

B. *Ask and answer what an item's country of origin is.*

  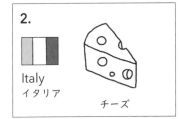

e.g. A：これは　どこの　ビールですか。

B：ちゅうごくのです。

1. A： ....

B： ....

2. A： ....

B： ....

スイス	Switzerland	イタリア	Italy
カメラ	camera	チーズ	cheese
ぎゅうにく	beef		
くつ	shoes		

V *Ask the price of more than one item.* Make up dialogues following the pattern of the example and based on the information provided. Change the pronoun to fit each item.

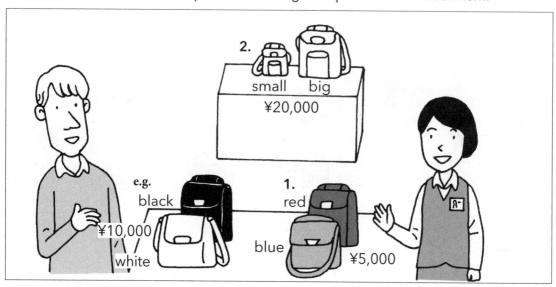

e.g. スミス　　　　：この　しろい　かばんは　いくらですか。

　　みせの　ひと：10,000 えんです。

　　スミス　　　　：この　くろい　かばんも　10,000 えんですか。

　　みせの　ひと：はい、それも　10,000 えんです。

1. スミス　　　　：..

　　みせの　ひと：..

　　スミス　　　　：..

　　みせの　ひと：..

2. スミス　　　　：..

　　みせの　ひと：..

　　スミス　　　　：..

　　みせの　ひと：..

VI *State what you want to buy and the quantity.* Make up sentences following the pattern of the example and based on the information provided.

e.g. スミス：その　みかんを　みっつ　ください。

1. スミス：..

2. スミス：..

3. スミス：..

4. スミス：..

VII *Ask the price of an item and where it was made. State how many you want.* Make up dialogues following the pattern of the example. Substitute the underlined parts with the alternatives given.

    e.g. スミス　　　　：すみません。その　<u>ワイン</u>は　いくらですか。

    みせの　ひと：1,200 えんです。

    スミス　　　　：それは　どこの　<u>ワイン</u>ですか。

    みせの　ひと：<u>フランス</u>のです。

    スミス　　　　：じゃ、それを　<u>2ほん</u>　ください。

1. スミス　　　：...（コーヒーカップ）

   みせの　ひと：...

   スミス　　　：...（コーヒーカップ）

   みせの　ひと：...（イギリス）

   スミス　　　：..（むっつ）

VOCABULARY

みかん	mikan orange		コーヒーカップ	coffee cup
あかワイン	red wine (In the case of wine, red wine is not			
	あかい　ワイン, but あかワイン. Likewise,			
	white wine is しろワイン.)			

2. スミス　　　：.. （タオル）

　　みせの　ひと：..

　　スミス　　　：.. （タオル）

　　みせの　ひと：.. （イタリア）

　　スミス　　　：.. （4まい）

Ⅷ Listen to the audio and choose the correct answers.　　　　　　　　　　🔊 059

　1. Where is the beer from?

　　ⓐにほん　　　　　ⓑアメリカ　　　ⓒドイツ

　2. How much does the beer cost?

　　ⓐ 300えん　　　ⓑ 200えん　　ⓒ 100えん

　3. How many bottles did the man buy?

　　ⓐ 1ぽん　　　　ⓑ 5ほん　　　ⓒ 10ぽん

SPEAKING PRACTICE

1. Smith is shopping in a clothing store.　　　　　　　　　　🔊 060

　スミス　　　　：すみません。あの　Tシャツは　いくらですか。

　みせの　ひと：どれですか。

　スミス　　　　：あの　あおい　Tシャツです。

　みせの　ひと：2,000えんです。

Smith:　　　　 Excuse me. How much is that T-shirt over there?
Shopkeeper:　Which one is it?
Smith:　　　　 That blue T-shirt.
Shopkeeper:　That one is 2,000 yen.

タオル　towel
どれ　　which one (of three or more things; see NOTES 1, p. 47)

2. Chan is shopping in a cake shop. 🔊 061

みせの　ひと：いらっしゃいませ。

チャン　　　：チーズケーキを　みっつと　アップルパイを　ふたつ　ください。

みせの　ひと：はい。2,500 えんです。

Shopkeeper: Hello, how are you today.
Chan: I would like three of the cheese cakes and two of the apple pies.
Shopkeeper: All right. That will be 2,500 yen.

3. Chan is asking something to a shopkeeper in a shopping mall. 🔊 062

チャン　　　：おてあらいは　どこですか。

みせの　ひと：あちらです。

チャン　　　：どうも。

Chan: Can you tell me where the restroom is?
Shopkeeper: It is over there.
Chan: Thanks.

NOTES

1. どれですか。
   どれ is used when asking about an item among three or more. どちら is used when asking about one of two items.

2. あちらです。
   あちら is the demonstrative pronoun used for a place distant from both the speaker and the listener. あちら is the polite form of the pronoun あそこ.

3. どうも。
   This is a colloquial shortening of どうも　ありがとう.

Active Communication

1. Ask people around you where an item they own is from (i.e., what its country of origin is).

2. If you're in Japan, go shopping and buy more than one of an item. Be sure to use the pattern "number of items ください."

VOCABULARY

チーズケーキ	cheese cake	どうも。	Thanks.
アップルパイ	apple pie		
おてあらい	restroom		
あちら	over there		

I Complete the dialogues by choosing words from the box below. Do not use the same word more than once.

なん　　だれ　　いつ　　どこ　　なんじ　　いくら

1. スミス：これは　（　　　　）の　ペンですか。

すずき：わたしのです。

2. ささき　：ロンドンは　いま　（　　　　）ですか。

なかむら：ごぜん　９じです。

3. スミス　：かいぎは　（　　　　）ですか。

なかむら：あしたの　４じからです。

4. スミス：あれは　（　　　　）ですか。

すずき：とけいです。

5. スミス　　　：それは　（　　　　）の　ワインですか。

みせの　ひと：にほんのです。

スミス　　　：（　　　　）ですか。

みせの　ひと：1,200 えんです。

II What do you say in the following situations?

1. You order curry and salad at a restaurant.

....

2. You want to know where the restrooms are.

....

3. In a shop, you want to see something located near the salesperson.

....

4. You ask a restaurant employee when the lunchtime begins and ends.

....

GETTING AROUND

Japan boasts one of the most convenient transportation systems in the world. All major cities from Kagoshima in southern Japan to Tokyo in the east and Hakodate in the north are connected by bullet train. Other train systems connect towns and outlying suburbs of cities. In large metropolitan areas such as Tokyo, Nagoya, and Osaka, there are also extensive subway systems. All modes of public transportation depart and arrive on exact schedules. Some trains show news and advertising in video formats.

Going Places (1): Where Are You Going?

TARGET DIALOGUE
🔊 063

Smith calls Chan at the Osaka branch office at her mobile phone.

チャン：はい、チャンです。

スミス：とうきょうししゃの　スミスです。おはようございます。

チャン：おはようございます。

スミス：あした　そちらに　いきます。かいぎは　１じからですね。

チャン：はい、１じからです。ひとりで　きますか。

スミス：いいえ、かとうさんと　いきます。

チャン：そうですか。では、あした。

スミス：しつれいします。

チャン：しつれいします。

■スミスさんは　あした　かとうさんと　おおさかししゃに　いきます。

Chan:　Hello, this is Chan.
Smith:　This is Smith, of the Tokyo branch. Good morning.
Chan:　Good morning.
Smith:　I will visit you tomorrow.
　　　　The meeting is from 1:00 P.M., right?
Chan:　Yes, it is from 1:00. Will you be coming alone?
Smith:　No, I'm going with Kato-san.
Chan:　I see. Well, we will see you tomorrow, then.
Smith:　Good bye.
Chan:　Good bye.

■Smith-san will go to the Osaka branch office with Kato-san tomorrow.

VOCABULARY

とうきょうししゃ	Tokyo branch
ししゃ	branch (office of a company)
おはようございます。	Good morning.
そちら	there [where you are]
に	to (particle; see GRAMMAR 2, p. 52)
いきます	go
ね	right?, isn't it? (particle; see NOTES 2, p. 51)
ひとりで	alone
きます	come
と	with, together with (particle; see GRAMMAR 4, p. 52)
では	well then
しつれいします。	Good bye.
おおさかししゃ	Osaka branch
おおさか	Osaka (city in western Japan)

NOTES

1. はい、チャンです。

   When answering the phone people often say はい before giving their name.

2. かいぎは　１じからですね。

   The particle ね comes at the end of a sentence or phrase and, like "isn't it?" in English, seeks confirmation from the other person. It is spoken with a rising intonation. ね is used when expressing admiration and praise, seeking agreement or empathy, and agreeing with what one's listener says, but in that case is pronounced with a falling intonation, sometimes drawing out the vowel: ねえ.

3. ひとりで　きますか。
   いいえ、かとうさんと　いきます。

   The Japanese verbs いきます and きます are always used from the point of view of the speaker. いきます expresses the idea of moving from where the speaker is now to some other place. きます, on the other hand, expresses the idea of moving toward the place where the speaker is now. Therefore, unlike in English, a speaker talking about going to the place where the listener is located, as in the above exchange, uses いきます rather than きます.

4. しつれいします。

   This expression is used as a form of "good-bye" when hanging up the phone or leaving a house or room. It is also used when entering a house or room, passing in front of someone, leaving in the middle of a gathering, and so on, to mean "excuse me."

KEY SENTENCES 🔊 064

1. スミスさんは　あした　ぎんこうに　いきます。
2. スミスさんは　せんしゅう　おおさかに　いきました。
3. スミスさんは　きのう　ともだちと　レストランに　いきました。
4. スミスさんは　きょねん　アメリカから　きました。

1. Smith-san is going to the bank tomorrow.
2. Smith-san went to Osaka last week.
3. Smith-san went to a restaurant with a friend yesterday.
4. Smith-san came from the United States last year.

GRAMMAR

1. Verbs (KS1, 2, 3, 4)

Japanese sentences end with a verb (or some other element followed by です, which behaves like a verb). The endings of verbs show the tense and whether the verb is affirmative or negative. Tenses of Japanese verbs can be divided roughly into two large categories:

(1) The present form (KS1)

The present form, or ます-form—so called because verbs in this tense end in ます—also expresses a future action.

VOCABULARY

せんしゅう	last week
いきました	went
きのう	yesterday
ともだち	friend

きょねん	last year
から	from (particle; see GRAMMAR 5, p. 52)
きました	came

(2) The past form

(KS2, 3, 4)

When expressing the past tense, ます changes to ました.

The chart below summarizes the tenses of Japanese verbs and shows the endings—affirmative and negative—that correspond to each.

Present form		Past form	
aff.	*neg.*	*aff.*	*neg.*
～ます	～ません	～ました	～ませんでした

To ask a question like "will you go?" that contains a verb, simply add か to the verb. Answers to such questions can be brief, as in the examples below.

e.g. スミスさんは　あした　きょうとに　いきますか。　Smith-san, will you go to Kyoto tomorrow?

はい、いきます。　　　　　　　　　　　　Yes, (I) will go.

いいえ、いきません。　　　　　　　　　　No, (I) will not go.

2. personは　place/eventに　いきます。

(KS1, 2, 3)

The role of the preposition "to" in English is played by the particle に in Japanese. に is placed after a noun that denotes a place or an event. It indicates the direction of movement with motion verbs such as いきます ("go"), きます ("come"), かえります ("return").

In this pattern, the particle へ (pronounced え) can also be used in place of に.

e.g. スミスさんは　パーティーに／へ　いきます。

Smith-san is going to the party.

3. Relative time expressions

(KS1, 2, 3, 4)

Relative time expressions like あした ("tomorrow"), らいしゅう ("next week"), こんげつ ("this month"), and きょねん ("last year") generally do not take particles.

4. personと

(KS3)

Use the particle と ("with") to indicate the person accompanied.

5. personは　placeから　きました。

(KS4)

When explaining that someone moved from one place to another, attach the particle から to the place of departure. どこから　きましたか means "Where did you come from?" and when Japanese ask non-Japanese this question, it usually means they want to know their country of origin.

WORD POWER

I Destinations

①くうこう　　②えき　　③ししゃ　　④こうえん　　⑤ともだちの うち

II Verbs

①いきます　　②きます

III Time expressions

	Last	This	Next
day	きのう	きょう	あした
week	せんしゅう	こんしゅう	らいしゅう
month	せんげつ	こんげつ	らいげつ
year	きょねん	ことし	らいねん

IV People

①ともだち　　②どうりょう　　③じょうし　　④かぞく　　⑤がくせい

VOCABULARY

くうこう	airport	らいしゅう	next week	らいねん	next year
えき	station	せんげつ	last month	どうりょう	colleague, coworker
こうえん	park	こんげつ	this month	じょうし	boss, superior
うち	house, home	らいげつ	next month	かぞく	family
こんしゅう	this week	ことし	this year	がくせい	student

EXERCISES

I *Practice conjugating verbs.* Repeat the verbs below and memorize their forms—present and past, affirmative and negative.

	Present form		Past form	
	aff.	*neg.*	*aff.*	*neg.*
go	いきます	いきません	いきました	いきませんでした
come	きます	きません	きました	きませんでした

II Make up sentences following the patterns of the examples. Substitute the underlined part with the alternatives given.

A. *State where someone will go.*

e.g. スミスさんは　ぎんこうに　いきます。

1. .... （くうこう）

2. .... （かんこく）

3. .... （コンサート）

B. *State when someone will go to a particular place.*

e.g. スミスさんは　あした　きょうとに　いきます。

1. .... （らいしゅう）

2. .... （らいげつ）

3. .... （あさって）

C. *State when someone went to a particular place.*

e.g. スミスさんは　きのう　ホンコンに　いきました。

1. .... （せんしゅう）

2. .... （せんげつ）

3. .... （おととい）

VOCABULARY

かんこく	South Korea, ROK	おととい	day before yesterday
きょうと	Kyoto		
あさって	day after tomorrow		
ホンコン	Hong Kong		

Ⅲ Make up dialogues following the patterns of the examples. Substitute the underlined part with the alternatives given.

A. *Ask and answer whether someone will go to a particular place.*

e.g. A：スミスさんは　あした　<u>きょうと</u>に　いきますか。

B：はい、いきます。

1. A： ....

（とうきょうえき）

B： ....

2. A： ....

（ぎんざの　デパート）

B： ....

B. *Ask and answer whether someone will go to a particular place.*

e.g A：スミスさんは　あした　<u>ぎんこう</u>に　いきますか。

B：いいえ、いきません。

1. A： ....

（おおさかししゃ）

B： ....

2. A： ....

（くうこう）

B： ....

C. *Ask and answer whether someone went to a particular place.*

e.g. A：スミスさんは　きのう　<u>おおさかししゃ</u>に　いきましたか。

B：はい、いきました。

1. A： ....

（パーティー）

B： ....

2. A： ....

（ともだちの　うち）

B： ....

VOCABULARY

とうきょうえき	Tokyo Station
ぎんざ	Ginza (district in Tokyo)

D. *Ask and answer whether someone went to a particular place.*

    e.g. A：スミスさんは　きのう　<u>たいしかん</u>に　いきましたか。

        B：いいえ、いきませんでした。

    1. A：＿＿＿＿＿＿＿＿＿＿＿＿＿＿＿＿＿＿＿＿＿（ジム）

        B：＿＿＿＿＿＿＿＿＿＿＿＿＿＿＿＿＿＿＿＿＿＿＿

    2. A：＿＿＿＿＿＿＿＿＿＿＿＿＿＿＿＿＿＿＿（ぎんこう）

        B：＿＿＿＿＿＿＿＿＿＿＿＿＿＿＿＿＿＿＿＿＿＿＿

Ⅳ Make up dialogues following the patterns of the examples. Substitute the underlined part with the alternatives given.

    A. *Ask and answer where someone will go.*

    e.g. A：スミスさんは　あした　どこに　いきますか。

        B：<u>のぞみデパート</u>に　いきます。

    1. A：＿＿＿＿＿＿＿＿＿＿＿＿＿＿＿＿＿＿＿＿＿＿＿

        B：＿＿＿＿＿＿＿＿＿＿＿＿＿＿＿（ほっかいどう）

    2. A：＿＿＿＿＿＿＿＿＿＿＿＿＿＿＿＿＿＿＿＿＿＿＿

        B：＿＿＿＿＿＿＿＿＿＿＿＿＿＿（ともだちの　うち）

    B. *Ask and answer when someone will go to a particular place.*

    e.g. A：かとうさんは　いつ　おおさかししゃに　いきますか。

        B：<u>らいしゅう</u>　いきます。

    1. A：＿＿＿＿＿＿＿＿＿＿＿＿＿＿＿＿＿＿＿＿＿＿＿

        B：＿＿＿＿＿＿＿＿＿＿＿＿＿＿＿＿＿＿＿（あした）

    2. A：＿＿＿＿＿＿＿＿＿＿＿＿＿＿＿＿＿＿＿＿＿＿＿

        B：＿＿＿＿＿＿＿＿＿＿＿＿＿＿＿＿＿（らいげつ）

| ほっかいどう | Hokkaido (island in northern Japan) |

V *State whom someone will go somewhere with.* Make up sentences following the pattern of the example. Substitute the underlined word with the alternatives given.

e.g. チャンさんは <u>ともだちと</u> レストランに いきます。

1. .... （なかむらさん）

2. .... （エマさん）

3. .... （どうりょう）

VI *Ask and answer whom someone will go somewhere with.* Make up dialogues following the pattern of the example. Substitute the underlined part with the alternatives given.

e.g. A：スミスさんは あした だれと のぞみデパートに いきますか。
　　 B：<u>かとうさんと</u> いきます。

1. A： ....

　 B： .... （エマさん）

2. A： ....

　 B： .... （じょうし）

VII Make up sentences following the patterns of the examples. Substitute the underlined parts with the alternatives given.

A. *State who came to a particular place.*

e.g. <u>スミスさんは</u> <u>きょねん</u> にほんに きました。

1. .... （ブラウンさん、せんげつ）

2. .... （アレンさん、おととい）

3. ....
　　　　　　　　　　　　　　　　　　　　　　　 （ハリスさん、せんしゅう）

B. *State where someone came from.*

e.g. <u>スミスさんは</u> きょねん <u>アメリカ</u>から きました。

1. .... （チャンさん、ホンコン）

2. .... （エマさん、フランス）

3. .... （ホフマンさん、ドイツ）

VOCABULARY

アレン　　　Allen (surname)

VIII *State when, where, and with whom someone will travel/traveled to a destination.* Make up sentences following the pattern of the example and based on the information provided.

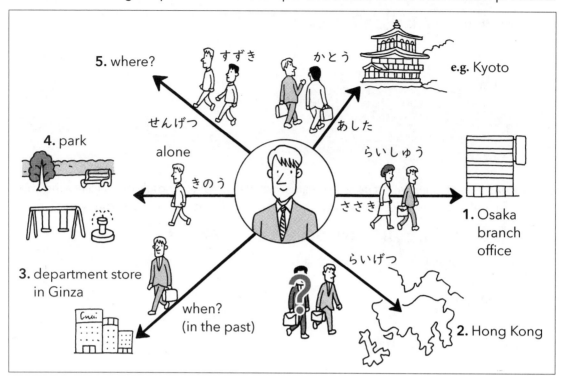

e.g. スミスさんは <u>あした　かとうさんと　きょうとに　いきます</u>。

1. ....

2. ....

3. ....

4. ....

5. ....

IX *Talk about when and with whom you are going somewhere.* Make up dialogues following the pattern of the example. Substitute the underlined parts with the alternatives given.

Smith is talking on the phone with a person from the Yokohama branch office.

e.g. よこはまししゃの　ひと：スミスさんは　いつ　よこはまししゃに　きますか。

スミス　　　　　　　　　：<u>あした</u>　いきます。

よこはまししゃの　ひと：だれと　きますか。

スミス　　　　　　　　　：<u>ささきさんと</u>　いきます。

よこはまししゃの　ひと：そうですか。

VOCABULARY

よこはま　　　　Yokohama (city near Tokyo)

1. よこはまししゃの　ひと：...

   スミス　　　　　　　　：...（らいしゅう）

   よこはまししゃの　ひと：...

   スミス　　　　　　　　：...（すずきさん）

   よこはまししゃの　ひと：...

2. よこはまししゃの　ひと：...

   スミス　　　　　　　　：...（あさって）

   よこはまししゃの　ひと：...

   スミス　　　　　　　　：...（かとうさん）

   よこはまししゃの　ひと：...

X Listen to the audio and fill in the blanks based on the information you hear.　🔊 069-071

1. スミスさんは　あさって　..........................と　..........................に　いきます。

2. スミスさんは　きのう　..........................と　..........................に　いきました。

3. エマさんは　きょねん　..........................から　きました。

SPEAKING PRACTICE

1. From today, Raja is starting an internship at ABC Foods.　🔊 072

   ささき　　　　　　　　：こちらは　インターンの　ラジャさんです。
   ラジャ　　　　　　　　：はじめまして。ラジャです。インドから　きました。
   　　　　　　　　　　　　とうきょうだいがくの　がくせいです。
   　　　　　　　　　　　　きょうから　よろしく　おねがいします。
   かいしゃの　ひとたち：よろしく　おねがいします。

   Sasaki:　　　　This is Raja-san, our intern.
   Raja:　　　　　Nice to meet you. My name is Raja. I am from India.
   　　　　　　　　I am a student at the University of Tokyo.
   　　　　　　　　[From today] I look forward to working with you.
   Company staff:　Nice to meet you!

VOCABULARY	
インターン	intern
の	(particle; see NOTES 1, p. 60)
ひとたち	people
～たち	(plural for people)

2. At a bus stop, Smith asks the driver a question before boarding. 🔊 073

スミス	：すみません。この　バスは　しぶやに　いきますか。
バスの　うんてんしゅ	：いいえ、いきません。
スミス	：どの　バスが　いきますか。
バスの　うんてんしゅ	：6 ばんの　バスが　いきます。
スミス	：ありがとうございます。

Smith: Excuse me. Does this bus go to Shibuya?
Bus driver: No, it doesn't go to Shibuya.
Smith: Which bus goes there?
Bus driver: The No. 6 bus goes there.
Smith: Thank you.

NOTES

1. インターンの　ラジャさん

This particle の here expresses apposition, not possession or affiliation, and it means Raja is an intern.

2. どの　バス

どれ is used alone to mean "which," but if "which" is to be followed by a noun, then どの is used.

e.g. どれ   which one
　　 どの　バス   which bus

3. どの　バス　いきますか。
6 ばんの　バスが　いきます。

The particle が, the subject marker, is used instead of the topic marker は after interrogatives like どれ and どの. が is repeated in replies to questions of the どれが or どの…が pattern, as in the exchange here.

Active Communication

Ask people around you where they are going tomorrow, next week, next month, and so on.

VOCABULARY

バス	bus	が	(particle; see NOTES 2, above)
しぶや	Shibuya (district in Tokyo)	〜ばん	number… (suffix for number)
うんてんしゅ	driver		
どの	which (of three or more things)		

Going Places (2): I'm Going by Shinkansen

TARGET DIALOGUE 🔊 074

Smith is carrying a suitcase. Nakamura notices and calls out to him.

なかむら：あ、スミスさん、しゅっちょうですか。

スミス　：ええ、かとうさんと　おおさかししゃに　いきます。
　　　　　きんようびに　とうきょうに　かえります。

なかむら：ひこうきで　いきますか。

スミス　：いいえ、しんかんせんで　いきます。

なかむら：そうですか。いってらっしゃい。

■ スミスさんは　かとうさんと　しんかんせんで　おおさかに
　いきます。きんようびに　とうきょうに　かえります。

Nakamura: Ah! Smith-san, are you going on a business trip?
Smith:　　Yes. I'm going to the Osaka branch office with Kato-san. I'll be back to Tokyo on Friday.
Nakamura: Are you going by airplane?
Smith:　　No. We're going by Shinkansen.
Nakamura: I see. Have a good trip.

■Smith-san will go to Osaka with Kato-san by Shinkansen.
They will return to Tokyo on Friday.

VOCABULARY

あ	ah, oh (see NOTES 1, p. 62)	ひこうき	airplane
しゅっちょう	business trip	で	by means of (particle; see GRAMMAR 2, p. 62)
ええ	yes (a softer way of saying はい)		
きんようび	Friday	しんかんせん	superexpress train, Shinkansen
に	at, in, on (particle; see GRAMMAR 1, p. 62)	いってらっしゃい。	Have a good trip., Have a good day.
かえります	return, come back		

61

NOTES

1. あ、スミスさん、しゅっちょうですか。

   あ is an utterance expressing having just noticed something. It is also used to get someone's attention.

2. しゅっちょうですか。

   Nakamura asks if Smith is going on a business trip because he is carrying a suitcase and is clearly on his way somewhere. She means, "Are you going on business?"

KEY SENTENCES
 075

> **1.** エマさんは　4がつに　にほんに　きました。
> **2.** スミスさんは　しんかんせんで　おおさかに　いきます。
> **3.** かいぎは　よっかですか、ようかですか。
>
> 1. Emma-san came to Japan in April.
> 2. Smith-san is going to Osaka by Shinkansen.
> 3. Is the meeting on the 4th or on the 8th?

GRAMMAR

1. Specific time expressions   (KS1)

When stating the time of a certain action, unlike relative time expressions (see L6, GRAMMAR 3, p. 52), specific time expressions take the particle に.

e.g. 5じに	at 5:00
どようびに	on Saturday
12にちに	on the twelfth
2025ねんに	in 2025

2. transportationで   (KS2)

When indicating means of movement, the particle で is attached to the noun indicating the means of transportation.

e.g. バスで　　　by bus
　　 タクシーで　by taxi

But to say "by foot," use あるいて, e.g., あるいて　きました, (I) walked here.
To ask the means by which someone will go somewhere, use なんで.

e.g. なんで　いきますか。　　How will you go?
　　 バスで　いきます。　　　I'll go by bus.

Since なんで means "Why?" in colloquial speech, なにで can be used in place of なんで to avoid confusion.

3. noun 1は　noun 2ですか、noun 3ですか。   (KS3)

This is the expression for confirming which of two alternatives (noun 2 or noun 3) is correct. The intonation rises for か in each case.

VOCABULARY

4がつ（しがつ）	April	ようか	8th, eighth (of the month)
よっか	4th, fourth (of the month)		

WORD POWER

I Verb

 076

かえります

II Dates

 077

Years		
1998 ねん	せん　きゅうひゃく　きゅうじゅう　はち　ねん	the year 1998
2022 ねん	にせん　にじゅう　に　ねん	the year 2022

Days of the week	
にちようび	Sunday
げつようび	Monday
かようび	Tuesday
すいようび	Wednesday
もくようび	Thursday
きんようび	Friday
どようび	Saturday

Months			
いちがつ	January	しちがつ	July
にがつ	February	はちがつ	August
さんがつ	March	くがつ	September
しがつ	April	じゅうがつ	October
ごがつ	May	じゅういちがつ	November
ろくがつ	June	じゅうにがつ	December

Days of the month					
ついたち	1st	じゅういちにち	11th	にじゅういちにち	21st
ふつか	2nd	じゅうににち	12th	にじゅうににち	22nd
みっか	3rd	じゅうさんにち	13th	にじゅうさんにち	23rd
よっか	4th	じゅうよっか	14th	にじゅうよっか	24th
いつか	5th	じゅうごにち	15th	にじゅうごにち	25th
むいか	6th	じゅうろくにち	16th	にじゅうろくにち	26th
なのか	7th	じゅうしちにち	17th	にじゅうしちにち	27th
ようか	8th	じゅうはちにち	18th	にじゅうはちにち	28th
ここのか	9th	じゅうくにち	19th	にじゅうくにち	29th
とおか	10th	はつか	20th	さんじゅうにち	30th
				さんじゅういちにち	31st

NOTE: Months and dates are written in hiragana here, but elsewhere in the book numerals are used to write them, e.g., １がつ for "January," １１にち for "the eleventh," etc.

VOCABULARY

～ねん	the year...
～ようび	day of the week
～がつ	month
～にち	day

Ⅲ Means of transportation

🔊 078

①でんしゃ

②ちかてつ

③くるま

④タクシー

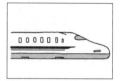
⑤しんかんせん

⑥ひこうき

⑦バイク

⑧じてんしゃ

EXERCISES

Ⅰ *State when an event will be held.* Make up sentences following the pattern of the example. Substitute the underlined part with the alternatives given.

e.g. かいぎは　<u>すいようび</u>です。

1. .... （げつようび）

2. .... （４がつ　はつか）

Ⅱ Make up dialogues following the patterns of the examples. Substitute the underlined parts with the alternatives given.

A. *Ask and answer when an event will be held.*

e.g. A：おまつりは　<u>なんがつ</u>ですか。
B：<u>９がつ</u>です。

1. A： .... （なんにち）
   B： .... （１７にち）

2. A： .... （なんようび）
   B： .... （にちようび）

VOCABULARY

でんしゃ	train	バイク	motorbike	なんにち	what day
ちかてつ	subway	じてんしゃ	bicycle	なんようび	what day of the week
くるま	car	（お）まつり	festival		
タクシー	taxi	なんがつ	what month		

B. *Ask and answer the questions about events.*

e.g. A：<u>たんじょうび</u>は　いつですか。

B：<u>8がつ　19にち</u>です。

1. A：＿＿＿＿＿＿＿＿＿＿＿＿＿＿＿＿＿　（かいぎ）

B：＿＿＿＿＿＿＿＿＿＿＿＿＿＿＿（7がつ　ついたち）

2. A：＿＿＿＿＿＿＿＿＿＿＿＿＿＿＿＿（パーティー）

B：＿＿＿＿＿＿＿＿＿＿＿＿＿（らいしゅうの　どようび）

3. A：＿＿＿＿＿＿＿＿＿＿＿＿＿＿＿＿＿　（プレゼン）

B：＿＿＿＿＿＿＿＿＿＿＿＿＿（こんしゅうの　きんようび）

4. A：＿＿＿＿＿＿＿＿＿＿＿＿＿＿＿＿（コンサート）

B：＿＿＿＿＿＿＿＿＿＿＿＿＿＿（9がつ　19にち）

C. *Ask and answer when an event will be held.*

e.g. A：<u>なつやすみ</u>は　いつから　いつまでですか。

B：<u>9がつ　ふつか</u>から　<u>なのか</u>までです。

1. A：＿＿＿＿＿＿＿＿＿＿＿＿＿＿＿＿＿（しゅっちょう）

B：＿＿＿＿＿＿＿＿＿＿＿＿＿＿＿＿＿

（げつようび、もくようび）

2. A：＿＿＿＿＿＿＿＿＿＿＿＿＿＿＿＿（りょこう）

B：＿＿＿＿＿＿＿＿＿＿＿＿＿＿＿＿＿

（4がつ　29にち、5がつ　いつか）

たんじょうび	birthday		りょこう	trip
なつやすみ	summer vacation			
なつ	summer			
やすみ	vacation			

Ⅲ Make up sentences or dialogues following the patterns of the examples and based on the information provided.

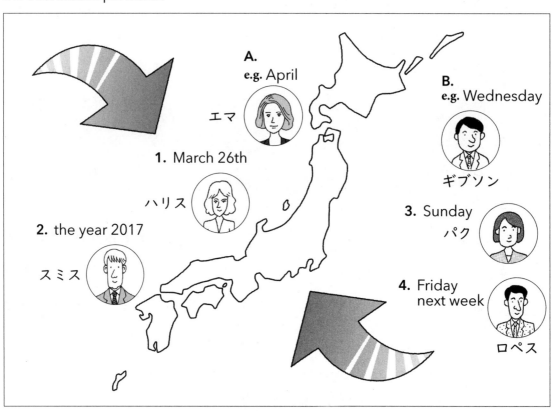

A. *State when someone came to a particular place.*

e.g. <u>エマさん</u>は　<u>4がつ</u>に　にほんに　きました。

1. ....

2. ....

B. *Ask and answer when someone will come to Japan.*

e.g. A：<u>ギブソンさん</u>は　いつ　にほんに　きますか。
　　B：<u>すいようび</u>に　きます。

3. A：...

　　B：...

4. A：...

　　B：...

IV *State how someone got home.* Make up sentenes following the pattern of the example. Substitute the underlined part with the alternatives given.

    e.g. スミスさんは　<u>ちかてつで</u>　うちに　かえりました。

    1. ....（タクシーで）

    2. ....（でんしゃで）

    3. ....（あるいて）

V *Ask and answer how someone will go to Osaka.* Make up dialogues following the pattern of the example. Substitute the underlined part with the alternatives given.

    e.g. A：スミスさんは　なんで　おおさかに　いきますか。

          B：<u>くるまで</u>　いきます。

    1. A：..

          B：..（しんかんせん）

    2. A：..

          B：..（ひこうき）

VOCABULARY

あるいて　　on foot, walking
なんで　　by what means

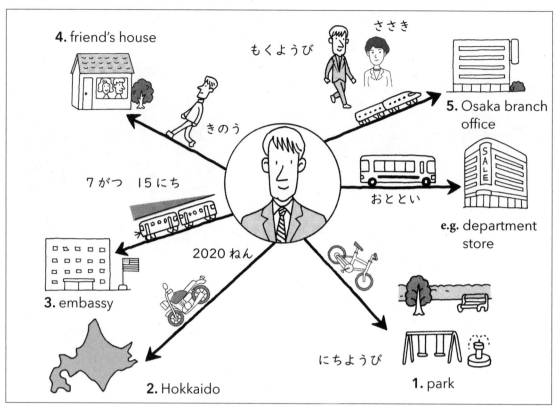

VI *State when and how someone traveled.* Make up sentences following the pattern of the example and based on the information provided.

4. friend's house

もくようび

ささき

5. Osaka branch office

きのう

7がつ 15にち

おととい

e.g. department store

2020 ねん

3. embassy

にちようび

2. Hokkaido

1. park

e.g. スミスさんは　<u>おととい　バスで　デパートに</u>　いきました。

1.

2.

3.

4.

5.

Ⅶ *Describe a schedule.* Make up sentences following the pattern of the example and based on the information provided in the page from Smith's weekly planner.

e.g.	Mon.	12:00	Go to Tokyo Hotel (by taxi, with Suzuki-san)
	Tue.		
1.	Wed.		Go to Osaka branch office (by airplane, alone)
	Thu.		
2.	Fri.	1:00	Go to Nozomi Department Store
		4:00	Go to Yokohama branch office (with Sasaki-san)
		6:00	Go to the American Embassy
	Sat.		
3.	Sun.	9:00 a.m.	Go to the park (with friends)
		7:00 p.m.	Go to Suzuki-san's house (with colleagues)

e.g. スミスさんは　げつようびの　12じに　すずきさんと　タクシーで
とうきょうホテルに　いきます。

1. ....

....

2. ....

....

3. ....

....

Ⅷ *Ask whether the event time is one or another day/hour.* Make up dialogues following the pattern of the example. Substitute the underlined parts with the alternatives given.

e.g. A：かいぎは　よっかですか、ようかですか。
B：よっかです。

1. A：... （みっか、むいか）

B：... （みっか）

2. A：... （4:00、5:00）

B：... （5:00）

とうきょうホテル　Tokyo Hotel (fictitious hotel name)
ホテル　　　　　　hotel

Ⅸ *Talk about when and how to travel.* Make up dialogues following the pattern of the example and based on the information provided.

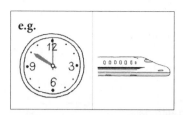

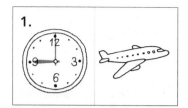

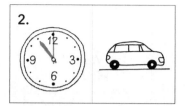

Smith is talking over the phone with Chan of the Osaka branch office.

e.g. チャン：らいしゅうの　げつようびに　そちらに　いきます。

スミス：なんじに　きますか。

チャン：10 じに　いきます。

スミス：なんで　きますか。

チャン：しんかんせんで　いきます。

スミス：そうですか。

1. チャン：..

スミス：..

チャン：..

スミス：..

チャン：..

スミス：..

2. チャン：..

スミス：..

チャン：..

スミス：..

チャン：..

スミス：..

X Listen to the audio and choose the correct answers. 079, 080

1. When and how will Emma go to Osaka?

    1)   ⓐげつようび   ⓑもくようび   ⓒすいようび

    2)   ⓐ    ⓑ 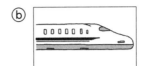   ⓒ

2. What time is the meeting?

    ⓐ１じ   ⓑ７じ

SPEAKING PRACTICE

1. Kato and Smith arrive at the Osaka branch office and Chan shows them to the meeting room. 081

チャン：(Opening the door.) どうぞ。

かとう：しつれいします。(Enters the room.)

スミス：しつれいします。(Enters the room.)

チャン：どうぞ　おかけください。

スミス：ありがとうございます。

Chan: Please go on in.
Kato: Thank you. (Excuse me.)
Smith: Thank you. (Excuse me.)
Chan: Please have a seat.
Smith: Thank you.

2. Nakamura and Raja are talking during their break. 082

なかむら：ラジャさんは　いつ　にほんに　きましたか。

ラジャ　：きょねんの　９がつに　きました。

なかむら：そうですか。なつやすみに　インドに　かえりますか。

ラジャ　：いいえ、かえりません。ともだちと　ほっかいどうに　いきます。

Nakamura: Raja-san, when did you come to Japan?
Raja: I came in September last year.
Nakamura: Ah, I see. Will you go back to India during the summer vacation?
Raja: No, I won't go back. I'm going to Hokkaido with a friend.

VOCABULARY

しつれいします。   Excuse me.
おかけください。   Please have a seat.

3. Smith and Emma are working.

083

スミス：かいぎは　いつですか。

エマ　：らいげつの　ようかです。

スミス：え？　よっかですか、ようかですか。

エマ　：ようかです。

スミス：ようかですね。

Smith: When is the meeting?
Emma: It's on the 8th of next month.
Smith: What? Is it the 4th or the 8th?
Emma: It's the 8th.
Smith: Right, the 8th.

NOTES

1. え？　よっかですか、ようかですか。

え is an utterance expressing uncertainty about what one has heard. It may be used when one is surprised.

Active Communication

1. Ask people around you when their birthdays are.

2. Ask people around you when their summer vacations are.

VOCABULARY

え   (see NOTES 1, above)

EATING OUT

The most famous type of Japanese food worldwide may be sushi, but numerous other dishes include tempura, shabu-shabu, yakitori, and soba. These dishes can be enjoyed in a wide range of establishments, from high-end restaurants to simple stalls people stop by on their way home from work. There are also places for eating and drinking late into the night, among which the izakaya are especially popular. Many restaurants around the cities, especially Tokyo, serve authentic world cuisines, so you can even get a sense of world travel by eating at the restaurants from different countries.

Doing Things (1): I'm Going to Eat Tempura

TARGET DIALOGUE

🔊 084

Smith and Sasaki are talking during their break.

ささき：しゅうまつに　なにを　しますか。

スミス：どようびに　ぎんざで　すずきさんと　てんぷらを　たべます。

ささき：そうですか。いいですね。

スミス：ささきさんは？

ささき：にちようびに　ともだちと　かぶきを　みます。

スミス：いいですね。

■スミスさんは　どようびに　ぎんざで　すずきさんと　てんぷらを
　たべます。
　ささきさんは　にちようびに　ともだちと　かぶきを　みます。

Sasaki: What are you going to do over the weekend?
Smith: On Saturday, I'm going to eat tempura in Ginza with Suzuki-san.
Sasaki: Really. That sounds nice.
Smith: How about you, Sasaki-san?
Sasaki: On Sunday, I'm going to see kabuki
        with a friend.
Smith: Oh, that sounds great.

■ Smith-san is going to eat tempura in Ginza
  with Suzuki-san on Saturday.
  Sasaki-san is going to see kabuki
  with a friend on Sunday.

VOCABULARY

しゅうまつ	weekend	で	at, in, on (particle; see GRAMMAR 2, p. 75)	いいですね。	That's good. (see NOTES 1, p. 75)
なに	what				
を	(particle; see GRAMMAR 1, p. 75)	てんぷら	tempura	かぶき	kabuki (see NOTES 3, p. 75)
		たべます	eat		
します	do			みます	see

NOTES

1. いいですね。
   This is the phrase that is used to express admiration or praise of the words or actions of someone.

2. ささきさんは？
   Spoken with a rising intonation, this means, "How about you, Sasaki-san, what are you going to do?"

3. かぶき
   Kabuki is a traditional performing art performed by male actors.

KEY SENTENCES 085

1. スミスさんは　あした　テニスを　します。
2. スミスさんは　きのう　レストランで　ばんごはんを　たべました。
3. エマさんは　パーティーで　なにも　たべませんでした。

1. Smith-san will play tennis tomorrow.
2. Smith-san ate supper at a restaurant yesterday.
3. Emma-san did not eat anything at the party.

GRAMMAR

1. person は　noun を　verb。 (KS1, 2)

Placed after a noun, the particle を, the object marker, indicates that the noun is the object of the sentence. を is used with verbs like みます("see"), よみます("read"), のみます("drink"), かいます("buy") and a host of others.

2. place/event で (KS2, 3)

The particle で is used when indicating the place or event in which a certain action is taken. It has the meaning of "at," "in," "on" in English. Word order in general: person は　time (に)　place/event で　noun を　verb.

3. なにも　in a negative sentence (KS3)

なにも is always used in negative statements such as わたしは　なにも　たべませんでした, meaning "I didn't eat anything." Likewise, だれも　いきませんでした means "Nobody went."

VOCABULARY

テニスを　します	play tennis	たべませんでした	did not eat
たべました	ate		
なにも　たべませんでした	didn't eat anything		
なにも　～ません	nothing (see GRAMMAR 3, above)		

WORD POWER

Ⅰ Food and drink
 086

①あさごはん ④ラーメン ⑦てんぷら ⑩おちゃ
②ひるごはん ⑤(お)すし ⑧スープ ⑪みず
③ばんごはん ⑥ステーキ ⑨にほんしゅ ⑫アイスクリーム

Ⅱ Verbs
087

①たべます ②のみます ③かいます ④よみます ⑤ききます

⑥みます ⑦テニスを します ⑧べんきょうを します ⑨かいものを します ⑩しごとを します

NOTE: For more on the "noun を します" verb type, see APPENDIX D, p. 246.

VOCABULARY

ひるごはん	lunch	おちゃ	green tea	ききます	listen to
ラーメン	ramen (Chinese noodle)	みず	water	べんきょうを します	study
(お)すし	sushi	アイスクリーム	ice cream	かいものを します	shop
ステーキ	steak	のみます	drink	しごとを します	work
スープ	soup	かいます	buy		
にほんしゅ	sake (Japanese rice liquor)	よみます	read		

III Numbers of people

088

☺	ひとり
☺☺	ふたり
☺☺☺	さんにん（3にん）
☺☺☺☺	よにん（4にん）
☺☺☺☺☺	ごにん（5にん）
?	なんにん

EXERCISES

I *Practice conjugating verbs.* Repeat the verbs below and memorize their forms—present and past, affirmative and negative.

	Present form		Past form	
	aff.	*neg.*	*aff.*	*neg.*
eat	たべます	たべません	たべました	たべませんでした
drink	のみます	のみません	のみました	のみませんでした
buy	かいます	かいません	かいました	かいませんでした
read	よみます	よみません	よみました	よみませんでした
listen to	ききます	ききません	ききました	ききませんでした
see	みます	みません	みました	みませんでした
do	します	しません	しました	しませんでした

ひとり	one person
ふたり	two people
～にん	…people
なんにん	how many people

II Make up sentences following the patterns of the examples. Substitute the underlined part with the alternatives given.

A. *State what someone will see.*

e.g. すずきさんは　<u>テレビ</u>を　みます。

1. ....（えいが）

2. ....（かぶき）

B. *State what someone will listen to.*

e.g. すずきさんは　<u>おんがく</u>を　ききます。

1. ....（ラジオ）

2. ....（ニュース）

III Make up sentences or dialogues following the patterns of the examples and based on the information provided.

A. *State what someone will do.*

e.g. スミスさんは　ステーキを　たべます。

1. ....

2. ....

3. ....

4. ....

VOCABULARY

えいが	movie
おんがく	music
ラジオ	radio
ニュース	news

B. *Ask and answer what someone will do.*

e.g. Ａ：スミスさんは　なにを　たべますか。

Ｂ：ステーキを　たべます。

1. Ａ：..

Ｂ：..

2. Ａ：..

Ｂ：..

3. Ａ：..

Ｂ：..

4. Ａ：..

Ｂ：..

Ⅳ Make up sentences following the patterns of the examples. Substitute the underlined part with the alternatives given.

A. *State where someone will drink something.*

e.g. すずきさんは　<u>うちで</u>　ビールを　のみます。

1. ....（レストラン）

2. ....（ホテルの　バー）

B. *State where someone will buy something.*

e.g. すずきさんは　<u>コンビニで</u>　みずを　かいます。

1. ....（スーパー）

2. ....（くうこう）

VOCABULARY

| バー | bar |
| コンビニ | convenience store |

Ⓥ Make up sentences or dialogues following the patterns of the examples and based on the information provided.

e.g. レストラン	1. としょかん	2. かいしゃ	3. コンビニ	4. こうえん
			sandwich	

A. *State where someone will do something.*

　　e.g. スミスさんは　レストランで　ばんごはんを　たべます。

　　1. ....

　　2. ....

　　3. ....

　　4. ....

B. *Ask and answer where someone will do something.*

　　e.g. A：スミスさんは　どこで　ばんごはんを　たべますか。

　　　　 B：レストランで　たべます。

　　1. A：...

　　　　 B：...

　　2. A：...

　　　　 B：...

　　3. A：...

　　　　 B：...

　　4. A：...

　　　　 B：...

VI *Ask and answer what someone did at an event.* Make up dialogues following the pattern of the example. Substitute the underlined parts with the appropriate forms of the alternatives given.

    e.g. A：おまつりで　なにを　<u>たべました</u>か。

        B：なにも　<u>たべませんでした</u>。

    1. A： .... （かいます）

        B： .... （かいます）

    2. A： .... （のみます）

        B： .... （のみます）

VII *Answer how many are in your party at a restaurant.* Make up dialogues following the pattern of the example and based on the information provided.

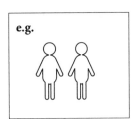 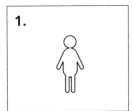 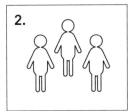 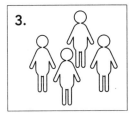

    e.g. A：なんめいさまですか。

        B：ふたりです。

    1. A：なんめいさまですか。

        B： ....

    2. A：なんめいさまですか。

        B： ....

    3. A：なんめいさまですか。

        B： ....

VOCABULARY

| なんめいさまですか。 How many people?（polite expression of なんにんですか）

VIII *Talk about what you did, where, and with whom.* Make up dialogues following the pattern of the example. Substitute the underlined parts with the alternatives given.

e.g. かとう：しゅうまつに　なにを　しましたか。

スミス：<u>ともだちと</u>　<u>ゴルフ</u>を　しました。

かとう：どこで　しましたか。

スミス：<u>はこね</u>で　しました。

かとう：そうですか。

1. かとう：_____

スミス：_____

（グリーンさん、テニス）

かとう：_____

スミス：_____

（ホテルの　テニスコート）

かとう：_____

2. かとう：_____

スミス：_____

（すずきさん、かいもの）

かとう：_____

スミス：_____

（ぎんざの　デパート）

かとう：_____

IX Listen to the audio and fill in the blanks based on the information you hear. 🔊 089

1. エマさんは　ぎんざで　_____を　かいました。

2. エマさんは　_____で　ひるごはんを　たべました。

VOCABULARY

ゴルフを　します	play golf
はこね	Hakone (popular travel destination southwest of Tokyo)
テニスコート	tennis court

SPEAKING PRACTICE

1. Suzuki phones a tempura restaurant called "Tenmasa." 🔊090

> みせの　ひと：てんまさでございます。
>
> すずき　　　　：よやくを　おねがいします。
>
> みせの　ひと：はい、ありがとうございます。
>
> すずき　　　　：どようびの　7じに　おねがいします。
>
> みせの　ひと：なんめいさまですか。
>
> すずき　　　　：ふたりです。
>
> みせの　ひと：はい、わかりました。では、おなまえと　おでんわばんごうを
> 　　　　　　　おねがいします。

Restaurant employee: This is Tenmasa.
Suzuki: I'd like to make a reservation.
Restaurant employee: Thank you.
Suzuki: Please make the reservation for 7:00 P.M. on Saturday.
Restaurant employee: How many people in your party?
Suzuki: For two, please.
Restaurant employee: Yes, well then. Please give me your name and your telephone number.

2. On Monday morning, Nakamura is talking to Smith. 🔊091

> なかむら：きのう　なにを　しましたか。
>
> スミス　：フリーマーケットに　いきました。
>
> なかむら：なにを　かいましたか。
>
> スミス　：なにも　かいませんでした。

Nakamura: What did you do yesterday?
Smith: I went to a flea market.
Nakamura: What did you buy?
Smith: I didn't buy anything.

Active Communication

1. Talk to people around you about your plans for the weekend.

2. Tell people around you about what you did the previous weekend.

VOCABULARY

てんまさ	Tenmasa (fictitious restaurant name)
～でございます	(polite form of ～です)
よやく	reservation
わかりました	understood, I see, I understand
わかります	understand, see, get it
おなまえ	your name
おでんわばんごう	your phone number
フリーマーケット	flea market

Doing Things (2): Do You Often Come Here?

TARGET DIALOGUE

🔊 092

Smith and Suzuki have arrived at a tempura restaurant in Ginza.

みせの　ひと　：いらっしゃいませ。

すずき　　　　：すずきです。

みせの　ひと　：すずきさまですね。どうぞ　こちらへ。

スミス　　　　：いい　みせですね。
　　　　　　　　すずきさんは　よく　この　みせに　きますか。

すずき　　　　：ええ、ときどき　きます。
　　　　　　　　せんしゅうは　ここで　グリーンさんに　あいました。

スミス　　　　：え、ほんとうですか。

(Branch president Green comes into the restaurant.)

スミス・すずき：あ、グリーンさん！

■ スミスさんと　すずきさんは　ぎんざの　てんぷらやで
グリーンさんに　あいました。

Restaurant employee:	Welcome.
Suzuki:	I am Suzuki.
Restaurant employee:	Thank you, Mr. Suzuki. This way, please.
Smith:	It's a nice restaurant. Do you often come here?
Suzuki:	Yes, I come here sometimes. Last week, I met Green-san here.
Smith:	Really?

Smith and Suzuki:　Oh, Green-san!

■ Smith-san and Suzuki-san met Green-san at the tempura restaurant in Ginza.

VOCABULARY

すずきさま	Mr. Suzuki		ここ	here
～さま	Mr., Mrs., Ms., Miss (more polite than さん)		に	(particle; see GRAMMAR 1, 2, p. 85)
どうぞ　こちらへ。	Please come in.		あいます	meet
いい	nice, good		ほんとうですか。	Really?
ね	(particle; see L6, NOTES 2, p. 51)		てんぷらや	tempura restaurant
よく	often		～や	(suffix for shop or restaurant)
ときどき	sometimes			

NOTES

1. せんしゅうは　ここで　グリーンさんに　あいました。

The particle は in せんしゅうは identifies せんしゅう as the topic from among the times Suzuki has come to this restaurant.

KEY SENTENCES

 093

1. スミスさんは　あした　たなかさんに　あいます。
2. スミスさんは　すずきさんに　レストランの　ばしょを　おしえました。
3. スミスさんは　まいにち　コーヒーを　のみます。
4. エマさんは　あまり　テレビを　みません。

1. Smith-san will meet Tanaka-san tomorrow.
2. Smith-san told Suzuki-san the location of the restaurant.
3. Smith-san drinks coffee every day.
4. Emma-san does not watch television very often.

GRAMMAR

1. person 1は　person 2に　verb。 (KS1)

The particle に can also serve as an object marker, as in the example here, where たなかさん is the object of the verb あいます("meet"). Essentially, に indicates the person or thing an action is directed at.

2. person 1は　person 2/placeに　nounを　verb。 (KS2)

With verbs like でんわばんごうを　おしえます("tell someone's telephone number"), メールを　おくります("send e-mail"), and でんわを　します("telephone"), に indicates the receiver of the action.

3. Habitual action (KS3)

The present form of verbs also expresses habitual actions when they are used with adverbs of frequency or words used with every time, such as まいにち ("every day"), まいしゅう ("every week"), and まいあさ ("every morning").

4. あまり／ぜんぜん　in a negative sentence (KS4)

The adverb あまり occurs in negative sentences, meaning "not often", "not very." ぜんぜん is also used in negative sentences, meaning "not at all."

VOCABULARY

ばしょ	location
おしえます	tell, teach
まいにち	every day
あまり… 〜ません	not often, not very

WORD POWER

I Verbs

 094

①でんわを　　②おくります　　③あいます　　④ききます　　⑤おしえます
します

II Family

 095

①たなかさんの　ごかぞく　　⑤かぞく　　　　⑨ささきさんの　ごしゅじん
②たなかさんの　おとうさん　⑥ちち　　　　　⑩おっと／しゅじん
③たなかさんの　おかあさん　⑦はは
④たなかさんの　おくさん　　⑧つま／かない

でんわを　します	telephone	おとうさん	(another person's) father	つま／かない	(my) wife
おくります	send	おかあさん	(another person's) mother	ごしゅじん	(another person's)
ききます	ask	おくさん	(another person's) wife		husband
ごかぞく	(another person's) family	ちち	(my) father	おっと／しゅじん	(my) husband
ご〜	(honorific prefix)	はは	(my) mother		

Ⅲ Time expressions

🔊 096

	Day	Morning	Evening	Week
Every	まいにち	まいあさ	まいばん	まいしゅう

Ⅳ Adverbs

🔊 097

Frequency

100%	いつも	always
.	よく	often
	ときどき	sometimes
	あまり…～ません	not often
0%	ぜんぜん…～ません	not at all

EXERCISES

Ⅰ *Practice conjugating verbs.* Repeat the verbs below and memorize their forms—present and past, affirmative and negative.

	Present form		Past form	
	aff.	*neg.*	*aff.*	*neg.*
telephone	でんわを します	でんわを しません	でんわを しました	でんわを しませんでした
send	おくります	おくりません	おくりました	おくりませんでした
meet	あいます	あいません	あいました	あいませんでした
ask	ききます	ききません	ききました	ききませんでした
tell, teach	おしえます	おしえません	おしえました	おしえませんでした

Ⅱ Make up sentences following the patterns of the examples. Substitute the underlined part with the alternatives given.

A. *State whom someone will telephone.*

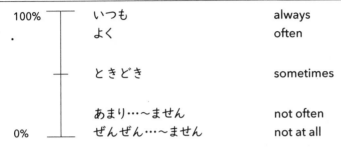

e.g. スミスさんは たなかさんに でんわを します。

1. ....（おかあさん）

2. ....（ささきさん）

3. ....（たいしかん）

B. *State to whom someone will send an e-mail.*

e.g. スミスさんは　たなかさんに　メールを　おくります。

1. ....（おとうさん）

2. ....（かとうさん）

3. ....（のぞみデパート）

Ⅲ *Ask and answer who will telephone, or e-mail whom.* Make up dialogues following the patterns of the examples and based on the information provided.

e.g. 1. なかむらさん	1） おおさかししゃの チャンさん	2） のぞみデパートの しゃちょう	e.g. 2. ぎんこう	3） ぎんざの　ホテル	4） にほんごの がっこう
					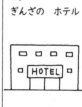

1. e.g. 1. A：スミスさんは　だれに　でんわを　しますか。
　　　　 B：なかむらさんに　します。

　　1）A：..

　　　 B：..

　　2）A：..

　　　 B：..

　e.g. 2. A：スミスさんは　どこに　でんわを　しますか。
　　　　 B：ぎんこうに　します。

　　3）A：..

　　　 B：..

　　4）A：..

　　　 B：..

メール	e-mail	にほんご	Japanese	がっこう	school
しゃちょう	president (of a company)	〜ご	language		

2. **e.g. 1.** A：スミスさんは　だれに　メールを　おくりますか。
B：<u>なかむらさん</u>に　おくります。

1) A： ....

B： ....

2) A： ....

B： ....

e.g. 2. A：スミスさんは　どこに　メールを　おくりますか。
B：<u>ぎんこう</u>に　おくります。

3) A： ....

B： ....

4) A： ....

B： ....

Ⅳ Make up sentences following the patterns of the examples and based on the information provided.

A. *State who asked whom for what.*

e.g. スミスさんは　なかむらさんに　<u>でんわばんごう</u>を　ききました。

1. ....

2. ....

B. *State who told whom what.*

e.g. なかむらさんは　スミスさんに　<u>でんわばんごう</u>を　おしえました。

1. ....

2. ....

V *Describe a schedule.* Make up sentences following the pattern of the example and based on the information in the page from Smith's weekly planner.

e.g.	Mon.	4:00	とうきょうえき	すずきさん
1.	Tue.	10:00	のぞみデパート	たなかさん
2.	Wed.	7:00	レストランローマ	ロンドンぎんこうの　ブラウンさん
3.	Thu.	11:00	さっぽろししゃ	ししゃの　ひと

e.g. スミスさんは　げつようびの　4じに　とうきょうえきで

すずきさんに　あいます。

1. ....

2. ....

3. ....

VI *State what someone does regularly.* Make up sentences following the pattern of the example and based on the information provided.

e.g. every day

1. every morning
ヨーグルト

2. every evening
おくさん
ビール

3. every week
おかあさん

e.g. かとうさんは　まいにち　さんぽを　します。

1. ....

2. ....

3. ....

VII *Ask and answer about how often something is done.* Make up dialogues following the pattern of the example and based on the information provided.

e.g. often

1. sometimes

2. not often

3. not at all
やさい
ジュース

レストランローマ	Restaurant Rome (fictitious restaurant name)	ヨーグルト	yogurt
ローマ	Rome	さんぽを　します	take a walk
さっぽろししゃ	Sapporo branch	やさいジュース	vegetable juice
さっぽろ	Sapporo (city on the island of Hokkaido)	やさい	vegetable

e.g. A：スミスさんは　よく　<u>ほん</u>を　<u>よみます</u>か。

　　 B：はい、<u>よく　よみます</u>。

1. A：..

　　 B：はい、..

2. A：..

　　 B：いいえ、..

3. A：..

　　 B：いいえ、..

Ⅷ *State what you want to order and the quantity.* Make up sentences following the pattern of the example and based on the information provided.

e.g. スミス：<u>ビールを　2ほん</u>　おねがいします。

1. スミス：...

2. スミス：...

3. スミス：...

| グラス | glass, wine glass |

IX *Talk about what you do and how often.* Make up dialogues following the pattern of the example. Substitute the underlined parts with the alternatives given.

e.g. すずき：こんどの　しゅうまつに　なにを　しますか。

エマ　：しぶやとしょかんに　いきます。

すずき：エマさんは　よく　しぶやとしょかんに　いきますか。

エマ　：はい、よく　いきます。

1. すずき：...

   エマ　：...（てんまさ）

   すずき：...（てんまさ）

   エマ　：...（ときどき）

2. すずき：...

   エマ　：...（こうえん）

   すずき：...（こうえん）

   エマ　：...（まいしゅう）

X Listen to the audio and fill in the blanks based on the information you hear.　🔊 098

Smith and Nakamura are talking together.

1. スミスさんは　なかむらさんに　のぞみデパートの

   でんわばんごうを　..。

2. なかむらさんは　スミスさんに　のぞみデパートの

   でんわばんごうを　..。

3. のぞみデパートの　でんわばんごうは　..　です。

| こんど | next, next time |
| しぶやとしょかん | Shibuya Library (fictitious library name) |

SPEAKING PRACTICE

1. Suzuki is in a restaurant with a friend and is about to order.

🔊 099

すずき　　　　：きょうの　おすすめは　なんですか。

みせの　ひと：こちらです。

すずき　　　　：じゃ、それを　2つ　おねがいします。

みせの　ひと：はい。おのみものは？

すずき　　　　：なまビールを　2つ　おねがいします。

みせの　ひと：はい。

Suzuki: What do you recommend today?
Restaurant employee: Here, how about this?
Suzuki: Okay. Please let us have that for two.
Restaurant employee: Fine. Would you like anything to drink?
Suzuki: Yes, please let us have two draft beers.
Restaurant employee: Yes, certainly.

2. Having finished their meal, they call the restaurant employee.

🔊 100

すずき　　　　：すみません。おかいけいを　おねがいします。

みせの　ひと：はい。

すずき　　　　：べつべつに　おねがいします。

みせの　ひと：はい。

Suzuki: Excuse me. May we have the bill, please?
Restaurant employee: Yes, certainly.
Suzuki: We would like to pay separately.
Restaurant employee: Yes [, that will be fine].

NOTES

1. べつべつに　おねがいします。

Expression used in a restaurant when each person wants to pay separately. べつべつで　おねがいします is also used.

Active Communication If you're in Japan, go to a restaurant and ask what they recommend on the menu; place an order.

VOCABULARY

おすすめ	recommendation
こちら	(polite word for これ)
（お）のみもの	beverage
なまビール	draft beer

（お）かいけい	bill, check
べつべつに	separately

I Complete the dialogues by choosing words from the box below. Do not use the same word more than once. Some are not needed.

なん　　なに　　だれ　　いつ　　どこ　　どの　　どれ

1. すずき：エマさんは　（　　　）　にほんに　きましたか。

   エマ　：きょねんの　10がつに　きました。

   すずき：（　　　）と　きましたか。

   エマ　：ひとりで　きました。

2. すずき：しゅうまつに　（　　　）を　しましたか。

   ラジャ：テニスを　しました。

   すずき：（　　　）で　しましたか。

   ラジャ：だいがくで　しました。

3. スミス　　　　：（　　　）　バスが　しぶやに　いきますか。

   うんてんしゅ：6ばんの　バスが　いきます。

4. スミス：しゅうまつに　はこねに　いきます。

   すずき：（　　　）で　いきますか。

   スミス：くるまで　いきます。

II What do you say in the following situations?

1. In a restaurant, you want to ask what the recommended dish of the day is.

   ....

2. You want to ask Smith-san if he often drinks beer.

   ....

3. You want to ask Emma-san when she will meet Chan-san.

   ....

4. You are now at the company. You ask your colleague, Suzuki-san, what time he came to the company today.

   ....

VISITING A JAPANESE HOME

Many people today live in Western-style houses or condominiums and the number who live in traditional-style dwellings has decreased, but even Western-style homes incorporate various Japanese features to suit local preferences and conditions. Shoes are not worn inside the home, so there is always space at the entrance for removing shoes. Many homes have rooms with tatami floors. The main form of seating in a tatami room is a square cushion called a zabuton. Even today, the Japanese-style room is considered a comforting and relaxing kind of space.

Describing Things: It's Delicious

TARGET DIALOGUE 101

Emma is visiting the Sasakis' home. She is enjoying their hospitality.

ささき：おちゃを　どうぞ。

エマ　：ありがとうございます。

ささき：おかしは　いかがですか。

エマ　：はい、いただきます。きれいな　おかしですね。
　　　　にほんの　おかしですか。

ささき：ええ、そうです。きょうとの　おかしです。

エマ　：とても　おいしいです。

■エマさんは　ささきさんの　うちで　きれいな　にほんの　おかしを
たべました。

Sasaki: Please, have some tea.
Emma: Thank you.
Sasaki: How about a sweet?
Emma: Yes, please. Isn't this a beautiful sweet! Is it a Japanese sweet?
Sasaki: Yes, it is. It's a sweet from Kyoto.
Emma: Hmm. It's really delicious.

■Emma-san ate a pretty Japanese sweet at Sasaki-san's house.

VOCABULARY

いかがですか。	How about ... ? (see NOTES 2, p. 97)	おいしい　delicious, tasty
いただきます	(see NOTES 3, p. 97)	
きれい（な）	pretty, beautiful, clean	
とても	very	

NOTES

1. おちゃを　どうぞ。

   "Thingを　どうぞ ("please help yourself to…")" is used to offer something to someone.

2. いかがですか。

   "Thingは　いかがですか" is often used when politely offering things like food or drink. It means "Would you like one?" or "How about some?"

3. はい、いただきます。

   This phrase is spoken when taking something that is offered. It implies both acceptance and gratitude.

KEY SENTENCES 102

1. この　ほんは　おもしろいです。
2. とうきょうの　ちかてつは　べんりです。
3. スミスさんは　あたらしい　パソコンを　かいました。
4. スミスさんは　きのう　ゆうめいな　レストランに　いきました。

1. This book is interesting.
2. Tokyo subways are convenient.
3. Smith-san bought a new computer.
4. Smith-san went to a famous restaurant yesterday.

GRAMMAR

1. Adjectives (1)
(KS1, 2, 3, 4)

Japanese adjectives can either modify nouns by directly preceding them, or act as predicates. In this they resemble English adjectives. There are two kinds of adjectives:
い-adjectives (KS1, KS3) and な-adjectives (KS2, KS4).

Modifying noun: adjective + noun		
い-adj.	おおきい　こうえん	big park
な-adj.	きれいな　はな	pretty flower

Unlike English, Japanese adjectives are conjugated. The present affirmative and negative forms are listed below.

	As predicate: adjective + です	
	aff.	*neg.*
い-adj.	おおきいです いいです	おおきくないです よくないです*
な-adj.	きれいです	きれいじゃありません きれいではありません**

* exceptional inflection
** more formal

VOCABULARY

おもしろい	interesting
べんり（な）	convenient
あたらしい	new, fresh
ゆうめい（な）	famous

WORD POWER

Ⅰ い-adjectives
🔊 103

①おおきい

②ちいさい

③たかい

④やすい

⑤あたらしい

⑥ふるい

⑦いい

⑧わるい

⑨あつい

⑩さむい

⑪あたたかい

⑫すずしい

⑬おもしろい

⑭おいしい

Ⅱ な-adjectives
🔊 104

①にぎやか（な）

②しずか（な）

③べんり（な）

④ゆうめい（な）

⑤きれい（な）

VOCABULARY

たかい	expensive	あつい	hot	にぎやか（な）	lively
やすい	inexpensive	さむい	cold	しずか（な）	quiet
ふるい	old	あたたかい	warm		
わるい	bad	すずしい	cool		

EXERCISES

Ⅰ *Practice conjugating* い*-adjectives.* Repeat the adjectives below and memorize their forms.

	As predicate: present form		Modifying
	aff.	*neg.*	**noun**
big, large	おおきいです	おおきくないです	おおきい
small	ちいさいです	ちいさくないです	ちいさい
expensive	たかいです	たかくないです	たかい
inexpensive	やすいです	やすくないです	やすい
new, fresh	あたらしいです	あたらしくないです	あたらしい
old	ふるいです	ふるくないです	ふるい
good, nice	いいです	よくないです	いい
bad	わるいです	わるくないです	わるい
hot	あついです	あつくないです	あつい
cold	さむいです	さむくないです	さむい
warm	あたたかいです	あたたかくないです	あたたかい
cool	すずしいです	すずしくないです	すずしい
interesting	おもしろいです	おもしろくないです	おもしろい
delicious	おいしいです	おいしくないです	おいしい

Ⅱ *State a characteristic of something.* Make up sentences following the pattern of the example. Substitute the underlined parts with the alternatives given.

e.g. この　ほんは　おもしろいです。

1. _____（この　カメラ、やすいです）

2. _____
　　　　　　　　　　　　　　（かとうさんの　うち、あたらしいです）

Ⅲ Make up dialogues following the patterns of the examples. Substitute the underlined parts with the appropriate forms of the alternatives given.

A. *Ask and answer about the characteristics of things.*

e.g. A : <u>その　ワイン</u>は　<u>たかいです</u>か。

B : はい、<u>たかいです</u>。

1. A : ....（この　パソコン、あたらしいです）

B : ....（あたらしいです）

2. A : ....（その　おべんとう、おいしいです）

B : ....（おいしいです）

B. *Ask and answer about the weather in a distant place.*

e.g. A : <u>とうきょう</u>は　<u>あつい</u>ですか。

B : いいえ、<u>あつくないです</u>。

1. A : ....（ロンドン、さむいです）

B : ....（さむいです）

2. A : ....（シドニー、すずしいです）

B : ....（すずしいです）

Ⅳ *Practice conjugating な-adjectives.* Repeat the adjectives below and memorize their forms.

	As predicate: present form		Modifying
	aff.	*neg.*	noun
lively	にぎやかです	にぎやかじゃありません	にぎやかな
quiet	しずかです	しずかじゃありません	しずかな
convenient	べんりです	べんりじゃありません	べんりな
famous	ゆうめいです	ゆうめいじゃありません	ゆうめいな
pretty, clean	きれいです	きれいじゃありません	きれいな

Ⅴ *Describe something.* Make up sentences following the pattern of the example. Substitute the underlined parts with the alternatives given.

e.g. <u>とうきょうの　ちかてつ</u>は　<u>べんりです</u>。

1. ....（ふじさん、ゆうめいです）

2. ....（この　はな、きれいです）

（お）べんとう	box lunch, bento	ふじさん	Mt. Fuji
シドニー	Sydney	はな	flower

VI Make up dialogues following the patterns of the examples. Substitute the underlined parts with the appropriate forms of the alternatives given.

A. *Ask and give one's opinion about a place.*

e.g. A：としょかんは　しずかですか。

B：はい、しずかです。

1. A：＿＿＿＿＿＿＿＿＿＿＿＿＿＿＿＿＿＿＿＿（ろっぽんぎ、にぎやかです）

B：＿＿＿＿＿＿＿＿＿＿＿＿＿＿＿＿＿＿＿＿（にぎやかです）

2. A：＿＿＿＿＿＿＿＿＿＿＿＿＿＿＿＿＿＿（おきなわの　うみ、きれいです）

B：＿＿＿＿＿＿＿＿＿＿＿＿＿＿＿＿＿＿＿＿（きれいです）

B. *Ask and give one's opinion about something.*

e.g. A：この　えは　ゆうめいですか。

B：いいえ、ゆうめいじゃありません。

1. A：＿＿＿＿＿＿＿＿＿＿＿＿＿＿＿＿＿＿（その　アプリ、べんりです）

B：＿＿＿＿＿＿＿＿＿＿＿＿＿＿＿＿＿＿＿＿（べんりです）

2. A：＿＿＿＿＿＿＿＿＿＿＿＿＿＿＿＿（あの　レストラン、しずかです）

B：＿＿＿＿＿＿＿＿＿＿＿＿＿＿＿＿＿＿＿＿（しずかです）

VII *Describe something someone has purchased.* Make up sentences following the pattern of the example and based on the information provided.

e.g. 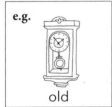	1. ケーキ 	2. セーター 	3. 
old	small	expensive	delicious

e.g. スミスさんは　ふるい　とけいを　かいました。

1. ＿＿＿＿＿＿＿＿＿＿＿＿＿＿＿＿＿＿＿＿＿＿＿＿＿＿＿＿＿＿＿＿＿＿＿＿

2. ＿＿＿＿＿＿＿＿＿＿＿＿＿＿＿＿＿＿＿＿＿＿＿＿＿＿＿＿＿＿＿＿＿＿＿＿

3. ＿＿＿＿＿＿＿＿＿＿＿＿＿＿＿＿＿＿＿＿＿＿＿＿＿＿＿＿＿＿＿＿＿＿＿＿

VOCABULARY

ろっぽんぎ	Roppongi (district in Tokyo)	アプリ	application
おきなわ	Okinawa (islands in southern Japan)	ケーキ	cake
うみ	ocean	セーター	sweater
え	painting, picture		

Ⅷ *Describe the place where someone went.* Make up sentences following the pattern of the example and based on the information provided.

famous

1.
quiet

2.
lively

e.g. スミスさんは　きのう　<u>ゆうめいな</u>　レストランに　いきました。

1. ....

2. ....

Ⅸ *Talk about one's opinion of a place.* Make up dialogues following the pattern of the example. Substitute the underlined parts with the alternatives given.

e.g. A：しゅうまつに　<u>にっこう</u>に　いきます。

B：<u>にっこう</u>は　どんな　ところですか。

A：<u>きれいな</u>　ところですよ。

1. A：.. （あさくさ）

B：.. （あさくさ）

A：.. （にぎやかな）

2. A：.. （おだいば）

B：.. （おだいば）

A：.. （おもしろい）

にっこう	Nikko (scenic area north of Tokyo)	おだいば	Odaiba (district in Tokyo)
どんな	what kind of		
ところ	place		
あさくさ	Asakusa (district in Tokyo)		

X *State something in a place you are visiting.* Smith visits the home of a friend. Praise something in the friend's house as if you are Smith.

e.g. big

1. interesting **2.** very old **3.** pretty

e.g. スミス：おおきい　うちですね。

1. スミス：...

2. スミス：...

3. スミス：...

XI *Talk about the weather.* Make up dialogues following the pattern of the example. Substitute the underlined parts with the alternatives given.

e.g. A：きょうは　<u>さむい</u>ですね。
　　 B：ええ、ほんとうに　<u>さむい</u>ですね。

1. A：...（あたたかい）

　　 B：...（あたたかい）

2. A：...（いい　てんき）

　　 B：...（いい　てんき）

XII Listen to the audio and fill in the blank based on the information you hear. 　🔊 105

　　 1. はこねは　............................　ところです。

VOCABULARY

ほんとうに　really
てんき　weather

SPEAKING PRACTICE

1. Emma visits the Sasakis' home. She rings the doorbell. 🔊 106

ささき：はい、どなたですか。

エマ　：エマです。

ささき：あ、ちょっと　まってください。

　　　　(*Opens the door.*) どうぞ。

エマ　：おじゃまします。

Sasaki: Yes. Who is it?
Emma: It's Emma.
Sasaki: Ah, just a minute. Please come in!
Emma: Thank you.

2. Smith is looking at rice bowls in an antique shop. 🔊 107

スミス　　　　：これは　いくらですか。

みせの　ひと：8,000 えんです。

スミス　　　　：ちょっと　たかいですね。

みせの　ひと：こちらは　6,500 えんです。

スミス　　　　：じゃ、それを　ください。

Smith: How much is this?
Shopkeeper: It's 8,000 yen.
Smith: It's a bit expensive.
Shopkeeper: This one is 6,500 yen.
Smith: Okay. I'll take that one.

NOTES

1. おじゃまします。
Customary expression used when entering private space as a guest.

Active Communication Tell people around you about where you come from and tell them what kind of place it is.

VOCABULARY

どなた	who (polite word for だれ)	おじゃまします。	May I come in? (see NOTES 1, above)
ちょっと	a little bit		
まってください	please wait		
まちます	wait		

Describing Impressions: It Was Beautiful

TARGET DIALOGUE 108

At the Sasakis' house, Emma is talking with the Sasakis.

エマ　：せんしゅう　ふじさんに　のぼりました。

ささき：どうでしたか。

エマ　：とても　きれいでした。

ささき：しゃしんを　とりましたか。

エマ　：ええ、これです。

　　　　(*Shows photos on her smart phone.*)

ささき：ほんとうに　きれいですね。どのくらい　あるきましたか。

エマ　：８じかんぐらい　あるきました。

　　　　たいへんでしたが、たのしかったです。

■エマさんは　ささきさんと　ささきさんの　ごしゅじんに

しゃしんを　みせました。

Emma: Last week, I climbed Mt. Fuji.
Sasaki: How was it?
Emma: It was really beautiful.
Sasaki: Did you take photos?
Emma: Yes. Here they are.
Sasaki: It really is beautiful.
　　　　How long did you walk?
Emma: I walked for about eight hours.
　　　　It was hard, but it was also
　　　　enjoyable.

■ Emma-san showed her photos
to the Sasakis.

VOCABULARY

のぼります	climb	あるきます	walk	が	but (particle; see
どうでしたか。	How was it?	８じかん	8 hours		GRAMMAR 2, p. 106)
どう	how (in question)	～じかん	(number of) hours	たのしかったです	it was fun, it was
きれいでした	it was beautiful	～ぐらい	about (amount) (see		enjoyable
しゃしん	photo		NOTES 1, p. 106)	たのしい	fun, pleasant,
とります	take (a photo)	たいへんでした	it was hard		enjoyable
どのくらい	how long	たいへん（な）	hard, tough	みせます	show

1. どのくらい　あるきましたか。

　　８じかんぐらい　あるきました。

Here, どのくらい means "how long." くらい may also be pronounced ぐらい. The ぐらい in Emma's response, ８じかんぐらい, is used with certain periods of time, with prices, and with amounts and means "about" or "approximately." ぐらい may also be pronounced くらい.

e.g. ５ふんぐらい　　　　about 5 minutes

　　　1,000えんぐらい　about 1,000 yen

　　　500にんぐらい　　about 500 people

KEY SENTENCES　　　　　　　　　　　　　　　　　　🔊 109

1. きのうは　さむかったです。
2. きのうの　おまつりは　にぎやかでした。
3. スミスさんは　デパートに　いきましたが、なにも　かいませんでした。

1. Yesterday, it was cold.
2. Yesterday's festival was lively.
3. Smith-san went to the department store, but he did not buy anything.

GRAMMAR

1. Adjectives (2)　　　　　　　　　　　　　　　　　　　(KS1, 2)

Japanese adjectives are conjugated not only for affirmative and negative but according to tense.

| | As predicate: adjective +です | | | |
| | Present form | | Past form | |
	aff.	neg.	aff.	neg.
い-adj.	おおきいです いいです	おおきくないです よくないです*	おおきかったです よかったです*	おおきくなかったです よくなかったです*
な-adj.	きれいです	きれいじゃありません	きれいでした	きれいじゃありませんでした

* exceptional inflection

2. clause 1が、clause 2。　　　　　　　　　　　　　　(KS3)

This が is a conjunction that joins two clauses. It can be translated as "but."

さむかったです　　it was cold

にぎやかでした　　it was lively

WORD POWER

Ⅰ い-adjectives

①たのしい

②つまらない

③むずかしい

④いそがしい

Ⅱ な-adjectives

①かんたん（な）

②たいへん（な）

③ひま（な）

Ⅲ Verbs

①のぼります

②あるきます

③（しゃしんを）
とります

④みせます

Ⅳ Events

①（お）まつり

②コンサート

③クラス

VOCABULARY

つまらない	boring, uninteresting	ひま（な）	free, not busy
むずかしい	difficult	クラス	class
いそがしい	busy		
かんたん（な）	easy, simple		

EXERCISES

Ⅰ Repeat the adjectives below and memorize their forms—present and past, affirmative and negative.

A. *Practice conjugating い-adjectives.*

	Present form		Past form	
	aff.	*neg.*	*aff.*	*neg.*
good, nice	いいです	よくないです	よかったです	よくなかったです
hot	あついです	あつくないです	あつかったです	あつくなかったです
cold	さむいです	さむくないです	さむかったです	さむくなかったです
interesting	おもしろいです	おもしろくないです	おもしろかったです	おもしろくなかったです
delicious	おいしいです	おいしくないです	おいしかったです	おいしくなかったです
fun, enjoyable	たのしいです	たのしくないです	たのしかったです	たのしくなかったです
boring	つまらないです	つまらなくないです	つまらなかったです	つまらなくなかったです
difficult	むずかしいです	むずかしくないです	むずかしかったです	むずかしくなかったです
busy	いそがしいです	いそがしくないです	いそがしかったです	いそがしくなかったです

B. *Practice conjugating な-adjectives.*

	Present form		Past form	
	aff.	*neg.*	*aff.*	*neg.*
pretty, clean, beautiful	きれいです	きれいじゃありません	きれいでした	きれいじゃありませんでした
lively	にぎやかです	にぎやかじゃありません	にぎやかでした	にぎやかじゃありませんでした
easy, simple	かんたんです	かんたんじゃありません	かんたんでした	かんたんじゃありませんでした
hard, tough	たいへんです	たいへんじゃありません	たいへんでした	たいへんじゃありませんでした
free, not busy	ひまです	ひまじゃありません	ひまでした	ひまじゃありませんでした

Ⅱ Make up sentences following the patterns of the examples. Substitute the underlined parts with the alternatives given, using the same grammatical forms as in the examples.

A. *Comment about the weather yesterday.*

e.g. きのうは　<u>さむかったです</u>。

1. ....（あついです）

2. ....（あたたかいです）

B. *Comment about something you did.*

e.g. きのうの　デートは　<u>たのしくなかったです</u>。

1. ....（おもしろいです）

2. ....（いいです）

| デート　date

C. *Comment about something you saw.*

e.g. きのうの　おまつりは　<u>きれいでした</u>。

1. .... （にぎやかです）

D. *Comment about something you saw.*

e.g. きのうの　おまつりは　<u>にぎやかじゃありませんでした</u>。

1. .... （きれいです）

Ⅲ Make up dialogues following the patterns of the examples. Substitute the underlined parts with the appropriate forms of the alternatives given.

A. *Ask and answer about something you experienced.*

e.g. なかむら：<u>えいがは</u>　<u>おもしろかったです</u>か。

　　エマ　　：はい、<u>おもしろかったです</u>。

　　スミス　：いいえ、<u>おもしろくなかったです</u>。

1. なかむら： .... （セール、やすいです）

　　エマ　　： .... （やすいです）

　　スミス　： .... （やすいです）

2. なかむら： ....

　　　　　　　　　　（にほんごの　クラス、むずかしいです）

　　エマ　　： .... （むずかしいです）

　　スミス　： .... （むずかしいです）

VOCABULARY

セール　sale

B. *Ask and answer about something you experienced.*

e.g. <u>very</u>　<u>not very</u>　　very　not very　　very　not very

e.g. かとう：<u>パーティー</u>は　どうでしたか。

エマ　：とても　<u>たのしかったです</u>。

スミス：あまり　<u>たのしくなかったです</u>。

1. かとう：..（コンサート）

　 エマ　：..（いいです）

　 スミス：..（いいです）

2. なかむら：..（テスト）

　 エマ　　：...（かんたんです）

　 スミス　：...（かんたんです）

Ⅳ *Contrast two things.* Make up sentences following the pattern of the example. Substitute the underlined parts with the appropriate forms of the alternatives given.

e.g. きのうは　<u>いそがしかったです</u>が、きょうは　<u>ひまです</u>。

1. ....（ひまです、いそがしいです）

2. ....（あついです、すずしいです）

3. ....（あたたかいです、さむいです）

Ⅴ *Talk about something you did.* Make up dialogues following the pattern of the example. Substitute the underlined parts with the appropriate forms of the alternatives given.

e.g. なかむら：スミスさん、しゅうまつに　なにを　しましたか。

スミス　：<u>ほっかいどう</u>で　<u>スキーを　しました</u>。

なかむら：どうでしたか。

スミス　：とても　<u>たのしかったです</u>。

テスト　　　　　　test
スキーを　します　ski

1. なかむら：...

   スミス　：...

   （あさくさ、てんぷらを　たべます）

   なかむら：...

   スミス　：...

   （おいしいです）

2. なかむら：...

   スミス　：...

   （ぎんざ、かぶきを　みます）

   なかむら：...

   スミス　：...

   （きれいです）

🔊 **Ⅵ** Listen to the audio and fill in the blanks based on the information you hear. 🔊114-116

1. おまつりは　とても ....。

2. ほっかいどうは　とても ....。

3. ステーキは　あまり ....。

SPEAKING PRACTICE

1. Emma is visiting the Sasakis' home. 🔊117

   エマ　：そろそろ　しつれいします。きょうは　どうも　ありがとうございました。

   ささき：どういたしまして。

   エマ　：とても　たのしかったです。

   ささき：わたしたちも　たのしかったです。また　きてください。

   Emma: I need to be going in a little while. Thank you very much [for today].
   Sasaki: You're welcome.
   Emma: I had a very nice time.
   Sasaki: And we enjoyed having you. Please come again.

VOCABULARY

そろそろ　しつれいします。	I need to be going in a little while.	わたしたち	we
		また　きてください。	Please come again.
そろそろ	in a little while	また	again
どうも　ありがとうございました。	(see NOTES 2, p. 112)	きてください	please come
どういたしまして。	You're welcome.		

2. On Monday morning, Smith and Nakamura are talking at the office. 🔊 118

スミス　　：しゅうまつに　はこねに　いきました。これ、はこねの　おみやげです。
　　　　　　どうぞ。

なかむら：ありがとうございます。はこねは　どうでしたか。

スミス　　：とても　よかったです。

Smith:　　　Over the weekend, I went to Hakone. This is a souvenir of Hakone. I hope you like it.
Nakamura:　Thank you. How was Hakone?
Smith:　　　It was very nice.

3. Nakamura received a souvenir from Smith the day before. 🔊 119

なかむら：スミスさん、きのうは　おみやげを　ありがとうございました。
　　　　　　とても　おいしかったです。

スミス　　：そうですか。よかったです。

Nakamura:　Thank you for the souvenir yesterday, Smith-san. It was really delicious.
Smith:　　　Good. I'm glad to hear that.

NOTES

1.　そろそろ　しつれいします。
Set phrase used when the time has come to leave a place you are visiting.

2.　どうも　ありがとうございました。
When expressing thanks for something that has ended, the past tense of ありがとうございます is used.

3.　これ、はこねの　おみやげです。
これは　はこねの　おみやげです is used when explaining what これ is in a situation where the listener's attention is already focused on これ. In contrast, the これ in これ、はこねの　おみやげです is used to focus the listener's attention on something before explaining what it is.

4.　よかったです。(SPEAKING PRACTICE 3)
This is used in the sense of "I'm glad to hear that," when hearing a positive response from someone to whom you have given a present or offered advice.

Active Communication
Ask people around you to give their impressions of places they have been, movies they have seen, and other experiences.

VOCABULARY

| （お）みやげ | souvenir |
| よかったです。 | I'm glad to hear that. (see NOTES 4, above) |

WEEKEND TRIPS

Tokyo is surrounded by a number of places to visit for pleasure within about two hours of the city. To the north is the historical site of Nikko; to the southwest are resort areas surrounding five large lakes in the foothills of Mt. Fuji; and to the south is Kamakura, the historic town that dates back to the twelfth century. The western part of the greater metropolitan area is the mountainous Okutama region known for its scenic rivers and gorges. Also close by is Yokohama, which preserves its heritage as a port first opened for world trade in the mid-nineteenth century, and Hakone, an easily accessible mountain vacation resort known for natural beauty, comfortable inns, and numerous hot-spring spas, called onsen.

Asking about Places: What Is at Nikko?

TARGET DIALOGUE

🔊 120

Nakamura and Raja are talking during their break.

なかむら：どようびに　エマさんと　にっこうに　いきます。

ラジャ　：そうですか。にっこうに　なにが　ありますか。

なかむら：おおきい　おてらや　じんじゃが　あります。
　　　　　おんせんも　あります。

ラジャ　：おんせんって　なんですか。

なかむら：(Shows him a smartphone and points.)

The Toshogu Shrine (Nikko)

　　　　　これです。にほんの　スパですよ。

ラジャ　：いいですね。

■なかむらさんは　どようびに　エマさんと　にっこうに　いきます。
　にっこうに　おおきい　おてらや　じんじゃが　あります。

Nakamura: On Saturday, I'm going to Nikko with Emma-san.
Raja:　　Are you? What is there [to see] at Nikko?
Nakamura: There are large temples, shrines, and other sights. There are also onsen.
Raja:　　What is an "onsen"?
Nakamura: This is an onsen. It's a Japanese spa.
Raja:　　Oh, that's great.

■Nakamura-san will go to Nikko with Emma-san
　on Saturday.
　There are large temples, shrines,
　and other sights at Nikko.

VOCABULARY

に	in, on, at (particle; see GRAMMAR 1, p. 115)	じんじゃ	Shinto shrine
が	(particle; see GRAMMAR 1, p. 115)	おんせん	hot spring
あります	be, exist (see GRAMMAR 1, p. 115)	〜って　なんですか。	What is a/an … ?
（お）てら	temple	スパ	spa
や	and, and so on (particle; see GRAMMAR 3, p. 115)	よ	(particle; see NOTES 2, p. 115)

1. おんせんって　なんですか。

 〜って　なんですか is the way part of something one has heard may be repeated in order to ask what it means.

2. にほんの　スパですよ。

 The particle よ is added to the end of a sentence to call attention to information the speaker thinks the other person does not know.

KEY SENTENCES

 121

1. 1かいに　うけつけが　あります。
2. うけつけに　おんなの　ひとが　います。
3. テーブルの　うえに　はなが　あります。
4. にっこうに　おてらや　じんじゃが　あります。

1. There is an information desk on the first floor.
2. There is a woman at the information desk.
3. There are flowers on the table.
4. At Nikko, there are temples, shrines, and other sights.

GRAMMAR

1. place に　noun が　あります／います。 (KS 1, 2, 3, 4)

Both verbs あります and います express "being." あります is used for inanimate things (books, buildings, trees, etc.), and います for animate things (people, animals, insects, etc.). Existence in or at a place is indicated by the particle に. When a subject is introduced for the first time, or when the speaker believes the information to be new to the listener, the subject marker が is used after the noun. が should be used, for instance, when stating that someone or something unknown to your listener is in or at a particular place.

2. Position words (KS3)

When using words indicating position such as うえ ("on", "above") and した ("under"), use the following order: noun 1 (thing/person/place) の noun 2 (position).

3. noun 1 や　noun 2 (KS4)

The particle や is used for "and" when listing two or more things or people and implying the existence of others. Another particle, と, also means "and" but it does not imply the existence of other people or things.

 e.g. 1かいに　ぎんこうと　コンビニが　あります。

 There is a bank and a convenience store on the first floor (and nothing else).

Note that unlike "and" in English, both や and と are used only to connect nouns. They cannot be used to connect verbs or clauses (see L4, GRAMMAR 4, p. 30).

おんなの　ひと	woman	
おんな	female, woman	
います	be, exist (see GRAMMAR 1, above)	
テーブル	table	

うえ	on, above

WORD POWER

I Parts of a building

 122

①うけつけ ②ゆうびんきょく ③かいぎしつ ④ちゅうしゃじょう

II Things in a hotel room

 123

①へや ③でんきポット ⑤つくえ ⑦ごみばこ ⑨ソファー
②れいぞうこ ④ベッド ⑥いす ⑧テーブル ⑩はな

ゆうびんきょく	post office	でんきポット	electric kettle	ごみばこ	trash basket
かいぎしつ	meeting room	ベッド	bed	ソファー	sofa
ちゅうしゃじょう	parking lot	つくえ	desk		
へや	room	いす	chair		

Ⅲ Features of a tourist site

 124

①（お）てら　②じんじゃ　③おんせん　④たき　⑤みずうみ

Ⅳ Positions

125

①うえ　②した　③なか

④まえ　⑤うしろ　⑥となり　⑦ちかく

EXERCISES

Ⅰ *Practice conjugating verbs.* Repeat the verbs below and memorize their forms—present and past, affirmative and negative.

	Present form		Past form	
	aff.	*neg.*	*aff.*	*neg.*
be	あります	ありません	ありました	ありませんでした
be	います	いません	いました	いませんでした

たき	waterfall	まえ	in front
みずうみ	lake	うしろ	behind
した	under	となり	next to
なか	inside	ちかく	vicinity, near

Ⅱ Make up sentences following the patterns of the examples. Substitute the underlined part with the alternatives given.

A. *State what is at a particular place.*

e.g. にっこうに　<u>おてら</u>が　あります。

1. .... （じんじゃ）

2. .... （みずうみ）

B. *State who is at a particular place.*

e.g. うけつけに　<u>おんなの　ひと</u>が　います。

1. .... （おとこの　ひと）

2. .... （たなかさん）

Ⅲ Make up dialogues following the patterns of the examples. Substitute the underlined parts with the alternatives given.

A. *Ask and answer what is at a particular place.*

e.g. A：<u>1かい</u>に　なにが　ありますか。
　　 B：<u>ぎんこう</u>が　あります。

1. A：.. （2かい）

　 B：.. （ゆうびんきょく）

2. A：.. （4かい）

　 B：.. （かいぎしつ）

B. *Ask and answer who is at a particular place.*

e.g. A：<u>うけつけ</u>に　だれが　いますか。
　　 B：<u>たなかさん</u>が　います。

1. A：.. （ちゅうしゃじょう）

　 B：.. （おんなの　ひと）

2. A：.. （3がい）

　 B：.. （スミスさん）

| おとこの　ひと | man |
| おとこ | male, man |

Ⅳ *State what is at a certain place.* Make up sentences following the pattern of the example. Substitute the underlined parts with the alternatives given.

e.g. <u>テーブルの　うえ</u>に　<u>はな</u>が　あります。

1. ....（つくえの　した、ごみばこ）

2. ....（れいぞうこの　なか、みず）

Ⅴ *Ask and answer what is at a certain place.* Make up dialogues following the pattern of the example. Substitute the underlined parts with the alternatives given.

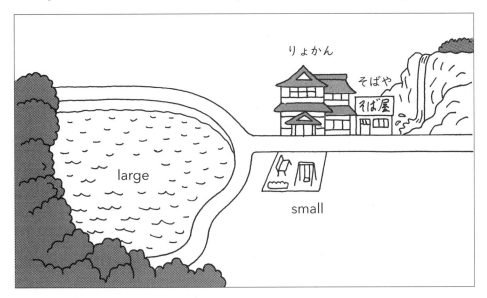

e.g. A：りょかんの　<u>ちかく</u>に　なにが　ありますか。
　　B：<u>おおきい　みずうみ</u>や　<u>たき</u>が　あります。

1. A：..（となり）
　　B：..（そばや）

2. A：..（まえ）
　　B：..（ちいさい　こうえん）

VOCABULARY

りょかん　Japanese inn
そばや　soba shop
そば　soba (buckwheat noodle)

Ⅵ Make up dialogues following the patterns of the examples. Substitute the underlined part with the alternatives given.

A. *Ask and answer what is at a certain place.*

e.g. A：<u>ひきだしの　なかに</u>　なにが　ありますか。

B：なにも　ありません。

1. A： _____ （つくえの　うえ）

B： _____

2. A： _____ （テーブルの　した）

B： _____

3. A： _____ （ポケットの　なか）

B： _____

B. *Ask and answer who is at a certain place.*

e.g. A：<u>となりの　へやに</u>　だれが　いますか。

B：だれも　いません。

1. A： _____ （4かい）

B： _____

2. A： _____ （かいぎしつ）

B： _____

3. A： _____ （コンビニの　まえ）

B： _____

VOCABULARY

ひきだし	drawer
ポケット	pocket
だれも… 〜ません	no one

VII *Talk about where you are going and what is there.* Make up dialogues following the pattern of the example. Substitute the underlined parts with the alternatives given.

e.g. かとう：にちようびに　くるまで　<u>はこね</u>に　いきます。

スミス：そうですか。<u>はこね</u>に　なにが　ありますか。

かとう：<u>みずうみや　おんせん</u>が　あります。

スミス：いいですね。

1. かとう： .... （かまくら）

   スミス： .... （かまくら）

   かとう： .... （じんじゃや　おてら）

   スミス： ....

2. かとう： .... （おだいば）

   スミス： .... （おだいば）

   かとう： .... （テーマパークや　おんせん）

   スミス： ....

VIII Listen to the audio and fill in the blanks based on the information you hear. 🔊 126-128

1. １かいに .... が　あります。

2. ２かいに .... が　あります。

3. ３がいに .... が　あります。

VOCABULARY

| かまくら | Kamakura (historic area south of Tokyo) |
| テーマパーク | theme park |

SPEAKING PRACTICE

1. Nakamura and Raja are talking during their break.　　🔊 129

なかむら：ラジャさんの　うちは　インドの　どこですか。

ラジャ　：ゴアです。

なかむら：どんな　ところですか。

ラジャ　：しずかな　ところです。

　　　　　　ふるい　きょうかいや　きれいな　ビーチが　あります。

なかむら：なにが　ゆうめいですか。

ラジャ　：カシューナッツが　ゆうめいです。

Nakamura: Where is your home in India, Raja-san?
Raja:　　　I come from Goa.
Nakamura: What kind of place is Goa?
Raja:　　　It's a quiet place. There are old churches, pretty beaches, and other sights.
Nakamura: What is it famous for?
Raja:　　　It's famous for cashew nuts.

NOTES

1. インドの　どこですか。
の　どこですか is used when asking for a more specific place within a larger area.

Active Communication Ask people around you what is in their hometowns or nearby their houses.

VOCABULARY

ゴア	Goa (state in India)
きょうかい	church
ビーチ	beach
カシューナッツ	cashew nuts

Asking for a Place: Where Is It?

TARGET DIALOGUE
🔊 130

Nakamura and Emma are in a souvenir shop in Nikko.

なかむら　　　：すみません。この　ちかくに　おいしい　おそばやさんが
　　　　　　　　ありますか。

みせの　ひと：ええ。そばいちが　おいしいですよ。

エマ　　　　　：どこに　ありますか。

みせの　ひと：あそこに　おてらが　ありますね。
　　　　　　　　そばいちは　あの　おてらの　まえです。

エマ　　　　　：そうですか。
　　　　　　　　それから、この　たきは　ここから　ちかいですか。
　　　　　　　　(Shows a photo.)

みせの　ひと：いいえ、ちょっと　とおいです。
　　　　　　　　バスで　15ふんぐらいです。

エマ　　　　　：そうですか。どうも　ありがとうございます。

■ そばいちは　おてらの　まえに　あります。

Nakamura:　　Excuse me. Is there a good soba shop nearby?
Salesperson:　Yes, there is. The Sobaichi shop is good.
Emma:　　　　Where is it?
Salesperson:　There is a temple over there, right?
　　　　　　　Sobaichi is in front of that
　　　　　　　temple.
Emma:　　　　I see. Also, is this waterfall
　　　　　　　[in this photo] somewhere
　　　　　　　near here?
Salesperson:　No, it is a little far from here.
　　　　　　　About 15 minutes by bus.
Emma:　　　　I see. Thank you very much.

■ Sobaichi is in front of the temple.

VOCABULARY

この　ちかく	vicinity, near here		それから	also
おそばやさん	soba shop (see NOTES 1, p. 124)		ちかい	near, close
そばいち	Sobaichi (fictitious soba shop)		とおい	far
あそこ	over there			

NOTES

1. おそばやさん

   Adding the suffix 〜さん after the 〜や denoting "shop" softens the tone.

2. そばいちが　おいしいですよ。

   When the particle が is used, as in 〜が　おいしいです, the part preceding が is information new to the listener. When the particle は is used as in 〜は　おいしいです, the following part (おいしいです) is information new to the listener.

KEY SENTENCES

 131

1. かいぎしつに　いすが　6つ　あります。
2. かいぎしつに　おきゃくさんが　4にん　います。
3. タクシーのりばは　えきの　まえに　あります。
4. スミスさんは　2かいに　います。
5. スミスさんの　うちは　えきから　ちかいです。

1. There are six chairs in the meeting room.
2. There are four guests in the meeting room.
3. The taxi stand is in front of the station.
4. Smith-san is on the second floor.
5. Smith-san's house is near the station.

GRAMMAR

1. placeに　nounが　number　あります／います。　(KS1, 2)

When wanting to say how many of a noun are in a certain place, the word order is "place に　thing/person が　number　あります／います." Also, there is no particle following the number (see L5, GRAMMAR 5, p. 39).

2. nounは　placeに　あります／います。　(KS3, 4)

When stating that what or who is in a certain place, use 〜が　あります／います, as in 1かいに　レストランが　あります. However, when stating where a certain thing or person is located, the thing or person becomes the topic of the sentence, and the particle が changes to は, as in レストランは　1かいに　あります.

① 1かいに　レストランが　あります。　　There is a restaurant on the first floor.
② レストランは　1かいに　あります。　　The restaurant is on the first floor.

When the existence of a certain thing and its location is clear, as in ②, "placeに　あります" at the end of the sentence can also be replaced with "placeです." (see L5, GRAMMAR 1, p. 39)
②' レストランは　1かいです。
For ①, however, が　あります cannot be replaced with です.

3. place 1は　place 2から　ちかい／とおいです。　(KS5)

This expression is used to describe subjectively the distance of one point and a different point.

| おきゃくさん | guest, customer |
| タクシーのりば | taxi stand |

WORD POWER

I **Things near a train station**

①タクシーのりば　③こうばん　⑤ほんや　⑦ラーメンや
②バスのりば　④びょういん　⑥パンや

II **Office supplies**

①けしゴム　③はさみ　⑤ひきだし
②えんぴつ　④クリアファイル　⑥キャビネット

VOCABULARY

バスのりば	bus terminal	パンや	bakery	えんぴつ	pencil
こうばん	police box	パン	bread	はさみ	scissors
びょういん	hospital, clinic	ラーメンや	ramen shop	クリアファイル	clear file
ほんや	bookstore	けしゴム	eraser	キャビネット	cabinet

Ⅲ **Demonstrative pronouns** 🔊 134　　Ⅳ **い-adjectives** 🔊 135

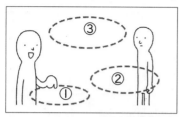

①ここ　②そこ　③あそこ

①ちかい

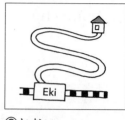

②とおい

EXERCISES

Ⅰ Make up sentences following the patterns of the examples. Substitute the underlined parts with the alternatives given.

A. *State how many of a certain object are in a certain place.*

e.g. ひきだしの　なかに　<u>ペン</u>が　<u>5ほん</u>　あります。

1. ....（めいし、6まい）

2. ....（クリップ、3つ）

3. ....（ファイル、たくさん）

B. *State how many people are in a certain place.*

e.g. こうえんに　<u>おんなの　ひと</u>が　<u>ふたり</u>　います。

1. ....（おとこの　ひと、3にん）

2. ....（おんなの　こ、ひとり）

3. ....（おとこの　こ、たくさん）

Ⅱ Make up dialogues following the patterns of the examples. Substitute the underlined parts with the alternatives given.

A. *Ask and answer how many of a certain object are on a certain place.*

e.g. A：テーブルの　うえに　<u>りんご</u>が　いくつ　ありますか。

　　 B：<u>2つ</u>　あります。

1. A：..（コップ、いくつ）

　 B：..（4つ）

そこ	there	おんなの　こ	girl	いくつ	how many
クリップ	paper clip	こ	child		
たくさん	many, much	おとこの　こ	boy		

2. A：_____ （フォーク、なんぼん）

   B：_____ （10 ぽん）

3. A：_____ （おさら、なんまい）

   B：_____ （5まい）

B. *Ask and answer how many people are in a certain place.*

e.g. A：レストランに　<u>おとこの　ひと</u>が　なんにん　いますか。

B：<u>ひとり</u>　います。

1. A：_____ （おんなの　ひと）

   B：_____ （ふたり）

2. A：_____ （おんなの　こ）

   B：_____ （4にん）

3. A：_____ （おとこの　こ）

   B：_____ （たくさん）

Ⅲ *State where a facility or store is located.* Look at the illustrations and make up sentences following the pattern of the example. Substitute the underlined parts with the alternatives given.

e.g. ちゅうしゃじょうは　<u>コンビニの　となり</u>に　あります。

1. _____

   （タクシーのりば、えきの　まえ）

2. _____

   （はなや、びょういんの　となり）

3. _____

   （こうばん、あそこ）

VOCABULARY

フォーク	fork
なんぼん	how many (long, thin objects)
なんまい	how many (flat objects)
はなや	florist

Ⅳ Make up dialogues following the patterns of the examples. Substitute the underlined parts with the alternatives given.

A. *Ask and answer where something is.*

e.g. A：<u>ちゅうしゃじょう</u>は　どこに　ありますか。

B：<u>コンビニの　となり</u>に　あります。

1. A：...（バスのりば）

B：...（えきの　まえ）

2. A：...（ほんや）

B：...

（ラーメンやの　となり）

3. A：...

（ロンドンぎんこうの　ファイル）

B：...（ここ）

4. A：...

（キャビネットの　かぎ）

B：...

（あの　ひきだしの　なか）

B. *Ask and answer where someone is.*

e.g. A：<u>スミスさん</u>は　どこに　いますか。

B：<u>2かい</u>に　います。

1. A：...（たなかさん）

B：...（しゃちょうしつ）

2. A：...（グリーンさん）

B：...（3がい）

3. A：...（ささきさん）

B：...（かいぎしつ）

V *State whether the place you are now is near/distant from a certain place.* Make up sentences following the pattern of the example. Substitute the underlined parts with the alternatives given.

e.g. としょかんは　えきから　ちかいです。

1. _____ （パンや、うち、ちかい）

2. _____ （ホテル、くうこう、とおい）

3. _____

（かとうさんの　うち、かいしゃ、とおい）

VI *Talk about how close a certain place is to where you are now.* Make up dialogues following the pattern of the example. Substitute the underlined parts with the alternatives given.

e.g. なかむら　　　　：たきは　ここから　ちかいですか。
　　ホテルの　ひと：いいえ、ちょっと　とおいです。
　　　　　　　　　　　バスで　15ふんぐらいです。
　　なかむら　　　　：そうですか。どうも　ありがとうございます。

1. なかむら　　　　：_____ （くまのじんじゃ）

　　ホテルの　ひと：_____

　　　　　　　　　　（いいえ、ちょっと　とおい）

　　　　　　　　　　（バスで　20ぷんぐらい）

　　なかむら　　　　：_____

2. なかむら　　　　：_____ （ボートのりば）

　　ホテルの　ひと：_____ （はい、ちかい）

　　　　　　　　　　（あるいて　5ふんぐらい）

　　なかむら　　　　：_____

3. なかむら　　　　：_____ （バスてい）

　　ホテルの　ひと：_____ （はい、ちかい）

　　　　　　　　　　（すぐ　そこ）

　　なかむら　　　　：_____

VOCABULARY

くまのじんじゃ	Kumano Shrine
ボートのりば	boat dock
バスてい	bus stop
すぐ　そこ	right [over] there

VII Listen to the audio and fill in the blanks based on the information you hear. 🔊136-138

1. ちゅうしゃじょうは _____ です。

2. こうばんは _____ です。

3. のぞみデパートの　ファイルは _____ です。

SPEAKING PRACTICE

1. Kato and Emma are working. 🔊139

かとう：のぞみデパートの　ファイルは　どこに　ありますか。

エマ　：ここに　あります。どうぞ。

Kato:　　Where is the file for Nozomi Department Store?
Emma:　It's here. Here you go.

2. Kato telephones Suzuki, who is out of the office. 🔊140

かとう：すずきさん、いま　どこですか。

すずき：いま　のぞみデパートに　います。

かとう：なんじごろ　かいしゃに　かえりますか。

すずき：3じに　かえります。

Kato:　　Where are you now Suzuki-san?
Suzuki:　I'm at the Nozomi Department Store now.
Kato:　　About what time will you get back to the office?
Suzuki:　I'll be back at 3 o'clock.

NOTES

1. なんじごろ　かいしゃに　かえりますか。

ごろ is used when talking about approximate time. However, it cannot be used, like ぐらい, to mean an approximate period of time. (see L11, NOTES 1, p. 106)

Active Communication　　If you are in Japan, go out on the street and ask various people if there is a station, department store, post office, etc. in the vicinity.

VOCABULARY

| 〜ごろ　about (time) (see NOTES 1, above)

Giving and Receiving: I Received It from My Friend

TARGET DIALOGUE
🔊 141

Nakamura and Emma are in Nikko. They have gotten off the bus near the waterfall.

エマ　　　：ちょっと　さむいですね。

なかむら：あ、スカーフが　ありますよ。

　　　　　　(Pulls a scarf out of her bag.)

　　　　　　これ、どうぞ。

エマ　　　：え、いいんですか。

なかむら：ええ、わたしは　さむくないですから。

エマ　　　：ありがとうございます。すてきな　スカーフですね。

なかむら：ええ、たんじょうびに　ともだちに　もらいました。

■なかむらさんは　エマさんに　スカーフを　かしました。

Emma: It's a bit cold here.
Nakamura: Oh, I have a scarf. Here you go.
Emma: Oh, are you sure?
Nakamura: Certainly. [Because] I am not cold.
Emma: Thank you very much. It's a lovely scarf!
Nakamura: Thank you. I received it from a friend on my birthday.

■Nakamura-san lent her scarf to Emma-san.

スカーフ	scarf
あります	have
いいんですか。	Are you sure? (see NOTES 1, p. 132)
から	because (particle; see NOTES 2, p. 132)

すてき（な）	lovely, nice
に	from (particle; see GRAMMAR 1, p. 132)
もらいます	receive
かします	lend, loan

NOTES

1. いいんですか。

   When someone makes an offer that is unexpected, this expression is used to confirm that he/she really meant it.

2. わたしは　さむくないですから。

   から is added after an explanatory phrase, signaling a reason for something. Here, the expression is used out of Nakamura's consideration for Emma. She wants to give a reason, reassuring Emma that she is really willing to lend her scarf and make it easier for Emma to accept her offer.

KEY SENTENCES 142

1. スミスさんは　なかむらさんに　はなを　あげました。
2. なかむらさんは　スミスさんに　はなを　もらいました。
3. スミスさんは　あした　かいぎが　あります。

1. Smith-san gave Nakamura-san some flowers.
2. Nakamura-san received flowers from Smith-san.
3. Smith-san has a meeting tomorrow.

GRAMMAR

1. person 1 は　person 2 に　noun を　あげます。 (KS1)

The sentence construction using the verb あげます is the same as the "person 1 は　person 2 に　noun を verb" construction explained in L9, GRAMMAR 2, p. 85. The particle に follows the person who received the thing; the thing that changes hands takes the particle を.

NOTE: あげます cannot be used in a sentence meaning "someone gives something to me (the speaker)"; in that case the verb くれます is used.

2. person 1 は　person 2 に　noun を　もらいます。 (KS2)

When using the verb もらいます ("receive"), the referent of the particle に is not the person receiving but the person giving. This に means "from."

3. person は　noun が　あります。 (KS3)

When using あります to mean "have" or "own," the noun takes the particle が. When stating how many of the noun, the number follows "noun が" and does not take a particle.

e.g. スミスさんは　あした　かいぎが　2つ　あります。　Smith-san has two meetings tomorrow.

| あげます | give |

WORD POWER

Ⅰ Verbs

 143

①あげます　②もらいます

③あります　④かします　⑤かります

Ⅱ Gifts

 144

①イヤリング　　⑤ブラウス　　　　　　⑧セーター　　⑪きょうとの　おみやげ
②ネックレス　　⑥バッグ　　　　　　　⑨マフラー
③ゆびわ　　　　⑦コンサートの　チケット　⑩ネクタイ
④スカーフ

Ⅲ Words that can be used with あります ("have")

 145

①（お）かね　　　　　②よてい　　　　　③やくそく　　　　　④じかん

VOCABULARY

かります (R2)	borrow	ブラウス	blouse	ネクタイ	tie	じかん	time
イヤリング	earrings	バッグ	bag	（お）かね	money		
ネックレス	necklace	チケット	ticket	よてい	schedule, plan		
ゆびわ	ring	マフラー	muffler, scarf	やくそく	appointment, promise		

133

EXERCISES

I *Practice conjugating verbs.* Repeat the verbs below and memorize their forms—present and past, affirmative and negative.

	Present form		Past form	
	aff.	*neg.*	*aff.*	*neg.*
give	あげます	あげません	あげました	あげませんでした
receive	もらいます	もらいません	もらいました	もらいませんでした
have	あります	ありません	ありました	ありませんでした
lend	かします	かしません	かしました	かしませんでした
borrow	かります	かりません	かりました	かりませんでした

II *State what someone gave to or received from another.* Make up sentences following the pattern of the example and based on the information provided.

e.g. interesting	**1.** pretty	**2.**	**3.** Australian
		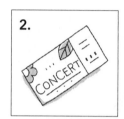	

e.g. スミスさんは　なかむらさんに　<u>おもしろい　ほん</u>を　あげました。
なかむらさんは　スミスさんに　<u>おもしろい　ほん</u>を　もらいました。

1. ....

....

2. ....

....

3. ....

....

III *State what someone lent to or borrowed from another.* Make up sentences following the pattern of the example. Substitute the underlined parts with the alternatives given.

e.g. なかむらさんは　スミスさんに　<u>かさ</u>を　かしました。
スミスさんは　なかむらさんに　<u>かさ</u>を　かりました。

1. ....（くるま）

....（くるま）

2. ....（おかね）

....（おかね）

Ⅳ Make up dialogues following the patterns of the examples and based on the information provided.

A. *Ask and answer whom someone gave something to.*

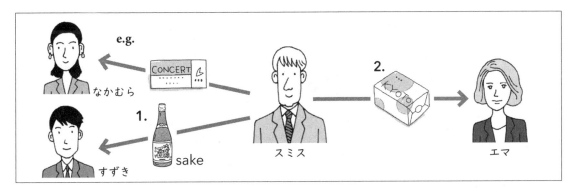

e.g. A：スミスさんは　だれに　コンサートの　チケットを　あげましたか。
B：なかむらさんに　あげました。

1. A：
   B：

2. A：
   B：

B. *Ask and answer what someone received from another.*

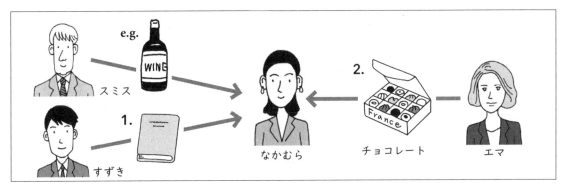

e.g. A：なかむらさんは　スミスさんに　なにを　もらいましたか。
B：ワインを　もらいました。

1. A：
   B：

2. A：
   B：

VOCABULARY

チョコレート　chocolate

V Make up sentences or dialogues following the patterns of the examples and based on the information provided.

	クリスマス	たんじょうび	バレンタインデー
リサ → スミス	**e.g. 1.**	**2.**	**e.g. 2.** nothing
スミス → リサ	**1.** scarf pretty	**3.**	**4.** nothing

A. *State who gave what to whom, and who received what from whom, on a specific day.*

e.g. 1. リサさんは　クリスマスに　スミスさんに　ネクタイを　あげました。

スミスさんは　クリスマスに　リサさんに　ネクタイを　もらいました。

1. ....

....

2. ....

....

3. ....

....

B. *Ask and answer what someone gave to another on a specific day.*

e.g. 1. A：リサさんは　クリスマスに　スミスさんに　なにを　あげましたか。

B：ネクタイを　あげました。

1. A：..

B：..

2. A：..

B：..

クリスマス	Christmas
バレンタインデー	Valentine's Day

3. A : ....

B : ....

C. *Ask and answer when someone received something from another.*

e.g. 1. A：スミスさんは　いつ　リサさんに　ネクタイを　もらいましたか。

B：クリスマスに　もらいました。

1. A : ....

B : ....

2. A : ....

B : ....

3. A : ....

B : ....

D. *Ask and answer what someone received from another on a specific day.*

e.g. 2. A：スミスさんは　バレンタインデーに　リサさんに　なにを

もらいましたか。

B：なにも　もらいませんでした。

4. A : ....

B : ....

Ⅵ *State someone's schedule.* Make up sentences following the pattern of the example. Substitute the underlined parts with the alternatives given.

e.g. スミスさんは　<u>あした</u>　<u>かいぎ</u>が　あります。

1. ....

（こんばん、ともだちと　やくそく）

2. ....

（あさっての　ごご、じかん）

3. ....

（らいしゅう、しゅっちょう）

こんばん　　　　this evening

Ⅶ *Ask and answer someone's schedule.* Make up dialogues following the pattern of the example. Substitute the underlined parts with the alternatives given.

e.g. たなか：スミスさん、<u>あした</u>は　いそがしいですか。

スミス：はい、いそがしいです。<u>かいぎ</u>が　ありますから。

1. たなか：...（あさって）

スミス：...

（おおきい　プレゼン）

2. たなか：...（きんようびの　よる）

スミス：...

（にほんごの　クラス）

Ⅷ *Talk about some item of a person's apparel.* Make up dialogues following the pattern of the example and based on the information provided.

lovely

nice / けっこんきねんび Wedding Anniversary

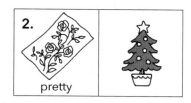
pretty

e.g. なかむら：<u>すてきな　ネックレス</u>ですね。

エマ　　：ええ、<u>たんじょうび</u>に　おっとに　もらいました。

なかむら：よく　にあいますね。

エマ　　：ありがとうございます。

1. なかむら：...

エマ　　：...

なかむら：...

エマ　　：...

2. なかむら：...

エマ　　：...

なかむら：...

エマ　　：...

よる	night	よく　にあいますね。	It suits you well.
けっこんきねんび	wedding anniversary	よく	well
けっこん	wedding, marriage	にあいます	suit, look good on
きねんび	anniversary		

Ⅸ Listen to the audio and answer the questions based on the information you hear. 146

   1. スミスさんは　たんじょうびに　なにを　もらいましたか。

     ....

   2. だれに　もらいましたか。

     ....

SPEAKING PRACTICE

1. The train lurches, and Emma steps on the foot of another person standing. 🔊 147

  おんなの　ひと：いたい！

  エマ　　　　　　：すみません。だいじょうぶですか。

  おんなの　ひと：ええ、だいじょうぶです。

  エマ　　　　　　：どうも　すみませんでした。

Woman: Ouch!
Emma: I'm sorry. Are you all right?
Woman: Yes, I'm fine.
Emma: I'm very sorry.

1. Compliment someone around you on something he/she is wearing.

2. Ask people around you if they have time tomorrow evening.

VOCABULARY

いたい！	Ouch!
だいじょうぶですか。	Are you all right?
すみませんでした。	I'm sorry (for what I did a while ago).

I Complete the sentences by choosing the most appropriate particle from the box below. The same particle may be used more than once. Some of the particles are not needed.

| が | を | に | で | と |

1. スミスさんは　なかむらさん　（　　　　）　ワインを　あげました。

2. なかむらさんは　スミスさん　（　　　　）　ワインを　もらいました。

3. スミスさんは　いま　きょうと　（　　　　）　います。

4. きょうとに　ふるい　おてら　（　　　　）　あります。

5. スミスさんは　きょうと　（　　　　）　おてらを　みます。

II Change the word in the parentheses to the form that is appropriate in the context of the sentence.

1. きのう　えいがを　みました。とても ＿＿＿＿＿＿＿＿＿＿＿＿。（おもしろい）

2. この　サンドイッチは　あまり ＿＿＿＿＿＿＿＿＿＿＿＿。（おいしい）

3. せんしゅうの　テストは　ぜんぜん ＿＿＿＿＿＿＿＿＿＿＿＿。
   （むずかしい）

4. きのうは ＿＿＿＿＿＿＿＿＿＿が、きょうは　いそがしいです。（ひま）

5. しゅうまつに ＿＿＿＿＿＿＿＿＿　レストランで　ばんごはんを　たべました。
   （ゆうめい）

III What do you say in the following situations?

1. You want to ask people who attended the party yesterday how the party was.

   ＿＿＿＿＿＿＿＿＿＿＿＿＿＿＿＿＿＿＿＿＿＿＿＿＿＿＿＿＿＿＿＿＿

2. You want to ask what there is to see at Nikko.

   ＿＿＿＿＿＿＿＿＿＿＿＿＿＿＿＿＿＿＿＿＿＿＿＿＿＿＿＿＿＿＿＿＿

3. You want to ask where the taxi stand is located.

   ＿＿＿＿＿＿＿＿＿＿＿＿＿＿＿＿＿＿＿＿＿＿＿＿＿＿＿＿＿＿＿＿＿

4. You want to ask what kind of place Shibuya is.

   ＿＿＿＿＿＿＿＿＿＿＿＿＿＿＿＿＿＿＿＿＿＿＿＿＿＿＿＿＿＿＿＿＿

5. You want to ask how many beers are in the refrigerator.

   ＿＿＿＿＿＿＿＿＿＿＿＿＿＿＿＿＿＿＿＿＿＿＿＿＿＿＿＿＿＿＿＿＿

MAKING LEISURE PLANS

Manga, anime, and computer games enjoyed by people from childhood to old age are now considered an important part of Japanese culture and have become quite popular around the world as well. The settings of these works are often real places or buildings around the country and they draw fans from around the country and the world. The photo is of buildings in Tokyo's Akihabara area, where numerous shops are clustered that sell figures and character goods relating to manga, anime, and games.

Talking about Preferences: I Like Japanese Anime

TARGET DIALOGUE 🔊 148

Smith's cousin Paul is visiting Japan.

スミス	：いとこの　ポールです。
ポール	：はじめまして。ポールです。よろしく　おねがいします。
	わたしは　にほんの　アニメが　すきです。
すずき	：どんな　アニメが　すきですか。
ポール	：ロボットの　アニメが　すきです。
すずき	：あ、わたしもです。かくのも　すきです。
	(Draws an illustration.)
スミス・ポール	：わあ！　すごい！　じょうずですね！

■ポールさんと　すずきさんは　ロボットの　アニメが　すきです。

Smith:　This is my cousin, Paul.
Paul:　　How do you do? I am Paul. Nice to meet you. I like Japanese anime.
Suzuki:　What kind of anime do you like?
Paul:　　I like mecha anime.
Suzuki:　Ah! I like them too.
　　　　　I also like drawing anime.
Smith and Paul: Wow!
　　　　　That's great. You're good!

■ Paul-san and Suzuki-san like mecha anime.

VOCABULARY

いとこ	cousin	かきます	draw	すごい！	That's great!
アニメ	anime, animation	の	(nominalizer; see	じょうず（な）	skilled, be good at
すき（な）	like, favorite		GRAMMAR 3, p. 144)		
ロボット	robot	わあ！	Wow! (exclamation of		
かく	draw		surprise)		

1. どんな　アニメが　すきですか。

    When asking what someone likes from a specific category, use "どんな　noun が　すきですか."

2. わたしもです。

    This means わたしも　ロボットの　アニメが　すきです. The expression わたしもです can be used when you want to say "I am the same [as the previous speaker]," whether it is affirmative or negative.

KEY SENTENCES

149

1. チャンさんは　ワインが　すきです。
2. チャンさんは　にほんごが　じょうずです。
3. スミスさんは　サッカーを　みるのが　すきです。

1. Chan-san likes wine.
2. Chan-san is good at Japanese.
3. Smith-san likes watching soccer matches.

GRAMMAR

1. person は　noun が　すきです。   (KS1)

   person は　noun が　じょうずです。   (KS2)

When using すきです (な-adjective with equivalent meaning to "like") and じょうずです ("be skilled"), the thing one likes or the skill takes the particle が, and is followed by すきです or じょうずです.

NOTE: じょうずです is always used to describe others. Japanese almost never use it to describe themselves or members of their families because it sounds like boasting. People therefore rarely ask じょうずですか meaning "Are you good at [such-and-such]."

2. Verb dictionary form   (KS3)

Japanese verbs are conjugated in various forms. Up to this point in this textbook, verbs have been introduced in the ます-form or its derivatives. In this lesson we will study a new form called the "dictionary form," which is so named because it is the form of the verb that is listed in dictionaries.

Japanese verbs are divided into three categories: Regular 1, Regular 2, and Irregular. The Irregular verbs are きます and します or compound verbs formed with these verbs. The Regular 2 verbs introduced through Lesson 14 are: たべます, みます, おしえます, みせます, います, あげます, かります. Regular 2 verbs introduced from Lesson 15 onward will be included in VOCABULARY, marked (R2), for each lesson.

To obtain the dictionary form of a Regular 1 verb, the sound before the ます changes as shown in the chart on the following page. To obtain the dictionary form of Regular 2 verbs, the rule is simpler: change ます to る. The dictionary form of Irregular verbs is shown in the chart on the following page.

サッカー	soccer, football
みる (R2)	see, watch

	Regular 1			Regular 2	
	ます-form	Dictionary form		ます-form	Dictionary form
buy	かいます	かう	see, watch	みます	みる
go	いきます	いく	be	います	いる
swim	およぎます	およぐ	eat	たべます	たべる
lend	かします	かす	tell, teach	おしえます	おしえる
wait	まちます	まつ	Irregular		
drink	のみます	のむ	come	きます	くる
return, go home	かえります	かえる	do	します	する

3. person は　verb [dictionary form] のが　すきです。　　　　　　(KS3)

By adding the nominalizer の to the dictionary form of the verb in place of a noun in the sentence "person は noun が　すきです," you can express what someone likes to do. Likewise you can express what someone is skillful at doing with "person は　verb [dictionary form] のが　じょうずです."

WORD POWER

I な-adjectives

 150

①すき（な）

②じょうず（な）

II Sports

151

①スキー

②サッカー

③やきゅう

④ダイビング

Ⅲ Dictionary form

 152

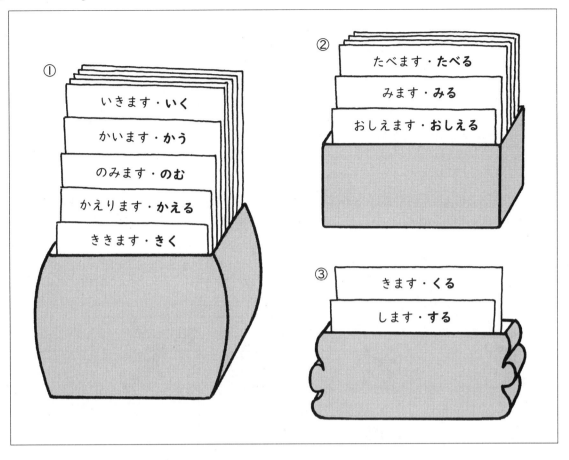

① いきます・**いく**
かいます・**かう**
のみます・**のむ**
かえります・**かえる**
ききます・**きく**

② たべます・**たべる**
みます・**みる**
おしえます・**おしえる**

③ きます・**くる**
します・**する**

Ⅳ Verbs

 153

①かきます

②はなします

③うたいます

④およぎます

⑤はしります

はなします	talk, speak
うたいます	sing
およぎます	swim
はしります	run

EXERCISES

Ⅰ *Practice conjugating な-adjectives.* Repeat the adjectives below and memorize their forms—present and past, affirmative and negative.

	Present form		Past form	
	aff.	*neg.*	*aff.*	*neg.*
like	すきです	すきじゃありません	すきでした	すきじゃありませんでした
be skilled	じょうずです	じょうずじゃありません	じょうずでした	じょうずじゃありませんでした

Ⅱ Make up sentences following the patterns of the examples and based on the information provided.

VOCABULARY

ゴルフ	golf
ダンス	dance
うた	song
ウイスキー	whiskey

A. *State what someone likes and is skilled at.*

    e.g. <u>かとうさん</u>は　<u>にほんしゅ</u>が　すきです。<u>ゴルフ</u>が　じょうずです。

    1. ....

    2. ....

    3. ....

B. *State what someone dislikes and is unskilled at.*

    e.g. <u>かとうさん</u>は　<u>コーヒー</u>が　すきじゃありません。

    <u>テニス</u>が　じょうずじゃありません。

    1. ....

....

    2. ....

....

    3. ....

....

Ⅲ *Ask for and give more information about what one likes.* Make up dialogues following the pattern of the example. Substitute the underlined parts with the alternatives given.

    e.g. エマ　　：すずきさんは　<u>スポーツ</u>が　すきですか。

    すずき：はい、すきです。

    エマ　　：どんな　<u>スポーツ</u>が　すきですか。

    すずき：<u>やきゅう</u>が　すきです。

    1. エマ　：..（くだもの）

    すずき：..

    エマ　：..（くだもの）

    すずき：..（りんご）

VOCABULARY

| スポーツ | sports |
| くだもの | fruits |

2. エマ　　：..（イタリアりょうり）

　　すずき：..

　　エマ　　：..（イタリアりょうり）

　　すずき：..（ピザ）

3. エマ　　：..（おんがく）

　　すずき：..

　　エマ　　：..（おんがく）

　　すずき：..（ジャズ）

Ⅳ　*Practice conjugating verbs.* Repeat the verbs below and memorize their dictionary forms.

	ます-form	Dictionary form			ます-form	Dictionary form
go	いきます	いく		swim	およぎます	およぐ
sing	うたいます	うたう		talk, speak	はなします	はなす
run	はしります	はしる		eat	たべます	たべる
take	とります	とる		see	みます	みる
drink	のみます	のむ		come	きます	くる
draw	かきます	かく		do	します	する

Ⅴ　*Practice making dictionary forms.* Change the following verbs to their dictionary forms.

e.g. たべます　→　たべる

1. うたいます　→　.......................................

2. はしります　→　.......................................

3. いきます　　→　.......................................

4. します　　　→　.......................................

5. およぎます　→　.......................................

6. はなします　→　.......................................

7. みます　　　→　.......................................

8. かきます　　→　.......................................

9. あるきます　→　.......................................

10. よみます　　→　.......................................

VOCABULARY

イタリアりょうり	Italian cuisine
りょうり	food, dish, cooking, cuisine
ピザ	pizza
ジャズ	jazz

VI *State what a person likes to do.* Make up sentences following the pattern of the example and based on the information provided.

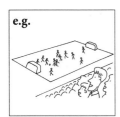   

e.g. サッカーを　みるのが　すきです。

1. ....

2. ....

3. ....

VII *Talk about what you like to do.* Make up dialogues following the pattern of the example. Substitute the underlined parts with the appropriate forms of the alternatives given.

e.g. かとう　　：グリーンさんは　おんがくを　きくのが　すきですか。

グリーン：ええ、すきです。かとうさんは？

かとう　　：わたしも　すきです。うたうのも　すきです。

グリーン：そうですか。いいですね。

1. かとう　　：..（はしります）

　　グリーン：..

　　かとう　　：..

　　　　　　　..（およぎます）

　　グリーン：..

2. かとう　　：..（えを　かきます）

　　グリーン：..

　　かとう　　：..

　　　　　　　..（びじゅつかんに　いきます）

　　グリーン：..

VOCABULARY

びじゅつかん　　art museum

Ⅷ Listen to the audio and fill in the blanks based on the information you hear. 🔊 154, 155

1. スミスさんは .... のが　すきです。

2. ブラウンさんは .... のが　じょうずです。

SPEAKING PRACTICE

1. Nakamura and Raja are talking during their break. 🔊 156

なかむら：ラジャさんは　スポーツが　すきですか。

ラジャ　：はい、すきです。

なかむら：どんな　スポーツが　すきですか。

ラジャ　：サッカーが　すきです。でも、じょうずじゃありません。

Nakamura: Do you like sports, Raja-san?
Raja:　　　Yes, I do.
Nakamura: What sports do you like?
Raja:　　　I like soccer. But I'm not good at playing it.

Active Communication

Imagine you are at a party. Introduce people around you to one another and give details about their interests and skills.

| でも | but |

Making an Invitation: Shall We Go Together?

TARGET DIALOGUE
🔊 157

Suzuki, Paul, and Smith are talking.

すずき：つぎの　にちようびに　あきはばらで　アニメの　イベントが
　　　　あります。おもしろい　イベントですから、いっしょに
　　　　いきませんか。

ポール：いいですね。ぜひ。イベントは　なんじからですか。

すずき：１じからです。ひるごはんも　いっしょに　たべましょう。
　　　　スミスさんも　いっしょに　どうですか。

スミス：すみません。アニメは　ちょっと…。

すずき：そうですか。

■ すずきさんと　ポールさんは　つぎの　にちようびに　アニメの
　イベントに　いきます。

Suzuki: Next Sunday there is an anime event in Akihabara. It's an interesting event, so shall we go [see it] together?
Paul: Sounds good. I'd love to. What time does the event start?
Suzuki: It starts at 1:00 p.m. Let's have lunch together too. Smith-san, how about you?
Smith: Sorry, anime is not really . . .
Suzuki: I see.

■ Next Sunday, Suzuki-san and Paul-san will go to the anime event.

VOCABULARY

つぎ	next	から	because, so (particle; see GRAMMAR 4, p. 152)	ぜひ	I'd love to, by all means
あきはばら	Akihabara (district in Tokyo)			たべましょう	let's eat
イベント	event			どうですか	how about you?
あります	there is, take place (see GRAMMAR 1, p. 152)	いっしょに	together	ちょっと…	(see GRAMMAR 2, p. 152)
		いきませんか	shall we go?		

NOTES

1. スミスさんも いっしょに どうですか。

   どうですか is the expression used to ask the listener's intention. Here Suzuki is asking whether Smith wants to come along on the visit to Akihabara.

KEY SENTENCES

🔊 158

1. どようびに あさくさで おまつりが あります。
2. しゅうまつに いっしょに えいがを みませんか。
3. いっしょに いきましょう。
4. いい てんきですから、こうえんで ひるごはんを たべませんか。

1. There is a festival in Asakusa on Saturday.
2. Shall we see a movie together on the weekend?
3. Let's go together.
4. The weather is nice, so shall we have lunch in the park?

GRAMMAR

1. placeで eventが あります。 (KS1)

あります can also be used in the sense of "take place" or "happen." The place where the event happens takes the particle で.

2. verb [ます-form stem] ませんか。 (KS2, 4)

When suggesting some action to someone, ask by changing the ます of the ます-form to ませんか. The ways of responding to that form of question are listed below.

(1) Agreeing

ええ／はい、ぜひ。	Yes, I'd love to.
いいですね。ぜひ。	Sounds good. I'd love to.
ええ／はい、そう しましょう。	Yes, let's do that.

(2) Declining

すみません。nounは ちょっと…。	I'm sorry, but noun is not really [to my taste].
ざんねんですが、nounは ちょっと…。	Unfortunately, noun is a little [inconvenient for me].

は ちょっと… is added when responding to an inconvenient date, time or day of the week, or to invitations you are reluctant to accept. The "is not really to my taste" or "is inconvenient for me" is omitted after ちょっと because of the Japanese tendency to avoid a clear refusal.

3. verb [ます-form stem]ましょう。 (KS3)

When making an invitation for the speaker and the listener to do something together, the ます of the ます-form changes to ましょう. This is generally expressed in English as "let's [verb] . . . ."

4. clause 1から、clause 2。 (KS4)

Clause 1 ending with から expresses the reason for clause 2.

VOCABULARY

みませんか	shall we see?	たべませんか	shall we eat?
いきましょう	let's go		

WORD POWER

Ⅰ Events
🔊 159

①はなびたいかい

②ゆきまつり

③サッカーの　しあい

Ⅱ Parts of a train station
🔊 160

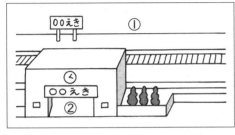

①ホーム　　②でぐち　　③にしぐち　　④ひがしぐち　　⑤きたぐち　　⑥みなみぐち

Ⅲ Physical condition
🔊 161

①おなかが　すきました

②のどが　かわきました

③つかれました

Ⅳ Variations on ます-form
🔊 162

	go	see	do	meet
V ます	いきます	みます	します	あいます
V ませんか	いきませんか	みませんか	しませんか	あいませんか
V ましょう	いきましょう	みましょう	しましょう	あいましょう

VOCABULARY

はなびたいかい	fireworks festival	でぐち	exit	みなみぐち	south exit
はなび	fireworks	にしぐち	west exit	みなみ	south
たいかい	festival, event	にし	west	おなかが　すきました。	I'm hungry.
ゆきまつり	snow festival	ひがしぐち	east exit	のどが　かわきました。	I'm thirsty.
ゆき	snow	ひがし	east	つかれました。	I'm tired.
しあい	game, match	きたぐち	north exit		
ホーム	platform	きた	north		

EXERCISES

Ⅰ *Invite someone to do something.* Make up sentences following the pattern of the example.

e.g. ひるごはんを　たべます。→　ひるごはんを　たべませんか。

1. おまつりに　いきます。→ ....

2. えいがを　みます。　　→ ....

3. しょくじを　します。　→ ....

4. コーヒーを　のみます。→ ....

Ⅱ Make up dialogues following the patterns of the examples and based on the information provided.

A. *Invite someone to do something and accept one's invitation.*

e.g.
tomorrow

1. にっこう
next month

2. しょくじ
this evening

3. サッカーの　しあい
next week

e.g. A：<u>あした　いっしょに　えいがを　みませんか</u>。

B：ええ、ぜひ。

1. A： ....

B： ....

2. A： ....

B： ....

3. A： ....

B： ....

VOCABULARY

しょくじを　します　have a meal

B. *Invite someone to do something and refuse one's invitation.*

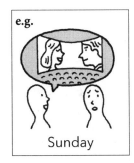

e.g.

Sunday

1. はこね

Saturday

2. かぶき

Friday

3. ひるごはん

weekend

e.g. A：にちようびに　いっしょに　えいがを　みませんか。

B：ざんねんですが、にちようびは　ちょっと…。

A：そうですか。じゃ、また　こんど。

1. A：...

B：...

A：...

2. A：...

B：...

A：...

3. A：...

B：...

A：...

VOCABULARY

ざんねんです　　it is unfortunate

また　こんど。　Next time., Another time.

Ⅲ Make up sentences or dialogues following the patterns of the examples and based on the information provided.

e.g. あさくさ	1. さっぽろ	2.	3. よこはま

Saturday	next month	this evening	Tuesday

A. *State when and where an event will take place.*

e.g. <u>どようびに　あさくさで　おまつり</u>が　あります。

1. ....

2. ....

3. ....

B. *Invite someone to an event and accept one's invitation.*

e.g. A : <u>どようびに　あさくさで　おまつり</u>が　あります。
　　　　いっしょに　いきませんか。
　　B : いいですね。ぜひ。

1. A : ....

　　 ....

　　B : ....

2. A : ....

　　 ....

　　B : ....

3. A : ....

　　 ....

　　B : ....

Ⅳ *Propose alternative options.* Make up dialogues following the pattern of the example. Substitute the underlined parts with the alternatives given.

e.g. A：しゅうまつに <u>あさくさで</u> <u>おまつり</u>が あります。

<u>どようび</u>に いっしょに いきませんか。

B：ざんねんですが、<u>どようび</u>は ちょっと…。

A：じゃ、<u>にちようび</u>は どうですか。

B：<u>にちようび</u>は じかんが あります。

A：じゃ、<u>にちようび</u>に いきましょう。

1. A： .... （かまくら、おまつり）

　 .... （にちようび）

　 B： .... （にちようび）

　 A： .... （どようび）

　 B： .... （どようび）

　 A： .... （どようび）

2. A： .... （しぶや、フリーマーケット）

　 .... （どようび）

　 B： .... （どようび）

　 A： .... （にちようび）

　 B： .... （にちようび）

　 A： .... （にちようび）

VOCABULARY

～は どうですか　how about . . .

Ⓥ *Give a reason and invite someone to do something.* Make up dialogues following the pattern of the example. Substitute the underlined parts with the appropriate forms of the alternatives given.

    e.g. A：<u>いい　てんきですから</u>、<u>こうえんで　ひるごはんを　たべませんか</u>。

       B：いいですね。そう　しましょう。

    1.　A：...

       （この　ちかくに　おいしい　そばやが　あります、いっしょに　いきます）

       B：...

    2.　A：...

       （にちようびは　スミスさんの　たんじょうびです、パーティーを　します）

       B：...

    3.　A：...

          （チケットが　２まい　あります、こんばん　えいがを　みます）

       B：...

Ⅵ *State a reason and invite someone to do something.* Make up dialogues following the pattern of the example. Substitute the underlined parts with the appropriate forms of the alternatives given.

    e.g. A：<u>おなかが　すきましたね</u>。<u>なにか　たべませんか</u>。

       B：ええ、そう　しましょう。

    1.　A：...

            （のどが　かわきました、なにか　のみます）

       B：...

    2.　A：...

            （つかれました、すこし　やすみます）

       B：...

VOCABULARY

パーティーを　します	have a party	やすみます	rest
なにか	something		
そう　しましょう。	Let's do that.		
すこし	a bit, a little		

VII *Invite someone to an event and propose a meeting time and place.* Make up dialogues following the pattern of the example. Substitute the underlined parts with the alternatives given.

e.g. すずき：にちようびに　<u>よこはま</u>で　<u>はなびたいかい</u>が　あります。

いっしょに　いきませんか。

スミス：いいですね。ぜひ。<u>はなびたいかい</u>は　なんじからですか。

すずき：<u>7じ</u>からです。<u>6じ</u>に　<u>よこはまえきの　にしぐち</u>で

あいましょう。

スミス：<u>6じ</u>に　<u>よこはまえきの　にしぐち</u>ですね。わかりました。

1. すずき：..

（しぶや、コンサート）

スミス：..

（コンサート）

すずき：..

（6じはん、5じはん、しぶやえきの　ひがしぐち）

スミス：..

（5じはん、しぶやえきの　ひがしぐち）

2. すずき：..

（しんじゅく、おまつり）

スミス：..

（おまつり）

すずき：..

（10じ、9じ、しんじゅくえきの　みなみぐち）

スミス：..

（9じ、しんじゅくえきの　みなみぐち）

VIII Listen to the audio and fill in the blanks based on the information you hear. 🔊163, 164

1. スミスさんは　こんばん　すずきさんと　しぶやで　..。

2. 1) ....に　あさくさで　おまつりが　あります。

2) スミスさんは　................................と　おまつりに　いきます。

しんじゅく　Shinjuku (district in Tokyo)

SPEAKING PRACTICE

1. Sasaki is having a party at her home.　🔊 165

   ささき：スミスさん、15にちの　にちようびに　うちで　パーティーを　します。
   　　　　きませんか。

   スミス：ありがとうございます。ぜひ。

   Sasaki: Smith-san, I am having a party at my house on Sunday, the 15th. Would you like to come?
   Smith:　Thank you. I'd love to.

2. Nakamura is going to play tennis on Saturday.　🔊 166

   なかむら：どようびに　スミスさんと　テニスを　します。

   　　　　　エマさんも　いっしょに　しませんか。

   エマ　　：ありがとうございます。ぜひ。

   Nakamura:　On Saturday, I'm going to play tennis with Smith-san. Would you like to join us, Emma-san?
   Emma:　　　Thank you. I'd love to.

NOTES

1. 15にちの　にちようび

   This の expresses apposition. When giving the date and the day of the week, it is expressed by "date の day of the week." The date is stated first and then the day of the week. They are usually connected with の.

2. きませんか。

   When the speaker invites someone to his/her home or an event he/she plans, きませんか is used.

3. ありがとうございます。ぜひ。

   When invited to the speaker's home, to an event the speaker has planned, or to join an event that is already decided, the affirmative response to the invitation is usually ありがとうございます。ぜひ.

Active Communication　Invite someone around you to an event.

Stating a Wish: I Want to Buy a Souvenir

TARGET DIALOGUE 🔊 167

Paul and Suzuki are discussing what to do on Sunday.

ポール：おとうとも　アニメが　すきですから、あきはばらで
　　　　おみやげを　かいたいです。

すずき：そうですか。じゃ、ひるごはんの　まえに、かいものを　しましょう。

ポール：ありがとうございます。

すずき：ポールさん、ホテルは　どこですか。

ポール：しんじゅくの　のぞみホテルです。

すずき：じゃ、10じに　ホテルの　ロビーで　あいましょう。

ポール：10じですね。わかりました。

■すずきさんと　ポールさんは　ひるごはんを　たべる　まえに
　かいものを　します。

Paul:　　My younger brother likes anime, too, so I'd like to buy him a souvenir at Akihabara.
Suzuki: I see. Before lunch, let's do some shopping.
Paul:　　Thank you.
Suzuki: Paul-san, where is your hotel?
Paul:　　It's the Nozomi Hotel in Shinjuku.
Suzuki: Then, let's meet at 10:00 in the lobby of your hotel.
Paul:　　At 10:00. I've got that.

■Suzuki-san and Paul-san will do some shopping before they have lunch.

VOCABULARY

おとうと	(my) younger brother	のぞみホテル	Nozomi Hotel (fictitious hotel name)
かいたいです	want to buy	ロビー	lobby
～の　まえに	before . . .	たべる　まえに	before eating
まえ	before		

KEY SENTENCES

 168

1.（わたしは）おいしい　おすしを　たべたいです。

2. スミスさんは　かいぎの　まえに　しりょうを　おくります。

3. スミスさんは　まいにち　ねる　まえに　ストレッチを　します。

1. (I) want to eat some good sushi.
2. Smith-san will send the material before the meeting.
3. Smith-san does stretching exercises every day before going to bed.

GRAMMAR

1.（わたしは）**verb** [ます-form stem]たいです／たくないです。 (KS1)

When a speaker states a wish, the ます is removed from the ます-form and たいです is added. The ～たいで
す is conjugated in the same way as い-adjectives.

 e.g. いきたいです。   (I) want to go.

  いきたくないです。 (I) don't want to go.

  いきたかったです。 (I) wanted to go.

  いきたくなかったです。 (I) didn't want to go.

 NOTE: Sometimes が is used as the object marker in place of を.

   e.g. ワインを／が　のみたいです。 (I) want to drink wine.

～たい expresses the wish of the speaker and cannot be used to express the wish of anyone other than the
speaker. か may be added to the end of the sentence to change it into a question, but it is not appropriate for use
when making an invitation. Also, it is considered impolite to use this expression when asking ～たいですか ("do
you want to do . . . ?") , especially to someone of higher status. When wishing to ask what someone wants to do,
it is safer to attach か to the ます-form of the verb (e.g., なにを　のみますか). Regarding future dreams or
hopes, however, it is acceptable to ask, even of a person of higher status ～たいですか.

2. personは　**noun**の　まえに　**verb**。 (KS2)

Expresses what is/was done before the noun (event, action, etc.).

3. personは　**verb 1** [dictionary form]　まえに　**verb 2**。 (KS3)

Indicates that the verb 2 action comes before the verb 1 action.

たべたいです	want to eat	ストレッチを　します	do stretching exercises
しりょう	material, data, documents		
ねる　まえに	before sleeping/going to bed		
ねます (R2)	sleep, go to bed		

WORD POWER

① Hobbies
🔊 169

①いけばな ②からて ③ピアノ ④ダンス

② Verbs
🔊 170

①ならいます ②りょうりを します ③あらいます ④シャワーを あびます

⑤しょくじを します ⑥はじめます ⑦かきます ⑧ねます

VOCABULARY

いけばな	flower arrangement	りょうりを します	cook	はじめます (R2)	start, begin
からて	karate	あらいます	wash	かきます	write
ピアノ	piano	シャワーを あびます (R2)			
ならいます	learn, take lessons in		take a shower		

EXERCISES

I *Practice conjugating verbs.* Repeat the verbs below and memorize their たい-forms—
present and past, affirmative and negative.

	Present form		Past form	
	aff.	*neg.*	*aff.*	*neg.*
want to buy	かいたいです	かいたくないです	かいたかったです	かいたくなかったです
want to eat	たべたいです	たべたくないです	たべたかったです	たべたくなかったです
want to see	みたいです	みたくないです	みたかったです	みたくなかったです
want to meet	あいたいです	あいたくないです	あいたかったです	あいたくなかったです
want to go	いきたいです	いきたくないです	いきたかったです	いきたくなかったです

II Make up sentences following the patterns of the examples.

A. *State what you want to do.*

e.g. おすしを　たべます。→　おすしを　たべたいです。

1. テレビを　みます。　　　→　...

2. たなかさんに　あいます。→　...

3. おみやげを　かいます。　→　...

4. おんせんに　いきます。　→　...

5. てがみを　かきます。　　→　...

B. *State what you don't want to do.*

e.g. おすしを　たべません。　→　おすしを　たべたくないです。

1. テレビを　みません。　　　→　...

2. たなかさんに　あいません。→　...

3. おみやげを　かいません。　→　...

4. おんせんに　いきません。　→　...

5. てがみを　かきません。　　→　...

| てがみ　letter

Ⅲ Make up dialogues following the patterns of the examples. Substitute the underlined part(s) with the appropriate forms of the alternatives given.

A. *Ask and answer where one wants to live.*

e.g. A：しょうらい　どんな　ところに　すみたいですか。

B：<u>うみの　ちかく</u>に　すみたいです。

1. A： ....

B： ....（あたたかい　ところ）

2. A： ....

B： ....（しずかな　まち）

B. *Ask for information.*

e.g. A：<u>にほんごを　べんきょうしたい</u>です。この　ちかくに
いい　<u>がっこう</u>が　ありますか。

B：ええ、<u>アジャルト・スクール</u>が　いいですよ。

1. A： ....

....（おはなみを　します、ところ）

B： ....（さくらこうえん）

2. A： ....

....（テニスを　ならいます、クラブ）

B： ....（みなとテニスクラブ）

3. A： ....

....（ふるい　かぐを　かいます、みせ）

B： ....（アンティークとうきょう）

VOCABULARY

しょうらい	in the future	さくらこうえん	Sakura Park (fictitious park name)
すみます	live	クラブ	club
まち	town	みなとテニスクラブ	Minato Tennis Club (fictitious club name)
べんきょうします	study (see APPENDIX D, p. 246)		
アジャルト・スクール	AJALT School (fictitious school name)	かぐ	furniture
		アンティークとうきょう	Antique Tokyo (fictitious shop name)
（お）はなみを　します	view cherry blossoms	アンティーク	antiques

Ⅳ *State what someone will do before a particular event.* Look at the illustration and make up sentences following the patterns of the examples. Substitute the underlined part with the alternatives given.

e.g. 1. ごご　１じから　かいぎが　あります。
　　　　かいぎの　まえに　<u>しょくじを　します</u>。

1. ....
　　　　　　　　　　　　　　　　　　　　（しりょうを　ダウンロードします）

2. ....
　　　　　　　　　　　　　　　　　　　　（コーヒーを　かいます）

e.g. 2. ごご　７じから　パーティーが　あります。
　　　　パーティーの　まえに　<u>ワインを　かいます</u>。

3. ....
　　　　　　　　　　　　　　　　　　　　（びよういんに　いきます）

4. ....
　　　　　　　　　　　　　　　　　　　　（シャワーを　あびます）

V Make up sentences following the patterns of the examples. Substitute the underlined part(s) with the appropriate forms of the alternatives given.

A. *State something that is done before doing something else.*

e.g. スミスさんは <u>ねる</u> まえに ストレッチを します。

1. スミスさんは ＿＿＿＿＿＿＿＿＿＿ まえに ニュースを チェックします。
　　　　（しごとを はじめます）

2. スミスさんは ＿＿＿＿＿＿＿＿＿＿ まえに シャワーを あびます。
　　　　（あさごはんを たべます）

3. スミスさんは ＿＿＿＿＿＿＿＿＿＿ まえに てを あらいます。
　　　　（りょうりを します）

B. *State something that was done before doing something else.*

e.g. <u>スミスさんは</u> <u>にほんに くる</u> まえに にほんごの べんきょうを はじめました。

1. ＿＿＿＿＿＿は ＿＿＿＿＿＿＿＿ まえに メールアドレスを
（すずきさん、メールを おくります）
チェックしました。

2. ＿＿＿＿＿＿は ＿＿＿＿＿＿＿＿ まえに おみやげを かいました。
（ポールさん、くにに かえります）

3. ＿＿＿＿＿＿は ＿＿＿＿＿＿＿＿ まえに ストレッチを しました。
（エマさん、およぎます）

VI Listen to the audio and fill in the blanks based on the information you hear. 🔊 171-173

1. チャンさんは まいあさ ＿＿＿＿＿＿＿ まえに ＿＿＿＿＿＿＿＿。

2. スミスさんは まいあさ ＿＿＿＿＿＿＿＿＿ まえに

＿＿＿＿＿＿＿＿＿。

3. すずきさんは もくようびに ＿＿＿＿＿＿＿＿＿ まえに

＿＿＿＿＿＿＿＿＿。

| チェックします | check |
| て | hand |

SPEAKING PRACTICE

1. An event ended, and Suzuki takes Paul back to the hotel.　🔊 174

すずき：すいようびの　よるは　いそがしいですか。

ポール：いいえ、いそがしくないです。

すずき：じゃ、いっしょに　ばんごはんを　たべませんか。

ポール：いいですね。ぜひ。

すずき：じゃ、また　すいようびに。

Suzuki:　Are you busy on Wednesday evening?
Paul:　No, I'm not busy.
Suzuki:　Well then, how about going out for dinner together?
Paul:　That would be very nice. I'd love to.
Suzuki:　Then, I'll see you on Wednesday.

2. Paul and Suzuki are at a Japanese restaurant. A plate of sashimi has been served. 🔊 175

ポール：きれいですね。

すずき：いただきます。

ポール：ちょっと　まってください。たべる　まえに　しゃしんを　とりたいです。

Paul:　Doesn't that look nice!
Suzuki:　Let's eat!
Paul:　Please wait a minute! Before we eat it, I want to take a picture.

NOTES

1. じゃ、また　すいようびに。
   すいようびに is a shortened version of すいようびに　あいましょう. When people part, they rarely say さようなら, usually using a phrase that refers to the next time they will meet.

   e.g. じゃ、また　あした。　See you tomorrow.

Active Communication

1. Get information about schools and teachers, or about a subject you want to take a lesson in.
2. Get information about things you want to buy and places you want to visit.

VOCABULARY

いただきます。 [said before eating]

CASUAL STYLE 1

WHAT IS THE CASUAL STYLE?

Japanese has a number of speech levels or styles that are used depending on degree of familiarity and status in vertical relationships. The style studied so far in this textbook is the so-called です ます-style that is most widely used in adult conversation.

Conversations in families or among friends follow the "casual style." People sometimes change their style of speech according to the circumstances, even when speaking to the same person, and a number of complex elements go into judging when and with whom to use casual style. Casual style, if used inappropriately, sounds very rude, and it should never be used carelessly where it does not belong. Here we introduce the casual style mainly for the purpose of hearing comprehension.

SAMPLE DIALOGUE 1 ──────────────────────────────── 🔊 176

A student in a university classroom finds a pen on the floor and speaks to her classmates:

はやし：これ、だれの　ペン？

やまだ：さあ。(*Turning toward Abe*) あべの？

あべ　：ううん、おれのじゃない。

はやし：ラジャさん、これって　ラジャさんの？

ラジャ：うん、ぼくの。ありがとう。

Hayashi: Whose pen is this?

Yamada: I don't know. Is it yours, Abe?

Abe: No, it's not mine.

Hayashi: Raja, is this yours?

Raja: Yes, it is. Thanks.

です ます style	Casual style
noun 1 は　noun 2 です。	**noun 1 は　noun 2。** です is omitted. When ね or よ are added, they become だね, だよ.
noun 1 は　noun 2 ですか。	**noun 1 は　noun 2 ？** か is omitted, and the question is expressed by rising intonation. は is often omitted and sometimes becomes って.
はい、noun 2 です。	**うん、noun 2。**
いいえ、noun 2 じゃありません。	**ううん、noun 2 じゃない。**
last name ＋さん **first name ＋さん**	"Last name + さん" and "first name + さん" can be used, but sometimes さん is replaced by くん or ちゃん. The first name or last name without a title, as well as nicknames, are also used.
わたし	Males often use ぼく or おれ. Females sometimes use あたし.

169

SAMPLE DIALOGUE 2 ———————————————— 🔊 177

Nakamura is talking to a friend named Chiba on the phone.

なかむら：あしたの　パーティー、いく？　　　Nakamura: Are you going to tomorrow's party?

ちば　　：うん、いく。　　　　　　　　　　Chiba:　　Yes, I am.

ですます style	Casual style
いきます。	いく。 The present affirmative form of verbs is expressed by the dictionary form.
パーティーに　いきますか。	パーティー、いく？ The particle に is often omitted when indicating a destination, but when the sentence involves someone relating to a benefactive expression, or when it indicates current location, it is not omitted. は and を are often omitted. で、と、and や are not omitted.

SAMPLE DIALOGUE 3 ———————————————— 🔊 178

Nakamura attended yesterday's party, but her friend Ono did not.

おの　　：きのうの　パーティー、どうだった？　　Ono:　　　How was yesterday's party?

なかむら：すごく　にぎやかだった。　　　　　Nakamura: It was very lively.

おの　　：りょうりは？　　　　　　　　　　Ono:　　　How about the food?

なかむら：おいしかったよ。　　　　　　　　Nakamura: It was good.

	Adjectives as predicates in casual style			
	Present form		Past form	
	aff.	*neg.*	*aff.*	*neg.*
い-adj.	おおきい いい	おおきくない よくない	おおきかった よかった	おおきくなかった よくなかった
な-adj.	きれい*	きれいじゃない	きれいだった	きれいじゃなかった

*In cases when ね or よ is added, in casual speech, they become きれいだね and きれいだよ.

BUSINESS TRIPS

Even in times when teleconferencing has become quite common, people in business recognize the value of face-to-face communication and travel frequently to meet in person with clients and associates. The Japanese archipelago stretches over a distance of 3,000 kilometers and the climate varies widely from Hokkaido in the north to Okinawa in the south. That diversity makes for great variety in the specialties of each area, whether fruit, vegetables, seafood, dairy or other products. Souvenirs sold in each part of the country feature local specialties, such as cookies made with butter from Hokkaido's famous dairy industry or sweets made with Okinawa-grown pineapple. People who go on business trips often purchase such souvenirs to share with their families or office mates.

Explaining Plans: I Will Go to Osaka and See Her

TARGET DIALOGUE　　　🔊 179

Emma speaks to Kato while he is working.

エマ　　：かとうさん、ちょっと　よろしいですか。

かとう：はい。

エマ　　：あした　おおさかに　いきます。

かとう：あ、パッケージフェアですね。

エマ　　：ええ。フェアの　あと、ししゃに　いって、チャンさんに
　　　　　あいます。あさって　こうじょうを　みて、
　　　　　4じの　ひこうきで　とうきょうに　かえります。

かとう：わかりました。きを　つけて。

■エマさんは　あした　おおさかに　いきます。

　あさって　こうじょうを　みて、とうきょうに　かえります。

Emma:　Kato-san. May I have a moment of your time?
Kato:　　Yes.
Emma:　Tomorrow, I will go to Osaka.
Kato:　　Ah, to the package fair, right?
Emma:　Yes. After the fair, I will go to the
　　　　branch office and see Chan-san.
　　　　The day after tomorrow I will see the
　　　　factory, and then I will take a 4:00
　　　　flight back to Tokyo.
Kato:　　I understand. Please take care.

■Emma-san will go to Osaka tomorrow.
The day after tomorrow she will see the
factory and then come back to Tokyo.

VOCABULARY

よろしい	be all right (polite expression of いい; see NOTES 1, p. 173)	パッケージ	package	こうじょう	factory
		フェア	fair	みて	see (て-form of みます)
		～の　あと	after . . .	きを　つけて。	Take care. (see NOTES 2, p. 173)
		あと	after		
パッケージフェア	package fair	いって	go (て-form of いきます)		

NOTES

1. ちょっと　よろしいですか。

This expression is used when addressing someone of higher status who is busy with something.

2. きを　つけて。

This means "take care" or "be careful" but when spoken to a person leaving on a trip, it is often used to hold the meaning of "Have a safe trip!"

KEY SENTENCES
 180

1. エマさんは　あした　おおさかししゃに　いって、
　　チャンさんに　あいます。

2. スミスさんは　かいぎの　あと、レポートを　かきました。

1. Emma-san will go to the Osaka branch office tomorrow and see Chan-san.
2. Smith-san wrote a report after the meeting.

GRAMMAR

1. Verb て-form   (KS1)

Japanese verbs are divided into three categories: Regular 1, Regular 2, and Irregular (see L15, GRAMMAR 2, p. 143). For Regular 1 verbs the て-form is obtained according to the sound immediately before ます as shown in the chart below. For Regular 2 verbs, the rule is simpler: change ます to て. The て-form of Irregular verbs is the same as for Regular 2 verbs.

Regular 1			Regular 2		
	ます-form	て-form		ます-form	て-form
buy	かいます	かって	eat	たべます	たべて
wait	まちます	まって	tell, teach	おしえます	おしえて
return, go home	かえります	かえって	show	みせます	みせて
go	いきます	いって*	see, watch	みます	みて
draw, write	かきます	かいて	be	います	いて
swim	およぎます	およいで	Irregular		
drink	のみます	のんで	come	きます	きて
lend	かします	かして	do	します	して

*Exceptional inflection

2. person は　verb 1 [て-form]、verb 2。   (KS1)

The て-form is used when stating several consecutive actions/acts. In this case the subject of the first action and of the next action is the same. Using the て-form, it is possible to link together two or three clauses; in that case the first and second verbs will be in the て-form. However, if the moods and tenses of the clauses are not the same, they cannot be linked using the て-form. For example, sentences such as the following cannot be linked using the て-form.

1. Statement: （わたしは）　チケットが　２まい　あります。I have two tickets.

2. Suggestion: あした　いっしょに　えいがを　みませんか。
　　　　　　　Shall we see a movie together tomorrow?

VOCABULARY

| レポート　　report

Further, when the first clause uses a verb of movement such as いきます, きます, or かえります, the location of the action of the second clause is assumed to be the same, even if not stated explicitly. For example: きのう ぎんざに　いって、ひるごはんを　たべました。("Yesterday I went to Ginza and ate lunch [there]") The place where I ate lunch was Ginza.

3. person は　noun の　あと、verb。   (KS2)

This expression is used when talking about an action following a noun (event, action, etc.). When emphasizing that the action comes after, not before, the particle で is added after あと.

WORD POWER

て-form   🔊 181

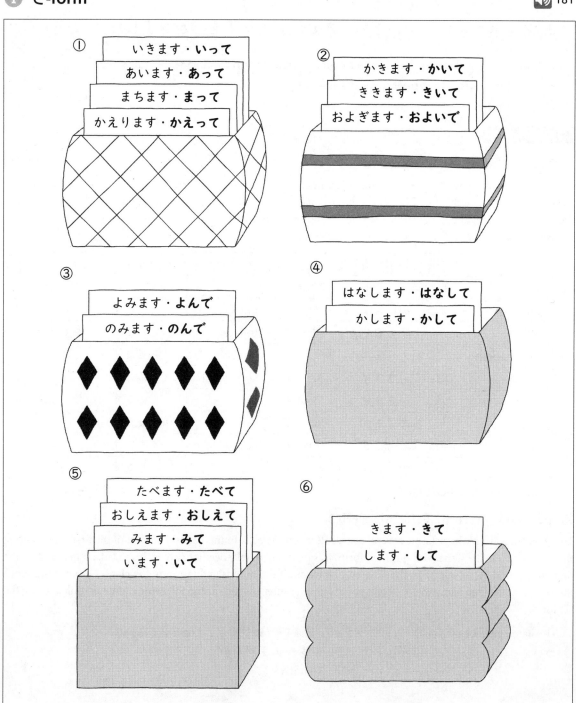

① いきます・**いって**
あいます・**あって**
まちます・**まって**
かえります・**かえって**

② かきます・**かいて**
ききます・**きいて**
およぎます・**およいで**

③ よみます・**よんで**
のみます・**のんで**

④ はなします・**はなして**
かします・**かして**

⑤ たべます・**たべて**
おしえます・**おしえて**
みます・**みて**
います・**いて**

⑥ きます・**きて**
します・**して**

EXERCISES

Ⅰ *Practice making* て*-forms.* Change the following verbs to their て-forms.

e.g. たべます → たべて

1. きます → ....

2. のみます → ....

3. かきます → ....

4. あいます → ....

5. かえります → ....

6. よみます → ....

7. みます → ....

8. ききます → ....

9. します → ....

10. いきます → ....

Ⅱ *State a sequence of actions.* Make up sentences following the pattern of the example and based on the information provided.

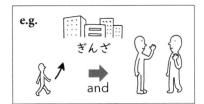
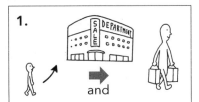

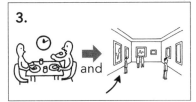

e.g. ぎんざに いきます。ともだちに あいます。
→ ぎんざに いって、ともだちに あいます。

1. デパートに いきます。かいものを します。

→ ....

2. ともだちに あいます。えいがを みます。

→ ....

3. レストランで ひるごはんを たべます。びじゅつかんに いきます。

→ ....

Ⅲ *Ask and answer what one will do.* Make up dialogues following the pattern of the example. Substitute the underlined parts with the appropriate forms of the alternatives given.

e.g. A：あした　なにを　しますか。

B：<u>はこねに　いって</u>、<u>テニスを　します</u>。

1. A：　_____

B：　_____

（ぎんざで　かいものを　します、えいがを　みます）

2. A：　_____

B：　_____

（よこはまに　いきます、サッカーの　しあいを　みます）

Ⅳ *Ask and answer what one did.* Make up dialogues following the pattern of the example. Substitute the underlined parts with the appropriate forms of the alternatives given.

e.g. A：きのう　なにを　しましたか。

B：<u>おおさかししゃに　いって</u>、<u>プレゼンを　しました</u>。

1. A：　_____

B：　_____

（くるまを　かります、ドライブを　します）

2. A：　_____

B：　_____

（ともだちに　あいます、いっしょに　すもうを　みます）

プレゼンを　します	give a presentation
ドライブを　します	go for a drive
すもう	sumo [wrestling]

Ⓥ *Invite someone to do something.* Combine the sentences following the pattern of the example.

　e.g. うちに　きませんか。ひるごはんを　たべませんか。
　　　→　うちに　きて、ひるごはんを　たべませんか。

　1. サンドイッチを　かいませんか。こうえんで　たべませんか。
　　　→ _____

　2. にっこうに　いきませんか。ゆうめいな　じんじゃを　みませんか。
　　　→ _____

Ⓥ *State what someone will do after a particular event.* Look at the illustrations and make up sentences following the patterns of the examples. Substitute the underlined parts with the appropriate forms of the alternatives given.

　e.g.1　ごご　１じから　かいぎが　あります。
　　　　かいぎの　あと、レポートを　かきます。

　1. _____
　　　_____ (やまもとさんに　あいます)

　e.g.2　きのう　パーティーが　ありました。
　　　　パーティーの　あと、タクシーで　うちに　かえりました。

　2. _____
　　　_____ (バーに　いって、ウイスキーを　のみます)

VOCABULARY

やまもと　Yamamoto (surname)

177

Ⅶ *Describe a schedule.* Make up sentences following the pattern of the example and based on the information provided in the schedule of Smith's business trip.

e.g.	Thursday	Osaka	Meeting	→ Call Green-san
1.	Friday	Kobe	Golf	→ Go to a friend's house
2.	Saturday	Kyoto	Have a meal with Yamamoto-san	→ See old temples and shrines

e.g. スミスさんは　もくようびに　おおさかに　いって、かいぎを　します。
かいぎの　あと、グリーンさんに　でんわを　します。

1. ....

....

2. ....

....

Ⅷ *Talk about a plan.* Make up dialogues following the pattern of the example. Substitute the underlined parts with the alternatives given.

e.g. かとう：　エマさん、フェアの　あと、なにを　しますか。
エマ　：　<u>こうべに　いって、ともだちに　あいます。</u>
かとう：　そうですか。

1. かとう：..

エマ　：..

（なら、ふるい　おてらを　みます）

かとう：..

2. かとう：..

エマ　：..

（ししゃ、チャンさんと　うちあわせを　します）

かとう：..

かいぎを　します	have a meeting
こうべ	Kobe (city near Osaka)
なら	Nara (old city in western Japan)
うちあわせを　します	have a preparatory meeting

IX Listen to the audio and fill in the blanks based on the information you hear. 🔊 182

エマさんは　どようびに　しんじゅくに　............................、

テレビを　............................。

SPEAKING PRACTICE

1. A meeting at the Osaka branch office has ended and Chan comes to talk to Emma. 🔊 183

チャン：エマさん、ステーキは　すきですか。

エマ　：はい、すきです。

チャン：じゃ、こうべに　いって、こうべビーフを　たべませんか。

エマ　：ありがとうございます。ぜひ。

Chan: Emma-san, do you like steak?
Emma: Yes, I do.
Chan: How would you like to go to Kobe and have some Kobe Beef?
Emma: Thank you very much. I'd love to.

2. Smith and Nakamura are talking at the office. 🔊 184

スミス　：ごご　6じから　かいぎが　あります。

　　　　　ばんごはんは　かいぎの　まえに　たべますか。あとで　たべますか。

なかむら：かいぎの　あとで　たべます。

Smith: There is a meeting from 6:00 P.M. Are you going to eat supper before the meet-
              ing? After the meeting?
Nakamura: I'll eat after the meeting.

NOTES

1. ステーキは　すきですか。
The use of は here indicates that of various kinds of food, the topic that has been brought up is "steak." When the word that is the topic has the particles が or を, they change to は. When the particle is other than が or を, は is added.

2. ばんごはんは　かいぎの　まえに　たべますか。
ばんごはん has been made the topic, so the particle を has changed to は, and ばんごはん comes at the head of the sentence.

Active Communication

Tell people around you what you did yesterday. Then talk about your plans for the coming weekend.

こうべビーフ　Kobe Beef (famous, high-quality beef)

LESSON 19

Making a Request: Please Give Her My Regards

TARGET DIALOGUE

🔊 185

After the package fair, Emma is in a taxi talking to Kato on the phone.

かとう：フェアは　どうでしたか。

エマ　：おもしろい　パッケージが　たくさん　ありました。
　　　　いろいろな　サンプルを　もらいましたから、
　　　　たくはいびんで　おくりました。

かとう：そうですか。じゃ、げつようびの　かいぎで
　　　　ほうこくしてください。

エマ　：はい、わかりました。

かとう：いまから　おおさかししゃですか。

エマ　：はい、そうです。

かとう：チャンさんに　よろしく　つたえてください。

エマ　：はい、つたえます。

■エマさんは　げつようびの　かいぎで　パッケージフェアについて
　ほうこくします。

Kato: How was the fair?
Emma: There were many interesting packages. I received various samples, so I sent them [back] by parcel delivery service.
Kato: Okay. Then, at the meeting on Monday, please report on your visit.
Emma: Yes, I understand.
Kato: Are you now headed to the Osaka branch office?
Emma: Yes, that's right.
Kato: Please give my regards to Chan-san.
Emma: Yes, I will relay your message.

■ Emma-san will report on the package fair at the meeting on Monday.

VOCABULARY

いろいろ（な）	various	■ほうこくします	report
サンプル	sample	よろしく　つたえてください。	Please give him/her my regards.
たくはいびん	parcel delivery service	つたえます (R2)	relay a message
ほうこくしてください	please report	～について	about . . .

1. よろしく　つたえてください。

   This is a set phrase requesting someone to relay your regards/greetings to someone who is not present.

KEY SENTENCES

🔊 186

1. ちょっと　まってください。
2. エマさんは　チャンさんに　メールで　しりょうを　おくりました。
3. つぎの　しんごうを　みぎに　まがってください。

1. Please wait a moment.
2. Emma-san sent Chan-san the material by e-mail.
3. Turn right at the next traffic light.

GRAMMAR

1. verb [て-form] ください。   (KS1, 3)

Adding ください after the て-form makes the polite form of an imperative.

2. means で   (KS2)

When stating a means of communication or transportation, add the particle で.

3. place/space を   (KS3)

In a sentence expressing a movement passing or moving through a place/space, the place/space is followed by the particle を.

WORD POWER

Ⅰ Verbs

🔊 187

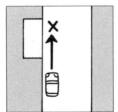
①まがります

②とめます

③いいます　　④もってきます

⑤とどけます

⑥まちます

しんごう	traffic light	まがります	turn	もってきます	bring
みぎ	right	とめます (R2)	stop	とどけます (R2)	deliver
まがってください	please turn	いいます	say		

Ⅱ Positions and directions 🔊 188

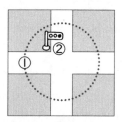 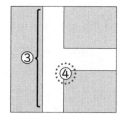 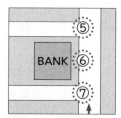 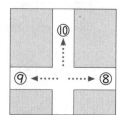

①こうさてん　　　③みち　　　　　⑤さき　　　　　⑧みぎ
②しんごう　　　　④かど　　　　　⑥まえ　　　　　⑨ひだり
　　　　　　　　　　　　　　　　⑦てまえ　　　　⑩まっすぐ

Ⅲ Means of delivery 🔊 189

①たくはいびん　　　②ゆうびん　　　③バイクびん

EXERCISES

Ⅰ *Practice conjugating verbs.* Repeat the verbs below and memorize their て-forms.

	ます-form	て-form
say	いいます	いって
wait	まちます	まって
turn	まがります	まがって
take	とります	とって
lend, loan	かします	かして
show	みせます	みせて
stop	とめます	とめて
tell, teach	おしえます	おしえて
deliver	とどけます	とどけて
bring	もってきます	もってきて

こうさてん	intersection	てまえ	just before	バイクびん	motorbike courier service
みち	road	ひだり	left		
かど	corner	まっすぐ	straight		
さき	beyond	ゆうびん	mail		

II *Make a request.* Make up sentences following the pattern of the example.

e.g. なまえを　かきます。　　→　なまえを　かいてください。

1. ちょっと　まちます。　　→ ....

2. しゃしんを　とります。　→ ....

3. もう　いちど　いいます。→ ....

4. ペンを　かします。　　　→ ....

5. パソコンを　とどけます。→ ....

III Make up sentences or dialogues following the patterns of the examples. Substitute the underlined parts with the appropriate forms of the alternatives given.

A. *Make a request.*

e.g. すみません。<u>あの　レストランの　なまえ</u>を　<u>おしえて</u>ください。

1. .... （メールアドレス、かきます）

2. .... （メニュー、みせます）

3. ....
　　　　　　　　　　　　　　（かいぎの　しりょう、もってきます）

B. *Make and accept a request to send something by a certain means.*

e.g. A：<u>スミスさん</u>に　<u>メール</u>で　<u>しりょう</u>を　おくってください。
　　B：はい、わかりました。

1. A：..
　　　　　　　　　　　　（のぞみデパート、ゆうびん、しょるい）

　　B：..

2. A：..
　　　　（おおさかししゃの　チャンさん、たくはいびん、この　にもつ）

　　B：..

3. A：..
　　　　　　　　　　　　（よこはまししゃ、バイクびん、カタログ）

　　B：..

VOCABULARY	
メニュー	menu
しょるい	documents
にもつ	package, luggage
カタログ	catalog

Ⅳ *Give directions to a taxi driver.* Make up sentences following the patterns of the examples. Substitute the underlined part(s) with the alternatives given.

A. e.g. <u>ぎんこうの　まえで</u>　とめてください。

1. .... （こうさてんの　てまえ）

2. .... （しんごうの　さき）

B. e.g. <u>つぎの　こうさてんを</u>　まっすぐ　いってください。

1. .... （この　みち）

2. .... （ぎんざどおり）

C. e.g. <u>デパートの　てまえを</u>　まがってください。

1. .... （スーパーの　てまえ）

2. .... （がっこうの　さき）

D. e.g. <u>つぎの　しんごうを</u>　<u>ひだり</u>に　まがってください。

1. .... （つぎの　こうさてん、ひだり）

2. .... （ふたつめの　かど、みぎ）

3. .... （はしの　てまえ、みぎ）

Ⅴ *Give directions to a taxi driver.* Tell the driver the route indicated by the arrows or to stop at the point indicated by the X.

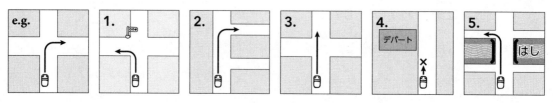

e.g. つぎの　こうさてんを　みぎに　まがってください。

1. ....

2. ....

3. ....

4. ....

5. ....

ぎんざどおり	Ginza Street
ふたつめ	second
～め	(suffix that attaches to a number and turns it into ordinal number)
はし	bridge

VI Make up dialogues following the patterns of the examples. Substitute the underlined parts with the alternatives given.

A. *Request that a purchase be delivered.*

e.g. スミス　　　　　：すみません。この　れいぞうこを　とどけてください。

みせの　ひと：はい。

スミス　　　　　：あしたの　ごご　おねがいします。

みせの　ひと：はい。わかりました。では、おなまえと　ごじゅうしょを
　　　　　　　　おねがいします。

1. スミス　　　　：＿＿＿＿＿＿＿＿＿＿＿＿＿＿＿＿（でんしレンジ）

みせの　ひと：＿＿＿＿＿＿＿＿＿＿＿＿＿＿＿＿＿＿＿＿

スミス　　　　：＿＿＿＿＿＿＿＿＿＿＿＿＿＿＿（きんようびに）

みせの　ひと：＿＿＿＿＿＿＿＿＿＿＿＿＿＿＿＿＿＿＿＿

＿＿＿＿＿＿＿＿＿＿＿＿＿＿＿＿＿＿＿＿＿＿＿

2. スミス　　　　：＿＿＿＿＿＿＿＿＿＿＿＿＿＿＿＿（ソファー）

みせの　ひと：＿＿＿＿＿＿＿＿＿＿＿＿＿＿＿＿＿＿＿＿

スミス　　　　：＿＿＿＿＿＿＿＿＿＿＿＿＿＿＿＿＿＿＿＿

（にちようびの　2じまでに）

みせの　ひと：＿＿＿＿＿＿＿＿＿＿＿＿＿＿＿＿＿＿＿＿

＿＿＿＿＿＿＿＿＿＿＿＿＿＿＿＿＿＿＿＿＿＿＿

VOCABULARY

| ごじゅうしょ | your address |
| まてに | by [specified time] |

B. *Give directions to a taxi driver.*

e.g. エマ　　　　　：<u>とうきょうタワー</u>の　ちかくまで　おねがいします。

うんてんしゅ：はい。

(after a while)

エマ　　　　　：つぎの　しんごうを　<u>ひだり</u>に　まがってください。

うんてんしゅ：はい。

エマ　　　　　：あの　<u>しろい　ビルの　まえ</u>で　とめてください。

うんてんしゅ：はい、わかりました。

(They have reached her destination.)

うんてんしゅ：4,000 えんです。

エマ　　　　　：はい。

うんてんしゅ：ありがとうございました。

エマ　　　　　：どうも。

1. エマ　　　　　：＿＿＿＿＿＿＿＿＿＿＿＿＿＿＿＿（えびすえき）

うんてんしゅ：＿＿＿＿＿＿＿＿＿＿＿＿＿＿＿＿

エマ　　　　　：＿＿＿＿＿＿＿＿＿＿＿＿＿＿＿＿（みぎ）

うんてんしゅ：＿＿＿＿＿＿＿＿＿＿＿＿＿＿＿＿

エマ　　　　　：＿＿＿＿＿＿＿＿＿＿＿＿＿（マンションの　まえ）

うんてんしゅ：＿＿＿＿＿＿＿＿＿＿＿＿＿＿＿＿

エマ　　　　　：＿＿＿＿＿＿＿＿＿＿＿＿＿＿＿＿

うんてんしゅ：＿＿＿＿＿＿＿＿＿＿＿＿＿＿＿＿

エマ　　　　　：＿＿＿＿＿＿＿＿＿＿＿＿＿＿＿＿

VII Listen to the audio and fill in the blanks based on the information you hear. 🔊190-192

Kato and Emma are talking.

1. エマさんは　となりの　へやから　いすを ＿＿＿＿＿＿＿＿＿。

2. エマさんは　たなかさんに　かいぎの　しりょうを ＿＿＿＿＿＿＿。

3. エマさんは　かとうさんに　ペンを ＿＿＿＿＿＿＿。

　　かとうさんは　エマさんに　ペンを ＿＿＿＿＿＿＿。

とうきょうタワー	Tokyo Tower	えびすえき	Ebisu Station
まで	to, as far as (particle)	えびす	Ebisu (district in Tokyo)
ビル	building	マンション	condominium

SPEAKING PRACTICE

1. Emma is staying at a hotel.

🔊 193

ホテルの　ひと：はい、ルームサービスです。

エマ　　　　　：すみません。もうふを　おねがいできますか。

ホテルの　ひと：はい、しょうちしました。

Hotel employee:　Hello. This is room service.
Emma:　　　　　Excuse me. May I ask for a blanket?
Hotel employee:　Yes, certainly.

2. Emma checks out of the hotel.

🔊 194

エマ　　　　　　：すみません。にもつを　５じまで　あずかってください。

フロントの　ひと：はい、しょうちしました。

Emma:　　　　　Excuse me. Please keep my bag [here] until 5:00 P.M.
Front desk clerk:　Yes, certainly.

NOTES

1. もうふを　おねがいできますか。

The expression "noun を　おねがいできますか" is more polite than the expression "noun を　おねがいします."

2. しょうちしました。

When asked to do something or relay information, しょうちしました ("certainly") is a more polite way of saying わかりました ("I understand").

Active Communication

If you're in Japan, give directions to a taxi driver or ask to have a package delivered in Japanese.

VOCABULARY

ルームサービス	room service		あずかります	keep, take care of
もうふ	blanket			
おねがいできますか。	May I ask [you to do this]?			
しょうちしました。	Yes, certainly.			

I Change the word in the parentheses to the form that is appropriate in the context of the sentence.

    1. デパートで　ケーキを ＿＿＿＿＿＿＿＿＿、ともだちの　うちに　いきました。

                                            （かいます）

    2. となりの　へやから　いすを ＿＿＿＿＿＿＿＿＿ください。（もってきます）

    3. くにに ＿＿＿＿＿＿＿＿＿ まえに　おみやげを　かいます。（かえります）

    4. わたしは　えを ＿＿＿＿＿＿＿のが　すきです。（かきます）

    5. のどが　かわきました。ビールを ＿＿＿＿＿＿＿たいです。（のみます）

II Look at the illustrations and complete the dialogue by filling in the blanks with the appropriate forms of the words given in the box. You may use the same word more than once.

します　　　じょうずです　　　すきです

たかはし：スミスさんは　テニスが　（**1.** ＿＿＿＿＿＿＿＿＿）か。

スミス　：ええ、でも　あまり　（**2.** ＿＿＿＿＿＿＿＿＿）。

たかはし：あした　ともだちと　テニスを　（**3.** ＿＿＿＿＿＿＿＿＿）。

         スミスさんも　いっしょに　（**4.** ＿＿＿＿＿＿＿＿＿）か。

スミス　：ありがとうございます。ぜひ。

AT THE MUSEUM

Japan has many different kinds of museums showing everything from Western fine arts to Japanese ukiyoe prints and from state-of-the-art technology to yōkai fantasy creatures. Museums in the Tokyo area include the Tokyo National Museum, featuring historic and cultural treasures from Japan and other parts of Asia; the Ghibli Museum, Mitaka designed and supervised by genius anime creator Hayao Miyazaki; and the National Museum of Emerging Science and Innovation, where visitors can experience science and space through stereoscopic films and get a real sense of the technologies of the future. The photo shows part of the exhibits at the Edo-Tokyo Museum tracing the architecture and culture of Tokyo from the seventeenth century to the present.

Going Places (3): How Do You Go There?

TARGET DIALOGUE
🔊 195

Smith and Suzuki are meeting at the museum. Smith receives a phone call from Suzuki.

すずき：スミスさん、すみません。

　　　　ねぼうしました。いま　うちを　でました。

スミス：ここまで　どのくらい　かかりますか。

すずき：30 ぷんぐらい　かかります。

スミス：そうですか。じゃ、1 かいの　カフェに　います。

すずき：すみません。

■ すずきさんの　うちから　はくぶつかんまで　30 ぷんぐらい
　かかります。

Suzuki: I'm sorry, Smith-san. I've overslept. I've just now left home.
Smith: How long will it take you to get here?
Suzuki: It will take about 30 minutes.
Smith: I see. Then I'll be in the café on the first floor.
Suzuki: I'm sorry.

■ It takes about 30 minutes from Suzuki-san's house to the museum.

VOCABULARY

ねぼうします	oversleep	カフェ	café
を	(particle; see GRAMMAR 2, p. 191)	はくぶつかん	museum
でます (R2)	leave		
かかります	take [time]		

KEY SENTENCES

🔊 196

1. スミスさんは　とうきょうえきで　しんかんせんに　のります。

2. スミスさんは　ひろしまえきで　しんかんせんを　おります。

3. とうきょうから　ひろしままで　しんかんせんで　4じかん
かかります。

4. スミスさんは　ひろしまに　1しゅうかん　います。

---

1. Smith-san will take the Shinkansen from Tokyo Station.
2. Smith-san will get off the Shinkansen at Hiroshima Station.
3. It takes four hours from Tokyo to Hiroshima by Shinkansen.
4. Smith-san will be in Hiroshima for a week.

GRAMMAR

1. person は　place で　transportation に　のります。 (KS1)

When using のります ("get on"), the means of transportation toward which the action is taken takes the particle に. Likewise, the point of arrival for つきます ("arrive") takes に.

e.g. スミスさんは　8じに　かいしゃに　つきました。
Smith-san arrived at the office at 8:00.

2. person は　place で　transportation を　おります。 (KS2)

When using おります ("get off"), the means of transportation that is the point of departure of the action takes the particle を. Likewse, the point of departure of でます ("leave") takes the particle を.

e.g. スミスさんは　7じはんに　うちを　でました。
Smith-san left home at 7:30.

3. place 1 から　place 2 まで　(transportation で)　period　かかります。 (KS3)

The verb かかります means "take time" and is used when the speaker considers the time to be long. When the speaker does not feel the time to be long, "period です" is used. The amount of time is placed immediately before the verb かかります and no particle is needed after it. When the time given is approximate, ぐらい may be added.

e.g. うちから　かいしゃまで　40ぷんぐらい　かかります。
It takes about 40 minutes from my home to the office.

4. person は　place に　period　います。 (KS4)

The period spent in a certain place is placed immediately before the verb います, with no particle after it. When the time given is approximate, ぐらい may be added.

e.g. たなかさんは　ロンドンに　3ねんぐらい　いました。
Tanaka-san stayed in London for about three years.

VOCABULARY

のります	get on, take [train, bus, etc.]	1 しゅうかん	one week
ひろしまえき	Hiroshima Station	います (R2)	stay, be
ひろしま	Hiroshima (city in western Japan)		
おります (R2)	get off		

WORD POWER

I Verbs

🔊 197

    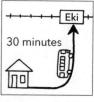

①のります ②おります ③でます ④つきます ⑤かかります

II Periods

🔊 198

	Minutes		Hours
5	ごふん（かん）	1	いちじかん
10	じゅっぷん（かん）	2	にじかん
15	じゅうごふん（かん）	3	さんじかん
20	にじゅっぷん（かん）	4	よじかん
25	にじゅうごふん（かん）	5	ごじかん
30	さんじゅっぷん（かん）	6	ろくじかん

	Days	Weeks	Months	Years
1	いちにち	いっしゅうかん	いっかげつ（かん）	いちねん（かん）
2	ふつか（かん）	にしゅうかん	にかげつ（かん）	にねん（かん）
3	みっか（かん）	さんしゅうかん	さんかげつ（かん）	さんねん（かん）
4	よっか（かん）	よんしゅうかん	よんかげつ（かん）	よねん（かん）
5	いつか（かん）	ごしゅうかん	ごかげつ（かん）	ごねん（かん）
6	むいか（かん）	ろくしゅうかん	ろっかげつ（かん）	ろくねん（かん）

(see also APPENDIX G, pp. 248, 249)

NOTE 1: The かん in parentheses in the charts above can be added or omitted, but かん is often added when the speaker wants to clearly state a period of time.

NOTE 2: When はん ("half") is added, the はん comes after the counter. かん indicated in parentheses is not added in this case.

e.g. さんじかんはん　　three and a half hours

いちねんはん　　one and a half years

EXERCISES

Ⅰ *Practice conjugating verbs.* Repeat the verbs below and memorize their dictionary forms and て-forms.

	ます-form	Dictionary form	て-form
get on, take	のります	のる	のって
get off	おります	おりる	おりて
leave	でます	でる	でて
arrive	つきます	つく	ついて
take (time)	かかります	かかる	かかって

Ⅱ *State where someone will get on and get off a means of public transportation.* Make up sentences following the pattern of the example and based on the information provided.

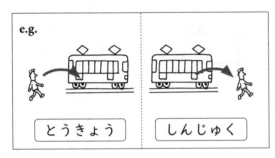

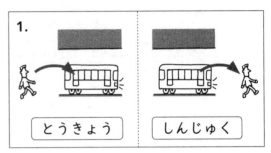

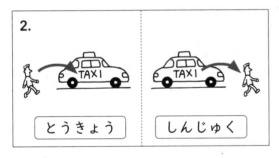

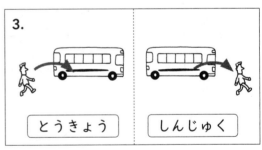

e.g. スミスさんは　とうきょうえきで　でんしゃに　のります。

　　　しんじゅくえきで　でんしゃを　おります。

1. ....

....

2. ....

....

3. ....

....

Ⅲ *State a person's departure and arrival time.* Make up sentences following the pattern of the example. Substitute the underlined parts with the alternatives given.

e.g. かとうさんは　<u>7じに　うちを</u>　でました。<u>8じに　かいしゃに</u>　つきました。

1. ....

（10じに　ホテル、11じに　くうこう）

2. ....

（あさ　とうきょう、1じごろ　きょうと）

Ⅳ Make up dialogues following the patterns of the examples and based on the information provided.

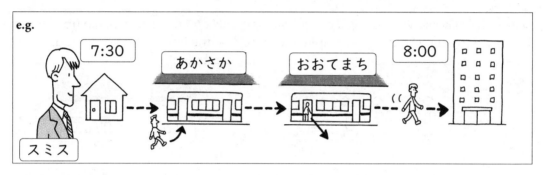

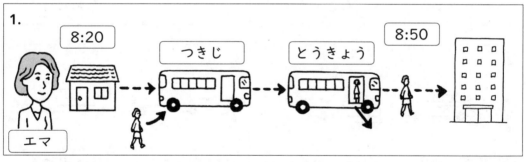

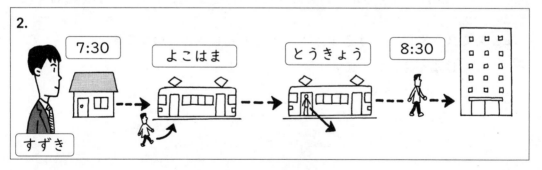

VOCABULARY

あかさか	Akasaka (district in Tokyo)
おおてまち	Otemachi (district in Tokyo)
つきじ	Tsukiji (district in Tokyo)

A. *Ask and answer how one commutes to work.*

e.g. たなか：スミスさんは　どうやって　かいしゃに　いきますか。

スミス：<u>あかさか</u>えきで　<u>ちかてつ</u>に　のって、<u>おおてまち</u>えきで

おります。

えきから　かいしゃまで　あるきます。

1. たなか：エマさんは

エマ　：

2. たなか：すずきさんは

すずき：

B. *Ask and answer what time one leaves home and what time one arrives at the office.*

e.g. たなか：まいにち　なんじに　うちを　でますか。

スミス：<u>7じはん</u>に　でます。

たなか：なんじに　かいしゃに　つきますか。

スミス：<u>8じ</u>に　つきます。

1. たなか：

エマ　：

たなか：

エマ　：

2. たなか：

すずき：

たなか：

すずき：

VOCABULARY

どうやって　　how, in what way

Ⓥ *Ask and answer how long it takes to get a particular place.* Make up dialogues following the pattern of the example and based on the information provided.

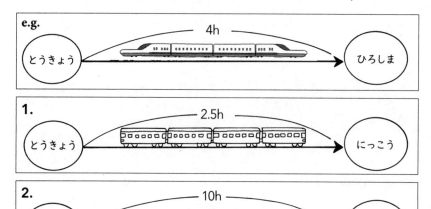

e.g. A：<u>とうきょうから　ひろしままで</u>　どのくらい　かかりますか。

B：<u>しんかんせんで　４じかん</u>ぐらい　かかります。

1. A：..

B：..

2. A：..

B：..

Ⓥ **Ⅵ** *Ask and answer how long one stayed in a particular place.* Make up dialogues following the pattern of the example. Substitute the underlined parts with the alternatives given.

e.g. スミス：たなかさんは　どのくらい　<u>ニューヨーク</u>に　いましたか。

たなか：<u>よっか</u>　いました。

1. スミス：..　（ホンコン）

たなか：..　（２しゅうかん）

2. スミス：..　（さっぽろ）

たなか：..　（５かげつ）

3. スミス：..　（ロンドン）

たなか：..　（３ねん）

VOCABULARY

| はねだくうこう | Haneda Airport |
| ニューヨーク | New York |

VII *Talk about a vacation plan.* Make up dialogues following the pattern of the example. Substitute the underlined parts with the alternatives given.

    e.g. すずき　：なつやすみに　なにを　しますか。

          なかむら：<u>ニューヨーク</u>に　いって、<u>ミュージカルを　みます</u>。

          すずき　：そうですか。どのくらい　<u>ニューヨーク</u>に　いますか。

          なかむら：<u>１しゅうかん</u>　います。

          すずき　：いいですね。

  1. すずき　：...

     なかむら：...

                                   （おきなわ、ダイビングを　します）

     すずき　：...
 （おきなわ）

     なかむら：...
 （むいか）

     すずき　：...

  2. すずき　：...

     なかむら：...

                             （きょうと、おてらを　みます）

     すずき　：...
 （きょうと）

     なかむら：...
 （いつか）

     すずき　：...

VIII Listen to the audio and fill in the blanks based on the information you hear. 🔊199-201

  1. チャンさんは　............に　うちを　でて、............に

     かいしゃに　つきます。

  2. とうきょうから　かまくらまで　............で　............ぐらい

     かかります。

  3. エマさんは　ほっかいどうに　............います。

    VOCABULARY

    | ミュージカル　　　　　　musical
    | ダイビングを　します　scuba dive

SPEAKING PRACTICE

1. Paul is at Akihabara Station.　🔊 202

　ポール　：とうきょうドームに　いきたいんですが。

　えきいん：5ばんせんの　でんしゃに　のって、すいどうばしで　おりてください。

　ポール　：すい…なんですか。

　えきいん：すいどうばしです。ここから　ふたつめです。

　ポール　：ありがとうございます。

Paul:	I would like to go to Tokyo Dome.
Station employee:	Take the train at Platform 5 and get off at Suidobashi.
Paul:	Sui . . . what?
Station employee:	Suidobashi. It's the second station from here.
Paul:	Thank you very much.

NOTES

1. とうきょうドームに　いきたいんですが。

とうきょうドームに　いきたいです indicates that the speaker wants to go to Tokyo Dome, but when changed to とうきょうドームに　いきたいんですが, the implication is that the speaker seeks advice and information about what train to take and from where. This …んですが is actually a preliminary, which would be followed by a question such as "which train should I take?" However, since it is clear to the listener from the situation what the speaker is asking for, the question part is omitted.

2. すい…なんですか。

When you have been unable to make out completely what the speaker said and you want it to be repeated, state the part that was audible and, after a brief pause, add なんですか.

Active Communication

If you're in Japan, ask a station employee the route and time required to get to a place you want to go to.

VOCABULARY

とうきょうドーム	Tokyo Dome	5ばんせん	Platform 5
いきたいんですが	I'd like to go	～ばんせん	platform …
えきいん	station employee	すいどうばし	Suidobashi (station in Tokyo)

LESSON 21

Asking Permission: May I Have It?

TARGET DIALOGUE
🔊 203

Smith and Suzuki are at at the museum.

スミス ：これは　むかしの　おかねですか。

すずき ：ええ、そうです。

あ、ここに　えいごの　パンフレットが　ありますよ。

スミス ：そうですね。

(Going over to a museum staff.) すみません。

この　パンフレットを　もらっても　いいですか。

はくぶつかんの　ひと：はい、どうぞ。

(Smith and Suzuki look around the exhibit.)

すずき ：つかれましたね。

スミス ：そうですね。あしが　いたいです。

(Sees an object that looks like a chair, and asks the museum staff.)

すみません。ここに　すわっても　いいですか。

はくぶつかんの　ひと：はい、どうぞ。

■スミスさんは　はくぶつかんで　えいごの　パンフレットを
　もらいました。

Smith:	Are these coins from a long time ago?
Suzuki:	Yes, that's right. Oh, there are English-language pamphlets over here.
Smith:	I see. Excuse me, may I have a copy of this pamphlet?
Museum staff:	Yes, please.
Suzuki:	It's tiring, isn't it?
Smith:	Yes, my legs hurt.
	Excuse me. Is it all right to sit down here?
Museum staff:	Yes, that's fine.

■ Smith-san got an English pamphlet at the museum.

VOCABULARY

むかし	a long time ago	あし	foot, leg	すわっても　いいですか	May I sit [here]?
えいご	English	いたい	hurt, sore, painful	すわります	sit down
パンフレット	pamphlet	に	on (particle; see		
もらっても　いいですか	May I have . . . ?		GRAMMAR 2, p. 200)		

199

KEY SENTENCES

 204

1. この　えの　しゃしんを　とっても　いいですか。
2. ここに　すわっても　いいですか
3. （わたしは）　あたまが　いたいです。

1. May I take a photo of this painting?
2. May I sit here?
3. I have a headache.

GRAMMAR

1. verb [て-form] も　いいですか。 (KS1, 2)

This expression is used when asking permission for something. When responding affirmatively, one says はい、どうぞ; when responding negatively, one says すみませんが、ちょっと….

2. place/thingに (KS2)

Actions such as かきます ("write, draw"), すわります ("sit down"), おきます ("put"), or とめます ("park") are performed with reference to a place or thing. When there is some result of the action, the noun indicating the place or thing takes the particle に.

   e.g. ここに　なまえを　かいてください。

     Please write your name here.

3. （わたしは）　body partが　いたいです。 (KS3)

This expression is used when stating that some part of the body hurts. The painful part of the body takes the particle が. The subject of the sentence is always the speaker, and わたしは is usually omitted.

（しゃしんを）とっても　いいですか	May I take [photos]?
あたま	head

WORD POWER

Ⅰ Verbs

🔊 205

①つかいます

②すわります

③はいります

④おきます

⑤あけます

⑥しめます

⑦つけます

⑧けします

Ⅱ Parts of the body

🔊 206

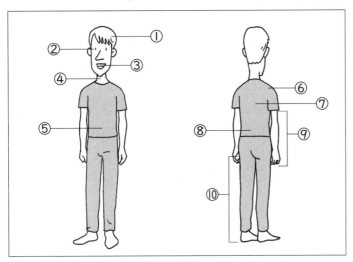

①あたま	③は	⑤おなか	⑦せなか	⑨て
②め	④のど	⑥かた	⑧こし	⑩あし

Ⅲ Symptoms

🔊 207

①あたまが いたいです。
②きぶんが わるいです。
③ねつが あります。

つかいます	use	つけます (R2)	turn on	おなか	stomach, belly	きぶんが わるい	feel sick, unwell
はいります	enter	けします	turn off	かた	shoulder	きぶん	feeling
おきます	put, place	め	eye	せなか	back	ねつが あります	have a fever
あけます (R2)	open	は	tooth	こし	lower back	ねつ	fever
しめます (R2)	close	のど	throat				

EXERCISES

I *Practice conjugating verbs.* Repeat the verbs below and memorize their て-forms.

	ます-form	て-form
use	つかいます	つかって
sit down	すわります	すわって
enter	はいります	はいって
put, place	おきます	おいて
open	あけます	あけて
close	しめます	しめて
turn on	つけます	つけて
turn off	けします	けして

II *Ask permission to do something.* Make up sentences following the pattern of the example.

    e.g. この　パンフレットを　もらいます。

        →　この　パンフレットを　もらっても　いいですか。

  1. まどを　あけます。

     →　...

  2. カーテンを　しめます。

     →　...

  3. でんきを　つけます。

     →　...

  4. あした　やすみます。

     →　...

  5. この　へやに　はいります。

     →　...

  6. ここに　にもつを　おきます。

     →　...

VOCABULARY

まど	window
カーテン	curtain
でんき	lights
やすみます	take a day off

III *Ask and grant permission to do something.* Make up dialogues following the pattern of the example and based on the information provided.

e.g. すずき　　　　　　　：<u>しりょうを　コピーしても</u>　いいですか。

　　としょかんの　ひと：はい、どうぞ。

1. すずき　　　　　　　：

　　としょかんの　ひと：

2. すずき　　　　　　　：

　　としょかんの　ひと：

3. すずき　　　　　　　：

　　としょかんの　ひと：

4. すずき　　　　　　　：

　　としょかんの　ひと：

VOCABULARY

コピーします　　make a copy
じゅうでんします　recharge

Ⅳ *Ask and refuse permission to do something.* Make up dialogues following the pattern of the example and based on the information provided.

e.g. スミス　　　　　：ここで　しょくじを　しても　いいですか。

　　おてらの　ひと：すみませんが、ちょっと…。

1. スミス　　　　　：＿＿＿＿＿＿＿＿＿＿＿＿＿＿＿＿＿＿＿＿

　　おてらの　ひと：＿＿＿＿＿＿＿＿＿＿＿＿＿＿＿＿＿＿＿＿

2. スミス　　　　　：＿＿＿＿＿＿＿＿＿＿＿＿＿＿＿＿＿＿＿＿

　　おてらの　ひと：＿＿＿＿＿＿＿＿＿＿＿＿＿＿＿＿＿＿＿＿

3. スミス　　　　　：＿＿＿＿＿＿＿＿＿＿＿＿＿＿＿＿＿＿＿＿

　　おてらの　ひと：＿＿＿＿＿＿＿＿＿＿＿＿＿＿＿＿＿＿＿＿

Ⅴ *Ask permission to do something.* Make up dialogues following the pattern of the example. Substitute the underlined parts with the alternatives given.

e.g. スミス　　　　　：すみません。かいぎしつで　べんきょうしても
　　　　　　　　　　　いいですか。

　　うけつけの　ひと：はい、どうぞ。

　　スミス　　　　　：4じまで　つかっても　いいですか。

　　うけつけの　ひと：はい、どうぞ。

　　スミス　　　　　：ありがとうございます。

にわ　garden, yard

1. スミス　　　　　　：_____
　　　　　　　　　　　　　　　　　　　　（ひるごはんを　たべます）

うけつけの　ひと：_____

スミス　　　　　　：_____（1：30）

うけつけの　ひと：_____

スミス　　　　　　：_____

2. スミス　　　　　　：_____
　　　　　　　　　　　　　　　　　　　　（ほんを　よみます）

うけつけの　ひと：_____

スミス　　　　　　：_____（7：30）

うけつけの　ひと：_____

スミス　　　　　　：_____

VI *State a request of another person.* Look at the illustrations and make up sentences following the pattern of the example. Substitute the underlined parts with the appropriate forms of the alternatives given.

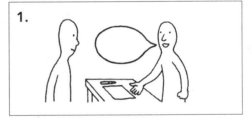

e.g. テーブルの　うえに　にもつを　おいてください。

1. _____（ここ、なまえを　かきます）

2. _____（その　いす、すわります）

3. _____
　　　　　　　　　　　（あの　ちゅうしゃじょう、くるまを　とめます）

VOCABULARY

とめます (R2)　park

Ⅶ *Ask for permission to borrow a pen.* Make up a dialogue based on the information provided.

1. みせの　ひと : ....

2. スミス　　　 : ....

3. スミス　　　 : ....

4. みせの　ひと : ....

5. スミス　　　 : ....

Ⅷ *State which part of your body hurts.* Make up sentences following the pattern of the example. Substitute the underlined part with the alternatives given.

e.g. （わたしは）　<u>あたま</u>が　いたいです。

1. ....（は）

2. ....（おなか）

3. ....（あし）

IX *Tell a doctor one's symptoms.* Make up dialogues following the pattern of the example and based on the information provided.

e.g. いしゃ：どう　しましたか。

チャン：<u>きぶんが　わるいです</u>。

1. いしゃ：..

 チャン：..

2. いしゃ：..

 チャン：..

3. いしゃ：..

 チャン：..

X Listen to the audio and fill in the blanks based on the information you hear. 🔊 208, 209

1. スミスさんは .... から .... を　つかいます。

2. Smith came to the Japanese-language school.

 スミスさんは　にほんごの　クラスの　パンフレットを .... 。

38 ど	38 degrees
～ど	... degree
いしゃ	medical doctor
どう　しましたか。	What seems to be the problem? (see NOTES 2, p. 208)

SPEAKING PRACTICE

1. Green is at the home appliances store.　　　　　　　　　　🔊 210

    グリーン　　　：すみません。この　テレビを　とどけてください。

    みせの　ひと：はい、ここに　ごじゅうしょと　おなまえを　おねがいします。

    グリーン　　　：ローマじで　かいても　いいですか。

    みせの　ひと：はい。

    Green:　　　　 Excuse me. Please deliver this TV [for me].
    Salesperson: Yes. Please fill in your address and name here.
    Green:　　　　 May I write it in romaji?
    Salesperson: Yes.

2. Green is at the clinic.　　　　　　　　　　　　　　　　🔊 211

    いしゃ　　：どう　しましたか。

    グリーン：すみません。えいごで　はなしても　いいですか。

    いしゃ　　：はい、どうぞ。

    Doctor:　What seems to be the problem?
    Green:　 Excuse me. May I speak in English?
    Doctor:　Yes. Go ahead.

NOTES

1. ローマじで　かいても　いいですか。

    When indicating the means of communication for writing or speaking (characters or language), use the particle で.

2. どう　しましたか。

    This is a doctor's standard query to a patient to learn what symptoms he/she has, meaning "what seems to be the problem?" It is also used when asking people in need and means "what is the matter?"

Active Communication

If you're in Japan, go to various stores or public institutions and ask permission to do something—to take a photograph, for example.

VOCABULARY

ローマじ　　romaji, romanized Japanese

Forbidding Actions: Please Don't Take Photos

TARGET DIALOGUE

🔊 212

Smith and Suzuki are at the museum.

スミス	：きれいな　きものですね。
すずき	：ほんとうに　きれいですね。
	これは　300ねんぐらいまえの　きものです。
スミス	：そうですか。いもうとに　みせたいです。
	(Takes a photo.)
はくぶつかんの　ひと	：すみません。ここで　しゃしんを　とらないでください。
スミス	：わかりました。すみません。
すずき	：スミスさん、あそこにも　きれいな　きものが
	ありますよ。
スミス	：あ、そうですね。いきましょう。

Smith:	Isn't that a beautiful kimono.
Suzuki:	Yes, it certainly is beautiful.
	This is a kimono from about 300 years ago.
Smith:	Is that so? I want to show this to my sister.
Museum staff:	Excuse me. Please do not take photos here.
Smith:	I understand. I'm sorry.
Suzuki:	Smith-san, over there, too, is another beautiful kimono.
Smith:	Ah, I see. Let's go.

VOCABULARY

きもの	kimono
～まえ	. . . ago
いもうと	(my) younger sister
とらないでください	please don't take [photos]

KEY SENTENCES

 213

1. ここは　でぐちですから、くるまを　とめないでください。
2. わさびを　いれないでください。
3. えきの　まえに　コンビニが　あります。
　　えきの　なかにも　（コンビニが）　あります。

1. This is the exit, so please do not park your car here.
2. Please do not add wasabi.
3. There is a convenience store in front of the station. There is another (convenience store) inside the station.

GRAMMAR

1. Verb ない-form　　　　　　　　　　　　　　　　　　　　　　　　(KS1, 2)

To form the ない-form of Regular 1 verbs, change the sound before ます, as shown in the chart below and add ない. The rule for Regular 2 verbs is simple; simply remove ます and add ない. The rule for Irregular verbs is irregular, as shown in the chart below.

	Regular 1				Regular 2	
	ます-form	ない-form			ます-form	ない-form
buy	かいます	かわない	see		みます	みない
go	いきます	いかない	be		います	いない
swim	およぎます	およがない	eat		たべます	たべない
lend	かします	かさない	tell, teach		おしえます	おしえない
wait	まちます	またない	Irregular			
drink	のみます	のまない	come		きます	こない
return, go home	かえります	かえらない	do		します	しない

2. verb [ない-form]でください。　　　　　　　　　　　　　　　　(KS1, 2)

This is the sentence pattern used when stating "please do not [do such and such]." This is a fairly strong expression which is used by managers or officials when giving instructions to people. When wishing to soften the expression, in most cases it is used along with some reason the action should not be taken (KS1). This expression can also be used when asking that a certain ingredient not be used in a dish (KS2).

3. placeにも　nounが　あります。　　　　　　　　　　　　　　　(KS3)

When the particle も is attached to a noun phrase indicating the location of something, the particle に is retained and も is added after it. Generally, when desiring to add the meaning of "also," the particles が, は, を can be replaced by も but for other particles, the も is simply added.

VOCABULARY

とめないでください	please don't park
わさび	wasabi
いれないでください	please don't add/put in
いれます (R2)	put in, add

WORD POWER

Ⅰ Verbs

🔊 214

①たちます

②さわります

③いれます

④たばこを
すいます

Ⅱ ない-form

🔊 215

すいます・**すわない**

かきます・**かかない**

はなします・**はなさない**

たちます・**たたない**

のみます・**のまない**

とります・**とらない**

あけます・**あけない**

しめます・**しめない**

とめます・**とめない**

きます・**こない**

します・**しない**

Ⅲ Restrictions

🔊 216

①たちいりきんし

②ちゅうしゃきんし

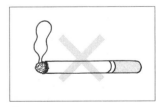
③きんえん

Ⅳ Adjective

🔊 217

あぶない

Ⅰ *Practice making ない-forms.* Change the following verbs to their ない-forms.

e.g. あいます → あわない

1. はなします → ....
2. みせます → ....
3. さわります → ....
4. およぎます → ....
5. かいます → ....

6. あげます → ....
7. たちます → ....
8. ききます → ....
9. きます → ....
10. します → ....

Ⅱ *Forbid someone to do something.* Make up sentences following the pattern of the example and based on the illustration provided.

e.g. まどを あけます。→ まどを あけないでください。

1. しゃしんを とります。 → ....
2. ドアを しめます。 → ....
3. でんきを けします。 → ....
4. かびんに さわります。 → ....

あぶない	dangerous
ドア	door
かびん	vase

III *Forbid someone to park with a reason.* Make up sentences following the pattern of the example. Substitute the underlined part with the alternatives given.

e.g. ここは　<u>いりぐち</u>ですから、くるまを　とめないでください。

1. ....　（でぐち）

2. ....　（みせの　まえ）

3. ....　（ちゅうしゃきんし）

IV *Forbid someone to do something with a reason.* Make up dialogues following the pattern of the example. Substitute the underlined parts with the appropriate forms of the alternatives given.

e.g. A：<u>ここは　たちいりきんし</u>ですから、<u>はいらない</u>でください。

B：はい、わかりました。すみません。

1. A：...
　　　　　　　　　　　　　　　（ここは　きんえん、たばこを　すいます）

B：...

2. A：...
　　　　　　　　　　　　　　　　　　　　（あぶない、たちます）

B：...

Ⅴ *State that the same thing is found in two places.* Make up sentences following the pattern of the example. Substitute the underlined parts with the alternatives given.

e.g. にっこうに　おんせんが　あります。
　　はこねにも　あります。

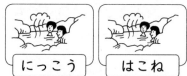

1. ....

　　　　　　　　　　　　　　　　　　　　　　（2かい、かいぎしつ、3がい）

2. ....

　　　　　　　　　　　（テーブルの　うえ、ビール、れいぞうこの　なか）

Ⅵ *Ask and answer that there is the same thing in two places.* Make up dialogues following the pattern of the example. Substitute the underlined parts with the alternatives given.

e.g. A：すみません。この　ちかくに　コンビニが　ありますか。
　　 B：ええ、えきの　まえに　あります。
　　　　それから、えきの　なかにも　ありますよ。
　　 A：そうですか。ありがとうございます。

1. A：...（こうえん）

　　 B：..

　　　　.......................................（びょういんの　まえ、がっこうの　となり）

　　 A：..

2. A：...（ちゅうしゃじょう）

　　 B：..

　　　　.......................................（あの　ビルの　となり、デパートの　ちか）

　　 A：..

VII *At a restaurant, ask that a specific ingredient not be put into the food.* Make up dialogues following the pattern of the example. Substitute the underlined parts with the alternatives given.

e.g. チャン ：<u>ハンバーガー</u>を　おねがいします。

みせの　ひと：はい。

チャン ：すみませんが、<u>ケチャップ</u>を　いれないでください。

みせの　ひと：はい、わかりました。

1. チャン ：＿＿＿＿＿＿＿＿＿＿＿＿＿＿＿＿ （おすし）

   みせの　ひと：＿＿＿＿＿＿＿＿＿＿＿＿＿＿＿＿＿

   チャン ：＿＿＿＿＿＿＿＿＿＿＿＿＿＿＿＿ （わさび）

   みせの　ひと：＿＿＿＿＿＿＿＿＿＿＿＿＿＿＿＿＿

2. チャン ：＿＿＿＿＿＿＿＿＿＿＿＿＿＿ （サンドイッチ）

   みせの　ひと：＿＿＿＿＿＿＿＿＿＿＿＿＿＿＿＿＿

   チャン ：＿＿＿＿＿＿＿＿＿＿＿＿＿＿ （マヨネーズ）

   みせの　ひと：＿＿＿＿＿＿＿＿＿＿＿＿＿＿＿＿＿

3. チャン ：＿＿＿＿＿＿＿＿＿＿＿＿＿ （チーズバーガー）

   みせの　ひと：＿＿＿＿＿＿＿＿＿＿＿＿＿＿＿＿＿

   チャン ：＿＿＿＿＿＿＿＿＿＿＿＿＿＿＿＿ （トマト）

   みせの　ひと：＿＿＿＿＿＿＿＿＿＿＿＿＿＿＿＿＿

VIII Listen to the audio and fill in the blanks based on the information you hear. 🔊218-220

1. ＿＿＿＿＿＿と　＿＿＿＿＿＿に　おてあらいが　あります。

2. ＿＿＿＿＿＿＿と　＿＿＿＿＿＿に　コンビニが　あります。

3. 3じから　＿＿＿＿＿が　ありますから、なかむらさんは　かいぎしつの

   エアコンを　＿＿＿＿＿＿＿。

VOCABULARY

ハンバーガー	hamburger	トマト	tomato
ケチャップ	ketchup		
マヨネーズ	mayonnaise		
チーズバーガー	cheese burger		

SPEAKING PRACTICE

1. Smith got tipsy at Sasaki's house yesterday and spilled red wine on her carpet.  221

   スミス：ささきさん、おはようございます。

   ささき：おはようございます。

   スミス：きのうは　すみませんでした。

   ささき：いいえ、どうぞ　きに　しないでください。

   Smith: Good morning, Sasaki-san.
   Sasaki: Good morning.
   Smith: I'm very sorry about yesterday.
   Sasaki: Oh, that's all right. Please don't worry about it.

2. Smith has a pain in his stomach and is being examined by a doctor. 222

   いしゃ：きょうは　おさけを　のまないでください。

   スミス：はい、わかりました。

   Doctor: Please do not have any alcohol today.
   Smith: Yes. I understand.

Active Communication

A stranger is trying to park in front of your house. What would you say?

VOCABULARY

きに　しないでください。	Please don't worry about it.
きに　します	worry about
（お）さけ	alcoholic drink, sake

AT WORK AND AFTER WORK

Businesspeople in Japan often go out to enjoy eating and drinking in the evening after work. This custom is a product of the belief that when they can get to know each other better it is easier to work together. There are also various traditional events that bring people together to savor some seasonal highlight. Among such events, people look forward especially to the "cherry blossom viewing" parties held to eat and drink beneath the cherry trees in spring, and these parties are held as regular annual events in some companies.

Explaining Actions: What Are You Doing Now?

TARGET DIALOGUE 🔊 223

Kato has asked Smith to prepare for a meeting.

かとう：もう　かいぎの　じゅんびは　できましたか。

スミス：すみません。まだです。かいぎしつは　よやくしましたが、
　　　　しりょうは　いま　つくっています。

かとう：そうですか。3じまでに　おわりますか。

スミス：はい、もうすぐ　できます。

(15 minutes later.)

スミス：かとうさん、しりょうが　できました。
　　　　チェックを　おねがいします。

かとう：はい。

Kato:　　Have you finished preparing for the meeting?
Smith:　I'm sorry. I have not finished yet. I reserved the meeting room,
　　　　but I am now preparing the materials.
Kato:　　I see. Will you finish by three o'clock?
Smith:　Yes, I will be ready soon.
Smith:　Kato-san, the materials are ready. Please check them.
Kato:　　All right.

もう	already	よやくします	make a reservation	もうすぐ	soon
じゅんび	preparation	つくっています	be making	チェック	check
できます (R2)	be done	つくります	make		
まだです	not yet	おわります	finish		

NOTES

1. もう　かいぎの　じゅんびは　できましたか。
   しりょうが　できました。

   When the information about what is done or finished in using the verb できます／おわります is new to the listener, the pattern of the second sentence is used: noun が　できました／おわりました. In the first sentence, Kato has already taken up the topic かいぎの　じゅんび, so the particle が is replaced with は. The もう ("already") can be placed at the beginning or later in the sentence.

KEY SENTENCES

 224

1. スミスさんは　いま　ひるごはんを　たべています。
2. スミスさんは　にほんごを　ならっています。
3. もう　レポートを　よみましたか。
4. グリーンさんは　てんぷらは　すきですが、おすしは　すきじゃありません。

1. Smith-san is eating his lunch now.
2. Smith-san is taking Japanese lessons.
3. Have you already read the report?
4. Green-san likes tempura, but he does not like sushi.

GRAMMAR

1. person は　verb [て-form] います。 （1）　　　　　　　(KS1, 2)

The present progressive form ("is doing") is formed by adding います to the verb て-form. (KS1)
The て-form います can also be used to express an action intentionally repeated over a certain period of time. (KS2)

2. もう　verb [ます-form stem] ましたか。　　　　　　　(KS3)

The past form of a verb may express not just the simple past but the completion of an action. Here, by adding もう, the speaker asks whether the action has already been completed.
To respond, the listener says:

　　はい、verb [ます-form stem] ました。　　Yes, I have . . . .
　　いいえ、まだです。　　　　　　　　　　No, not yet.

3. は for contrast　　　　　　　　　　　　　　　　　(KS4)

When contrasting two things, the particle は is added after both words. When the particle of the word with which the contrast is made is が or を, it is replaced with は. When the particle is any other than が or を, the particle は is added.

　　e.g. ワインを　のみます。ビールを　のみません。　　(I) drink wine. (I) don't drink beer.
　　　　→ワインは　のみますが、ビールは　のみません。　　(I) drink wine, but not beer.

　　　　たなかさんに　あいました。やまださんに　あいませんでした。
　　　　(I) met Tanaka-san. (I) didn't meet Yamada-san.
　　　　→たなかさんには　あいましたが、やまださんには　あいませんでした。
　　　　　(I) met Tanaka-san, but not Yamada-san.

VOCABULARY

たべています	be eating
ならっています	be taking lessons in

WORD POWER

Ⅰ Verbs

 225

①せつめいを　します

②そうじを　します

③おわります

④つくります

⑤できます

Ⅱ Lessons

 226

①しょどう

②ギター

③フランスご

VOCABULARY

せつめいを　します	explain	フランスご	French
そうじを　します	clean		
しょどう	calligraphy		
ギター	guitar		

EXERCISES

I *Practice conjugating verbs.* Repeat the verbs below and memorize their ています-forms—affirmative and negative.

	ます-form	ています-form	
		aff.	*neg.*
explain	せつめいを　します	せつめいを　しています	せつめいを　していません
make	つくります	つくっています	つくっていません
drink	のみます	のんでいます	のんでいません
talk	はなします	はなしています	はなしていません

II *State what someone is doing now.* Change the sentences following the pattern of the example.

> **e.g.** スミスさんは　そうじを　します。
>
> → 　スミスさんは　そうじを　しています。

1. スミスさんは　しんぶんを　よみます。

→ ....

2. スミスさんは　メールを　かきます。

→ ....

3. スミスさんは　コピーを　します。

→ ....

4. スミスさんは　たなかさんと　はなします。

→ ....

5. スミスさんは　オンラインかいぎを　します。

→ ....

6. スミスさんは　プロジェクトの　せつめいを　します。

→ ....

Ⅲ Make up dialogues following the patterns of the examples and based on the information provided.

A. *Ask and answer what one is doing now.*

e.g. 1. A：グリーンさんは　いま　なにを　していますか。

B：でんわを　しています。

1. A：

B：

2. A：

B：

3. A：

B：

4. A：

B：

5. A：

B：

B. *Answer what one is doing now.*

e.g. 2. Ａ：かとうさんは　いま　しりょうを　つくっていますか。

Ｂ：いいえ、プロジェクトの　せつめいを　しています。

6. Ａ：ささきさんは　いま　コーヒーを　のんでいますか。

Ｂ： ....

7. Ａ：エマさんは　いま　ささきさんと　はなしていますか。

Ｂ： ....

8. Ａ：なかむらさんは　いま　でんわを　していますか。

Ｂ： ....

Ⅳ *State what someone does every week.* Make up sentences following the pattern of the example. Substitute the underlined parts with the alternatives given.

e.g. スミスさんは　まいしゅう　にほんごを　ならっています。

1. ....

（なかむらさん、いけばな）

2. ....

（かとうさん、ギター）

3. ....

（エマさん、しょどう）

4. ....

（すずきさん、フランスご）

Ⅴ Make up dialogues following the patterns of the examples. Substitute the underlined parts with the appropriate forms of the alternatives given.

A. *Ask and answer whether one has completed an action.*

e.g. Ａ：もう　ひるごはんを　たべましたか。

Ｂ：はい、たべました。

1. Ａ： ....（レストラン、よやくします）

Ｂ： ....（よやくします）

2. Ａ： ....（レポート、かきます）

Ｂ： ....（かきます）

B. *Ask and answer whether one has completed an action.*

e.g. A：<u>そうじ</u>は　もう　おわりましたか。

B：いいえ、まだです。

1. A： ....（ダウンロード）

   B： ....

2. A： ....（かんじの　べんきょう）

   B： ....

C. *State that one is in the midst of something.*

e.g. A：<u>かいぎの　しりょう</u>は　もう　できましたか。

B：いま　<u>つくって</u>います。もうすこし　まってください。

1. A： ....（レポート）

   B： ....（かきます）

2. A： ....（プレゼンの　じゅんび）

   B： ....（します）

3. A： ....（ひるごはん）

   B： ....（つくります）

Ⅵ *State two contrasting things.* Make up sentences following the pattern of the example and based on the information provided.

すきです

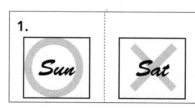
やすみです

します

いたいです

VOCABULARY

ダウンロード	download
かんじ	kanji
もうすこし	a little longer
スノーボードを　します	snowboard

e.g. こうちゃは　すきですが、コーヒーは　すきじゃありません。

1. ....

2. ....

3. ....

Ⅶ *Talk about what someone is doing where.* Make up dialogues following the pattern of the example. Substitute the underlined parts with the appropriate forms of the alternatives given.

e.g. チャン　　：なかむらさん、<u>エマさん</u>は　どこですか。

なかむら：<u>3がいの　かいぎしつ</u>です。

チャン　　：そうですか。

なかむら：<u>いま　のぞみデパートの　たなかさんに　あたらしい
　　　　　　しょうひんの　せつめいを　して</u>います。

チャン　　：わかりました。ありがとう。

1. チャン　　：...（すずきさん）

なかむら：...（1かいの　カフェ）

チャン　　：...

なかむら：...
　　　　　　　　　　　　　　　　　　　　　（おきゃくさんと　はなします）

チャン　　：...

2. チャン　　：...（スミスさん）

なかむら：...（6かいの　かいぎしつ）

チャン　　：...

なかむら：...
　　　　　　　　　　　　　　　　（プレゼンの　じゅんびを　します）

チャン　　：...

VOCABULARY

| しょうひん | product, goods |
| じゅんびを　します | prepare |

Ⅷ Listen to the audio and fill in the blanks based on the information you hear. 🔊 227-229

1. スミスさんは .... に　にほんごを ....。

2. スミスさんは　いま .... で　おきゃくさんと
........................。

3. エマさんは　いま　プレゼンの .... を ....。

SPEAKING PRACTICE

1. Smith is at the dry cleaners.　　　　　　　　🔊 230

スミス　　　　：これ、おねがいします。いつ　できますか。

みせの　ひと：すいようびの　ゆうがた　できます。

Smith:　　　　Here [is what I have today]. When will it be ready?
Laundry staff:　It will be ready Wednesday evening.

2. On a holiday, Chan calls Emma.　　　　　　🔊 231

エマ　：もしもし。

チャン：チャンです。いま　いいですか。

エマ　：すみません。いま　りょうりを　しています。

チャン：じゃ、また　あとで　でんわします。

エマ　：おねがいします。

Emma:　Hello?
Chan:　This is Chan. Can you talk now?
Emma:　I'm sorry. I'm cooking now.
Chan:　Okay. I'll call you back later.
Emma:　Please do!

ゆうがた	evening	あとで	later
もしもし。	Hello. (greeting when making or	でんわします	telephone, call (see APPENDIX D, p. 246)
	answering a telephone call) (see		
	NOTES 1, p. 227)		

3. Kato and Smith are talking during their break.　🔊 232

かとう：スミスさん、なにか　うんどうを　していますか。

スミス：ええ、ときどき　ジョギングを　しています。

かとう：しごとの　あとですか。

スミス：いいえ、あさ　はしっています。

Kato:　　Smith-san, are you doing any kind of exercise?
Smith:　Yes, sometimes I go jogging.
Kato:　　You do that after work?
Smith:　No, I go running in the morning.

NOTES

1. もしもし。
   When calling on the phone, this expression is used as a greeting by both the caller and the recipient of the call. It is not much used in a business environment.

2. いま　いいですか。
   This is the expression used to ask whether the person called is free to speak.

3. なにか　うんどうを　していますか。
   When なにか is used by itself, it means "something," but when it is used together with a noun, as in "なにか + noun," it means "some/any noun." なにか　うんどう means "any [kind of] exercise."

Active Communication　Imagine that you are involved in some activity that you can't break away from, and a call comes in on your cell phone. Explain to the person on the phone why it is inconvenient for you to talk at the moment.

VOCABULARY

うんどうを　します	do exercise
ジョギングを　します	jog

Work and Interests: I Work for an Apparel Maker

TARGET DIALOGUE 🔊 233

The staff of the office are together at an *izakaya* drinking place. Smith's younger sister Lisa, who is visiting Japan, joins them.

すずき：スミスさん、いもうとさんは　にほんごが　わかりますか。

スミス：はい、すこし　わかりますよ。

(*Lisa arrives and is talking as they are drinking.*)

すずき：リサさん、おしごとは？

リサ　：デザイナーです。ニューヨークの　アパレルメーカーに
　　　　つとめています。

すずき：おしごとは　たのしいですか。

リサ　：ええ、とても　たのしいです。
　　　　わたしの　ゆめは　じぶんの　ブランドを　つくることです。

すずき：そうですか。がんばってください。

リサ　：はい、ありがとうございます。

■ リサさんは　ニューヨークの　アパレルメーカーに　つとめています。
　ゆめは　じぶんの　ブランドを　つくることです。

Suzuki: Smith-san, does your sister understand Japanese?
Smith: Yes, she understands a little.
Suzuki: Lisa-san, may I ask what work you are doing?
Lisa: I am a designer. I work for an apparel maker in New York.
Suzuki: Do you enjoy your work?
Lisa: Yes, I really enjoy my work. My dream is to create my own brand.
Suzuki: Really. I hope it works out.
Lisa: Yes, thank you.

■ Lisa-san works for an apparel maker in New York. Her dream is to create her own brand of apparel.

VOCABULARY

いもうとさん	(another person's) younger sister	アパレルメーカー	apparel maker	ブランド	brand
わかります	understand	アパレル	apparel	こと	(nominalizer; see GRAMMAR 4, p. 229)
おしごと	your work	メーカー	maker	がんばってください。	I hope it works out.
デザイナー	designer	つとめています	work for, be employed	がんばります	do one's best
アパレルメーカー	apparel maker	ゆめ	dream		
		じぶんの	one's own		

KEY SENTENCES

1. スミスさんは　とうきょうに　すんでいます。
2. スミスさんは　にほんごが　わかります。
3. スミスさんは　チャンさんを　しっています。
4. スミスさんの　しゅみは　ほんを　よむことです。

1. Smith-san lives in Tokyo.
2. Smith-san understands Japanese.
3. Smith-san knows Chan-san.
4. Smith-san's hobby is reading.

GRAMMAR

1. person は　verb [て-form] います。 （2） (KS1, 3)

すんでいます, つとめています, and しっています are in the "て-form います" and express a present state.

2. person は　noun が　わかります。 (KS2)

Following the noun that is the object of the verb わかります ("understand"), the particle が is added, as in the case of すきです, じょうずです, いたいです (see L15, GRAMMAR 1, p. 143).

3. person は　noun を　しっています。 (KS3)

The verb しります ("know") is always used, not in the ます-form but in the form しっています. As distinct from other verbs, the possible replies to the question しっていますか ("do you know [about so-and-so]?") are as follows:

e.g. チャンさんを　しっていますか。　Do you know Chan-san?
　　はい、しっています。　　　　Yes, (I) know (her).
　　いいえ、しりません。　　　　No, (I) don't know (her).

しりません is appropriate when someone wants to know whether or not you know someone/something. The negative answer, when someone asks for further information, would be わかりません.

4. noun は　verb [dictionary form] ことです。 (KS4)

When you talk about your hobbies or dreams, the sentence pattern "noun 1 は　noun 2 です" or "noun は verb [dictionary form] ことです" can be used.

VOCABULARY

すんでいます	live
しっています	know
しゅみ	hobby, pastime

WORD POWER

Ⅰ Verbs
🔊 235

①すんでいます ②つとめています ③しっています ④わかります

Ⅱ Family
🔊 236

	Related to the speaker	Related to others
child	こども	おこさん
son	むすこ	むすこさん
daughter	むすめ	おじょうさん／むすめさん
older brother	あに	おにいさん
older sister	あね	おねえさん
younger brother	おとうと	おとうとさん
younger sister	いもうと	いもうとさん

EXERCISES

Ⅰ
Practice conjugating verbs. Repeat the verbs below and memorize their ています-forms—affirmative and negative.

	ます-form	ています-form	
		aff.	*neg.*
live	すみます	すんでいます	すんでいません
be employed	つとめます	つとめています	つとめていません
know	—*	しっています	しりません**

*ます-form is hardly ever used.
**The negative ています-form is しっていません, but this form is not used.

VOCABULARY

こども	child	おじょうさん	(another person's) daughter	あね	(my) older sister
おこさん	(another person's) child	むすめさん	(another person's) daughter	おねえさん	(another person's) older sister
むすこ	(my) son	あに	(my) older brother	おとうとさん	(another person's) younger brother
むすこさん	(another person's) son	おにいさん	(another person's) older brother		
むすめ	(my) daughter				

II *State where someone lives.* Make up sentences following the pattern of the example. Substitute the underlined parts with the alternatives given.

e.g. <u>やまもとさん</u>は　<u>きょうと</u>に　すんでいます。

1. ....（グリーンさん、しぶや）

2. ....（なかむらさん、しんじゅく）

III *Ask and answer where someone lives.* Make up dialogues following the pattern of the example. Substitute the underlined parts with the alternatives given.

e.g. A：<u>すずきさん</u>は　どこに　すんでいますか。
　　 B：<u>よこはま</u>に　すんでいます。

1. A：..（やまださん）

　 B：..（しぶや）

2. A：..（ホワイトさん）

　 B：..（ろっぽんぎ）

IV *State where someone is employed.* Make up sentences following the pattern of the example. Substitute the underlined parts with the alternatives given.

e.g. <u>たなかさん</u>は　<u>デパート</u>に　つとめています。

1. ....（やまださん、ぎんこう）

2. ....（スミスさん、ABC フーズ）

V *Ask and answer where someone is employed.* Make up dialogues following the pattern of the example. Substitute the underlined parts with the alternatives given.

e.g. A：<u>ブラウンさん</u>は　どこに　つとめていますか。
　　 B：<u>ロンドンぎんこう</u>に　つとめています。

1. A：..（ホワイトさん）

　 B：..（JBP ジャパン）

2. A：..（すずきさんの　おにいさん）

　 B：..（りょこうがいしゃ）

VOCABULARY

ホワイト	White (surname)
JBP ジャパン	JBP Japan (fictitious company name)
りょこうがいしゃ	travel agency

VI Make up sentences following the patterns of the examples and based on the information provided.

	Person	Residence	Employer
e.g.	あんどうさん	しながわ	JBP ジャパン
1.	グリーンさん	しぶや	ABC フーズ
2.	なかむらさんの　いもうとさん	さっぽろ	ぎんこう
3.	チャンさんの　おねえさん	ホンコン	デパート

A. *State where someone lives.*

e.g. あんどうさんは　しながわに　すんでいます。

1. ....

2. ....

3. ....

B. *State where someone is employed.*

e.g. あんどうさんは　JBP ジャパンに　つとめています。

1. ....

2. ....

3. ....

VII Make up dialogues following the patterns of the examples. Substitute the underlined part with the alternatives given.

A. *Ask and answer whether someone knows someone or something.*

e.g. A：ささきさんを　しっていますか。

B：はい、しっています。

1. A：...（ブラウンさん）

B：はい、...

2. A：...（たなかさんの　じゅうしょ）

B：はい、...

VOCABULARY

あんどう	Ando (surname)
しながわ	Shinagawa (district in Tokyo)

B. *Ask and answer whether someone knows someone or something.*

e.g. A：<u>ホワイトさん</u>を　しっていますか。

B：いいえ、しりません。

1. A：..

（チャンさんの　メールアドレス）

B：いいえ、..

2. A：..

（すずきさんの　でんわばんごう）

B：いいえ、..

Ⅷ Make up dialogues following the patterns of the examples. Substitute the underlined parts with the alternatives given.

A. *Talk about your work and whether you know a particular person.*

Smith meets various people for the first time at a party.

e.g. スミス　：<u>あんどうさん</u>、おしごとは？

あんどう：<u>エンジニア</u>です。JBP ジャパンに　つとめています。

スミス　：そうですか。じゃ、<u>よこはまししゃの　いとうさん</u>を
しっていますか。

あんどう：はい、しっています。

1. スミス：...（こじまさん）

こじま：...（かいしゃいん）

スミス：...

（おおさかししゃの　やましたさん）

こじま：...

2. スミス　：...（こばやしさん）

こばやし：...（べんごし）

スミス　：...

（ホンコンししゃの　ワンさん）

こばやし：...

VOCABULARY

エンジニア	engineer	やました	Yamashita (surname)
いとう	Ito (surname)	こばやし	Kobayashi (surname)
こじま	Kojima (surname)	べんごし	lawyer
かいしゃいん	company employee	ワン	Wang (surname)

B. *Talk about whether one knows someone and something.*

e.g. スミス ：JBP ジャパンの　<u>いとうさん</u>を　しっていますか。

なかむら：はい、しっています。

スミス　：じゃ、<u>いとうさんの　でんわばんごう</u>を　しっていますか。

なかむら：すみません。わかりません。

1. スミス　　：
　　　　　　　　　　　　　　　　　　　　　　　　　　　　　（ワンさん）

　なかむら：

　スミス　　：
　　　　　　　　　　　　　　　　　　　　（ワンさんの　メールアドレス）

　なかむら：

2. スミス　　：
　　　　　　　　　　　　　　　　　　　　　　　　　　（あんどうさん）

　なかむら：

　スミス　　：
　　　　　　　　　　　　　　　　（あんどうさんの　けいたいの　ばんごう）

　なかむら：

IX *State what language someone understands.* Make up sentences following the pattern of the example. Substitute the underlined part with the alternatives given.

e.g. スミスさんは　<u>にほんご</u>が　わかります。

1. 　　　　　　　　　　　　　　　　　　　　　　　　　　（フランスご）

2. 　　　　　　　　　　　　　　　　　　　　　　　　　　（かんじ）

X *Talk about knowing other languages.* Make up dialogues following the pattern of the example and based on the information provided.

e.g. スミス	1. かとう	2. ささき
〇フランスご ×ドイツご	〇えいご ×ちゅうごくご	〇ちゅうごくご ×かんこくご

VOCABULARY

けいたい	mobile phone
ドイツご	German
ちゅうごくご	Chinese
かんこくご	Korean

e.g. たなか：スミスさんは　フランスごが　わかりますか。

スミス：はい、わかります。

たなか：ドイツごも　わかりますか。

スミス：いいえ、わかりません。

1. たなか：

　　かとう：

　　たなか：

　　かとう：

2. たなか：

　　ささき：

　　たなか：

　　ささき：

Ⓧ *Ask and answer about someone's pastime.* Make up dialogues following the pattern of the example. Substitute the underlined parts with the appropriate forms of the alternatives given.

e.g. たなか：<u>スミスさんの</u>　しゅみは　なんですか。

スミス：<u>ほんを　よむ</u>ことです。

1. たなか：　　　　　　　　　　　　　　　　　　　　（エマさん）

　　エマ　：　　　　　　　　　　　　　　　　（しゃしんを　とります）

2. たなか　：　　　　　　　　　　　　　　　　　（なかむらさん）

　　なかむら：　　　　　　　　　　　　　　　　（ケーキを　つくります）

3. たなか：　　　　　　　　　　　　　　　　　　　（すずきさん）

　　すずき：　　　　　　　　　　　　　　　　　（えを　かきます）

Ⓧ Listen to the audio and fill in the blanks based on the information you hear. 🔊 237, 238

1. なかむらさんの　　　　　　　　　　　　は　さっぽろに

　　　　　　　　　　　　　　。ぎんこうに　　　　　　　　　　　　。

2. スミスさんは　　　　　　　　　は　わかりますが、　　　　　　　は

わかりません。

SPEAKING PRACTICE

1. Kato is talking with Raja.　　　　　　　　　　　　　　🔊 239

かとう：ラジャさんは　とうきょうだいがくですよね。

ラジャ：はい。

かとう：せんこうは　なんですか。

ラジャ：バイオテクノロジーです。

かとう：じゃ、もりせんせいを　しっていますか。

ラジャ：はい、よく　しっています。

Kato: You are studying at the University of Tokyo, right?
Raja: That's right.
Kato: What is your specialty?
Raja: My specialty is biotechnology.
Kato: Then do you know Professor Mori?
Raja: Yes, I know him well.

2. Smith wants to call Tanaka right away.　　　　　　🔊 240

スミス　　：なかむらさん、たなかさんの　けいたいの　ばんごうを　しっていますか。

なかむら：すみません。わかりません。すずきさんに　きいてください。

Smith:　　　Nakamura-san, do you know Tanaka-san's mobile phone number?
Nakamura:　I'm sorry. I don't know. Please ask Suzuki-san.

NOTES

1. とうきょうだいがくですよね。

Kato knows that Raja is a student, so he has omitted the word がくせい from his question, but his question is intended to confirm that Raja is a student at the University of Tokyo. よね is attached to a question when the speaker thinks that the listener has the correct information.

Active Communication

1. Next time you meet a Japanese person, tell him/her where you live and where you are employed. Then ask that person where he/she lives and is employed.

2. Talk about your hobbies.

VOCABULARY

よね	... right? (confirming expression) (combination of particles; see NOTES 1, above)	バイオテクノロジー	biotechnology
		もりせんせい	Professor Mori
		もり	Mori (surname)
せんこう	specialty, major	せんせい	(honorific used for teachers, doctors, etc.)

I Complete the sentences by choosing the most appropriate particle from the box below. The same particle may be used more than once. Some of the particles are not needed.

が	を	に	で	と

1. あねは　ぎんこう（　　　）　つとめています。

2. ここ（　　　）　にもつを　おいてください。

3. まいあさ　なんじに　うち（　　　）　でますか。

4. とうきょうえきで　しんかんせん（　　　）　のりました。

5. リサさんは　にほんご（　　　）　すこし　わかります。

II Change the word in the parentheses to the form that is appropriate in the context of the sentence.

1. A：すみません。この　ペンを ＿＿＿＿＿＿＿＿＿　も　いいですか。

   （つかいます）

   B：はい、どうぞ。

2. A：ここは　たちいりきんしですから、＿＿＿＿＿＿＿＿＿　でください。

   （はいります）

   B：はい。わかりました。

3. ささきさんは　いま　おきゃくさんと ＿＿＿＿＿＿＿＿＿ います。（はなします）

4. わたしの　しゅみは　えいがを ＿＿＿＿＿＿＿＿＿ ことです。　　（みます）

5. A：レポートは　もう　かきましたか。

   B：いま ＿＿＿＿＿＿＿＿＿ います。もうすこし　まってください。（かきます）

III What do you say in the following situations?

1. You want to ask how long it takes to go from Tokyo to Okinawa by air.

   ＿＿＿＿＿＿＿＿＿＿＿＿＿＿＿＿＿＿＿＿＿＿＿＿＿＿＿＿＿＿＿＿＿＿

2. You want to ask that tomato not be put into the sandwich.

   ＿＿＿＿＿＿＿＿＿＿＿＿＿＿＿＿＿＿＿＿＿＿＿＿＿＿＿＿＿＿＿＿＿＿

3. You want to ask what Smith-san is doing now.

   ＿＿＿＿＿＿＿＿＿＿＿＿＿＿＿＿＿＿＿＿＿＿＿＿＿＿＿＿＿＿＿＿＿＿

4. You want to ask Smith-san where his sister lives.

   ＿＿＿＿＿＿＿＿＿＿＿＿＿＿＿＿＿＿＿＿＿＿＿＿＿＿＿＿＿＿＿＿＿＿

CASUAL STYLE 2

SAMPLE DIALOGUE 1

A notebook with experimental data is sitting on Hayashi's desk.

ラジャ：それ、みても いい？	Raja: Can I have a look at that?
はやし：うん、いいよ。はい。(*Hands to Raja*)	Hayashi: Yeah, sure. Here.
ラジャ：これ、かりても いい？	Raja: Can I borrow this?
はやし：えー、ちょっと・・・。	Hayashi: Well, that's not quite . . .

ですます style	Casual style
みても いいですか。	みても いい？
	Expressions seeking permission for something are formed using the "て-form も いい？" (rising intonation). When permission is granted, the response is いいよ ("All right." "Sure.") or どうぞ. When wishing to gently refuse, the more vague えー、ちょっと・・・ is used. A firm refusal is expressed by saying だめ ("No." "That can't happen.").

SAMPLE DIALOGUE 2

242

Tomorrow the university club will have a party.

やまだ：あしたの パーティー、いく？	Yamada: Are you going to tomorrow's party?
ラジャ：うん、いく。	Raja: Yes. I'm going.
はやし：あたしは いかない。	Hayashi: I'm not going.
バイト あるから。	Because I have a part-time job.

ですます style	Casual style
いきません。	いかない。
	The present negative form of verbs is expressed by the ない-form.

SAMPLE DIALOGUE 3

🔊 243

Hayashi is planning to hold a party at her home next Saturday.

はやし：こんどの　どよう、 　　　　うち　こない？	Hayashi: Why don't you come over to my house next Saturday?
ラジャ：うん、いく。ありがとう。	Raja: Sure. I'll be there. Thanks!

ですます style	Casual style
きませんか。	こない？ Express an invitation by using the ない-form with rising intonation.

SAMPLE DIALOGUE 4

🔊 244

Hayashi brought along the latest edition of a really popular manga series.

はやし：もう　これ、よんだ？	Hayashi: Have you already read this?
ラジャ：うん、よんだ。	Raja: Yeah. I read it.
あべ　：おれは　まだ。かして。	Abe: I haven't. Can I borrow it? [lit. Lend me that.]
はやし：いいよ。	Hayashi: Sure.

ですます style	Casual style
よみました。	よんだ。 The past affirmative form of verbs is expressed by the た-form. See the APPENDIX D (pp. 244, 245) for the た-form. For the past negative form, the い of the ない-form changes to かった.
かしてください。	かして。 A request or instruction is expressed using the て-form alone. When agreeing to a request or instruction, respond with いいよ, わかった ("Got it."), ありがとう or something similar. When gently declining a request, say えー、ちょっと・・・. When refusing outright, いや（だ）("I don't want to") is often used.

APPENDIXES

List of Grammar Points

A. Particles

Particles	Examples	Unit	Lesson
の	こちらは　のぞみデパート<u>の</u>　たなかさんです。	1	1
	これは　だれ<u>の</u>　ペンですか。	1	2
	それは　わたし<u>の</u>じゃありません。	1	2
	かいぎは　あした<u>の</u>　4じからです。	2	3
	これは　フランス<u>の</u>　ワインです。	2	5
	こちらは　インターン<u>の</u>　ラジャさんです。	3	6
を	たなかさん<u>を</u>　おねがいします。	1	1
	これ<u>を</u>　ください。	2	4
	しゅうまつに　なに<u>を</u>　しますか。	4	8
	つぎの　しんごう<u>を</u>　みぎに　まがってください。	8	19
	ひろしまえきで　しんかんせん<u>を</u>　おります。	9	20
か	のぞみデパートの　たなかさんです<u>か</u>。	1	1
	かいぎは　よっかです<u>か</u>、ようかです<u>か</u>。	3	7
は	スミスさん<u>は</u>　アメリカじんです。	1	1
	てんぷら<u>は</u>　すきですが、おすし<u>は</u>　すきじゃありません。	10	23
から	かいぎは　あしたの　4じ<u>から</u>です。	2	3
	スミスさんは　きょねん　アメリカ<u>から</u>　きました。	3	6
	あしたは　いそがしいです。かいぎが　あります<u>から</u>。	6	14
	いい　てんきです<u>から</u>、こうえんで　ひるごはんを　たべませんか。	7	16
まで	しごとは　9じから　5じ<u>まで</u>です。	2	3
	とうきょうタワーの　ちかく<u>まで</u>　おねがいします。	8	19
も	これは　3,000えんです。あれ<u>も</u>　3,000えんです。	2	4
	エマさんは　パーティーで　なに<u>も</u>　たべませんでした。	4	8
	えきの　まえに　コンビニが　あります。えきの　なかに<u>も</u>　あります。	9	22
と	カレー<u>と</u>　サラダを　おねがいします。	2	4
	ともだち<u>と</u>　レストランに　いきました。	3	6
で	カード<u>で</u>　おねがいします。	2	4
	ひとり<u>で</u>　きますか。	3	6
	スミスさんは　しんかんせん<u>で</u>　おおさかに　いきます。	3	7
	レストラン<u>で</u>　ばんごはんを　たべました。	4	8
	どようびに　あさくさ<u>で</u>　おまつりが　あります。	7	16
	ばんごはんは　かいぎの　あと<u>で</u>　たべます。	8	18
に	スミスさんは　あした　ぎんこう<u>に</u>　いきます。	3	6
	エマさんは　4がつ<u>に</u>　にほんに　きました。	3	7
	スミスさんは　あした　たなかさん<u>に</u>　あいます。	4	9
	スミスさんは　すずきさん<u>に</u>　レストランの　ばしょを　おしえました。	4	9

		１かい<u>に</u>　うけつけが　あります。	6	12
		なかむらさんは　スミスさん<u>に</u>　はなを　もらいました。	6	14
		かいぎの　まえ<u>に</u>　しりょうを　おくります。	7	17
		とうきょうえきで　しんかんせん<u>に</u>　のります。	9	20
		ここ<u>に</u>　すわっても　いいですか。	9	21
		ニューヨークの　アパレルメーカー<u>に</u>　つとめています。	10	24
が		どの　バス<u>が</u>　いきますか。	3	6
		デパートに　いきました<u>が</u>、なにも　かいませんでした。	5	11
		１かいに　うけつけ<u>が</u>　あります。	6	12
		スミスさんは　あした　かいぎ<u>が</u>　あります。	6	14
		チャンさんは　ワイン<u>が</u>　すきです。	7	15
		とうきょうドームに　いきたいんです<u>が</u>。	9	20
		（わたしは）あたま<u>が</u>　いたいです。	9	21
		スミスさんは　にほんご<u>が</u>　わかります。	10	24
や		おおきい　おてら<u>や</u>　じんじゃが　あります。	6	12
ね		かいぎは　１じからです<u>ね</u>。	3	6
		いい　みせです<u>ね</u>。	4	9
よ		にほんの　スパです<u>よ</u>。	6	12
よね		ラジャさんは　とうきょうだいがくです<u>よね</u>。	10	24

B. Sentence patterns

N=noun, V=verb, A=adjective

Sentence patterns		Examples	Unit	Lesson
Nは　Nです		スミスさんは　アメリカじんです。	1	1
		しごとは　９じから　５じまでです。	2	3
		レストランは　５かいです。	2	5
		かいぎは　よっかですか、ようかですか。	3	7
Nを　ください		これを　ください。	2	4
		その　ワインを　２ほん　ください。	2	5
Nを　おねがいします		たなかさんを　おねがいします。	1	1
		カレーと　サラダを　おねがいします。	2	4
Nは　Nに／へ　V		スミスさんは　あした　ぎんこうに／へ　いきます。	3	6
Nは　Nから　V		スミスさんは　きょねん　アメリカから　きました。	3	6
Nは　Nを　V		スミスさんは　あした　テニスを　します。	4	8
		スミスさんは　ひろしまえきで　しんかんせんを　おります。	9	20
Nは　Nに　V		スミスさんは　あした　たなかさんに　あいます。	4	9
		スミスさんは　とうきょうえきで　しんかんせんに　のります。	9	20
Nは　Nに　Nを　V		スミスさんは　すずきさんに　レストランの　ばしょを　おしえました。	4	9
		スミスさんは　なかむらさんに　はなを　あげました。	6	14
		なかむらさんは　スミスさんに　はなを　もらいました。	6	14

Nは Aです	この ほんは おもしろいです。	5	10
Nに Nが あります ／います	1かいに うけつけが あります。	6	12
	うけつけに おんなの ひとが います。	6	12
Nは Nに あります ／います	タクシーのりばは えきの まえに あります。	6	13
	スミスさんは 2かいに います。	6	13
	スミスさんは ひろしまに 1しゅうかん います。	9	20
Nは Nが V	スミスさんは あした かいぎが あります。	6	14
	スミスさんは にほんごが わかります。	10	24
Nは Nが A	チャンさんは ワインが すきです。	7	15
	（わたしは） あたまが いたいです。	9	21
Nは Vのが A	スミスさんは サッカーを みるのが すきです。	7	15
Nで Nが あります	どようびに あさくさで おまつりが あります。	7	16
Vませんか	しゅうまつに いっしょに えいがを みませんか。	7	16
Vましょう	いっしょに いきましょう。	7	16
Vたいです	（わたしは）おいしい おすしを／が たべたいです。	7	17
Vて、V	エマさんは おおさかししゃに いって、チャンさんに あいます。	8	18
Vてください	ちょっと まってください。	8	19
Vても いいですか	この えの しゃしんを とっても いいですか。	9	21
Vないでください	わさびを いれないでください。	9	22
Vています	スミスさんは いま ひるごはんを たべています。	10	23
	スミスさんは にほんごを ならっています。	10	23
	スミスさんは とうきょうに すんでいます。	10	24
	スミスさんは チャンさんを しっています。	10	24
Nは Vことです	スミスさんの しゅみは ほんを よむことです。	10	24

C. Interrogatives

Interrogatives	Examples	Unit	Lesson
いくつ	テーブルの うえに りんごが <u>いくつ</u> ありますか。	6	13
いくら	これは <u>いくら</u>ですか。	2	4
いつ	かいぎは <u>いつ</u>ですか。	2	3
	なつやすみは <u>いつ</u>から <u>いつ</u>までですか。	3	7
	かとうさんは <u>いつ</u> おおさかししゃに いきますか。	3	6
だれ	これは <u>だれ</u>の ペンですか。	1	2

	スミスさんは　あした　だれと　のぞみデパートに　いきますか。	3	6
	スミスさんは　だれに　でんわを　しますか。	4	9
	うけつけに　だれが　いますか。	6	12
どう	ふじさんは　どうでしたか。	5	11
	スミスさんも　いっしょに　どうですか。	7	16
	どうしましたか。	9	21
どうやって	スミスさんは　どうやって　かいしゃに　いきますか。	9	20
どこ	これは　どこの　ビールですか。	2	5
	ワインショップは　どこですか。	2	5
	スミスさんは　あした　どこに　いきますか。	3	6
	どこから　きましたか。	3	6
	どこで　ばんごはんを　たべましたか。	4	8
どちら	スミスさん、おくには　どちらですか。	1	1
どなた	はい、どなたですか。	5	10
どの	どの　バスが　いきますか。	3	6
どのくらい	どのくらい　あるきましたか。	5	11
どれ	A：あの　Tシャツは　いくらですか。B：どれですか。	2	5
どんな	にっこうは　どんな　ところですか。	5	10
なに	しゅうまつに　なにを　しますか。	4	8
	にっこうに　なにが　ありますか。	6	12
なん	これは　なんですか。	1	2
	スミスさんは　なんで　おおさかに　いきますか。	3	7
なんじ	かいぎは　なんじから　なんじまでですか。	2	3
	いま　なんじですか。	2	3
	なんじに　いきますか。	3	7
なんがつ	おまつりは　なんがつですか。	3	7
なんにち	おまつりは　なんにちですか。	3	7
なんようび	おまつりは　なんようびですか。	3	7
なんにん	レストランに　おとこの　ひとが　なんにん　いますか。	6	13
なんめい	なんめいさまですか。	4	8
なんぼん	テーブルの　うえに　フォークが　なんぼん　ありますか。	6	13
なんまい	テーブルの　うえに　おさらが　なんまい　ありますか。	6	13

D. Verbs

This textbook introduces the ます-form, dictionary form, て-form, and ない-form for the conjugated forms of verbs. Other forms are the た-form, conditional form, volitional form, and imperative form, which will be introduced in Volume II and III.

	Regular 1	Regular 2	Irregular	
ます-form	かきます	たべます	きます	します
Dictionary form	かく	たべる	くる	する
て-form	かいて	たべて	きて	して
ない-form	かかない	たべない	こない	しない
た-form	かいた	たべた	きた	した
Conditional form	かけば	たべれば	くれば	すれば
Volitional form	かこう	たべよう	こよう	しよう
Imperative form	かけ	たべろ	こい	しろ

Regular 1 verbs					
～ます	Dictionary	～て	～ない	～た	Meaning
あいます	あう	あって	あわない	あった	meet
あずかります	あずかる	あずかって	あずからない	あずかった	keep
あらいます	あらう	あらって	あらわない	あらった	wash
あります	ある	あって	ない	あった	exist, have, take place
あるきます	あるく	あるいて	あるかない	あるいた	walk
いいます	いう	いって	いわない	いった	say
いきます	いく	いって	いかない	いった	go
うたいます	うたう	うたって	うたわない	うたった	sing
おきます	おく	おいて	おかない	おいた	put, place
おくります	おくる	おくって	おくらない	おくった	send
およぎます	およぐ	およいで	およがない	およいだ	swim
おわります	おわる	おわって	おわらない	おわった	finish
かいます	かう	かって	かわない	かった	buy
かえります	かえる	かえって	かえらない	かえった	return, come back
かかります	かかる	かかって	かからない	かかった	take [time]
かきます	かく	かいて	かかない	かいた	write, draw
かします	かす	かして	かさない	かした	lend, loan
がんばります	がんばる	がんばって	がんばらない	がんばった	do one's best
ききます	きく	きいて	きかない	きいた	listen to, ask
けします	けす	けして	けさない	けした	turn off
さわります	さわる	さわって	さわらない	さわった	touch
しります *	しる	しって	しらない	しった	know
（たばこを）すいます	すう	すって	すわない	すった	smoke
すみます	すむ	すんで	すまない	すんだ	live
すわります	すわる	すわって	すわらない	すわった	sit down
たちます	たつ	たって	たたない	たった	stand up
つかいます	つかう	つかって	つかわない	つかった	use
つきます	つく	ついて	つかない	ついた	arrive
つくります	つくる	つくって	つくらない	つくった	make
（しゃしんを）とります	とる	とって	とらない	とった	take (a photo)
ならいます	ならう	ならって	ならわない	ならった	learn, take lessons in
にあいます	にあう	にあって	にあわない	にあった	suit, look good on
のぼります	のぼる	のぼって	のぼらない	のぼった	climb

のみます	のむ	のんで	のまない	のんだ	drink
のります	のる	のって	のらない	のった	get on, take
はいります	はいる	はいって	はいらない	はいった	enter
はしります	はしる	はしって	はしらない	はしった	run
はなします	はなす	はなして	はなさない	はなした	talk, speak
まがります	まがる	まがって	まがらない	まがった	turn
まちます	まつ	まって	またない	まった	wait
もらいます	もらう	もらって	もらわない	もらった	receive
やすみます	やすむ	やすんで	やすまない	やすんだ	rest, take a day off
よみます	よむ	よんで	よまない	よんだ	read
わかります	わかる	わかって	わからない	わかった	understand

* This form is hardly ever used. Instead, しっています (the て-form) is used.

Regular 2 verbs					
～ます	Dictionary	～て	～ない	～た	Meaning
あけます	あける	あけて	あけない	あけた	open
あげます	あげる	あげて	あげない	あげた	give
（シャワーを）あびます	あびる	あびて	あびない	あびた	take a shower
います	いる	いて	いない	いた	be, exist, stay
いれます	いれる	いれて	いれない	いれた	put in, add
おしえます	おしえる	おしえて	おしえない	おしえた	tell, teach
おります	おりる	おりて	おりない	おりた	get off
かります	かりる	かりて	かりない	かりた	borrow
しめます	しめる	しめて	しめない	しめた	close
たべます	たべる	たべて	たべない	たべた	eat
つかれます	つかれる	つかれて	つかれない	つかれた	get tired
つけます	つける	つけて	つけない	つけた	turn on
（きを）つけます	つける	つけて	つけない	つけた	be careful
つたえます	つたえる	つたえて	つたえない	つたえた	relay a message
つとめます	つとめる	つとめて	つとめない	つとめた	work for, be employed
できます	できる	できて	できない	できた	be done
でます	でる	でて	でない	でた	leave
とどけます	とどける	とどけて	とどけない	とどけた	deliver
とめます	とめる	とめて	とめない	とめた	stop, park
ねます	ねる	ねて	ねない	ねた	sleep, go to bed
はじめます	はじめる	はじめて	はじめない	はじめた	start, begin
みせます	みせる	みせて	みせない	みせた	show
みます	みる	みて	みない	みた	see, watch

Irregular verbs					
～ます	Dictionary	～て	～ない	～た	Meaning
きます	くる	きて	こない	きた	come
もってきます	もってくる	もってきて	もってこない	もってきた	bring
します	する	して	しない	した	do
きに します	きに する	きに して	きに しない	きに した	worry about
じゅうでんします	じゅうでんする	じゅうでんして	じゅうでんしない	じゅうでんした	recharge
ダウンロードします	ダウンロードする	ダウンロードして	ダウンロードしない	ダウンロードした	download
チェックします	チェックする	チェックして	チェックしない	チェックした	check
ねぼうします	ねぼうする	ねぼうして	ねぼうしない	ねぼうした	oversleep
ほうこくします	ほうこくする	ほうこくして	ほうこくしない	ほうこくした	report
よやくします	よやくする	よやくして	よやくしない	よやくした	make a reservation

The verb します ("do") takes various nouns and expresses many meanings. The particle を is added to some nouns, and in other cases such as べんきょうします, コピーします, でんわします introduced in this textbook, they are used without attaching を.

うちあわせを します	have a preparatory meeting		ストレッチを します	do stretching exercises
うんどうを します	do exercise		スノーボードを します	snowboard
(お)はなみを します	view cherry blossoms		せつめいを します	explain
かいぎを します	have a meeting		そうじを します	clean
かいものを します	shop		ダイビングを します	scuba dive
コピーを します	make a copy		テニスを します	play tennis
ゴルフを します	play golf		でんわを します	telephone, call
さんぽを します	take a walk		ドライブを します	go for a drive
しごとを します	work		パーティーを します	have a party
じゅんびを します	prepare		プレゼンを します	give a presentation
ジョギングを します	jog		べんきょうを します	study
しょくじを します	have a meal		りょうりを します	cook
スキーを します	ski			

E. Adjectives

い-adjectives

あおい	blue		さむい	cold
あかい	red		しろい	white
あたたかい	warm		すずしい	cool
あたらしい	new, fresh		たかい	expensive
あつい	hot		たのしい	fun, pleasant, enjoyable
あぶない	dangerous		ちいさい	small
いい	nice, good		ちかい	near, close
いそがしい	busy		つまらない	boring, uninteresting
いたい	hurt, sore, painful		とおい	far
おいしい	delicious, tasty		ふるい	old
おおきい	large, big		むずかしい	difficult
おもしろい	interesting		やすい	inexpensive
くろい	black		わるい	bad

な-adjectives

いろいろ(な)	various		すてき(な)	lovely, nice
かんたん(な)	easy, simple		たいへん(な)	hard, tough
きれい(な)	pretty, beautiful, clean		にぎやか(な)	lively
しずか(な)	quiet		ひま(な)	free, not busy
じょうず(な)	skilled, be good at		べんり(な)	convenient
すき(な)	like, favorite		ゆうめい(な)	famous

F. Ko-so-a-do words

<Basic>

	こ-words	そ-words	あ-words	ど-words
thing	これ this one	それ that one	あれ that one over there	どれ which one (of three or more) どちら which one (of the two)
+ noun	この　ペン this pen	その　ペン that pen	あの　ペン that pen over there	どの　ペン which pen (of three or more) どちらの　ペン which pen (of the two)
place	ここ here	そこ there	あそこ over there	どこ where
direction	こちら this way	そちら that way	あちら that way over there	どちら which way
people	----	----	----	だれ who

<Polite>

	こ-words	そ-words	あ-words	ど-words
thing	こちら this one	そちら that one	あちら that one over there	どちら which one
+ noun	こちらの　ペン this pen	そちらの　ペン that pen	あちらの　ペン that pen over there	どちらの　ペン which pen
place	こちら here	そちら there	あちら over there	どちら where
direction	こちら this way	そちら that way	あちら that way over there	どちら which way
people	こちら this (person)	そちら that (person)	あちら that (person) over there	どなた who

G. Time expressions

Relative time

Day

おととい	day before yesterday
きのう	yesterday
きょう	today
あした	tomorrow
あさって	day after tomorrow

Morning

きのうの　あさ	yesterday morning
きょうの　あさ	this morning
けさ	this morning
あしたの　あさ	tomorrow morning

Evening

きのうの　ばん／よる	yesterday evening/night
ゆうべ	yesterday evening
こんばん	this evening
こんや	tonight
あしたの　ばん／よる	tomorrow evening/night

Week

せんせんしゅう	week before last
せんしゅう	last week
こんしゅう	this week
らいしゅう	next week
さらいしゅう	week after next

Month

せんせんげつ	month before last
せんげつ	last month
こんげつ	this month
らいげつ	next month
さらいげつ	month after next

Year

おととし	year before last
きょねん	last year
ことし	this year
らいねん	next year
さらいねん	year after next

Every: まい〜

まいあさ	every morning
まいばん	every evening, every night
まいにち	every day
まいしゅう	every week
まいつき／まいげつ	every month
まいとし／まいねん	every year

Specific time

いちじ	いっぷん	1:01	しちじ	ななふん	7:07
にじ	にふん	2:02	はちじ	はっぷん	8:08
さんじ	さんぷん	3:03	くじ	きゅうふん	9:09
よじ	よんぷん	4:04	じゅうじ	じゅっぷん	10:10
ごじ	ごふん	5:05	じゅういちじ	じゅういっぷん	11:11
ろくじ	ろっぷん	6:06	じゅうにじ	じゅうにふん	12:12

Refer to p. 63 for years, days of the week, months, and days of the month.

Periods

Minutes: 〜ふん／ぷん

いっぷん（かん）	(for) 1 minute	はっぷん（かん）	(for) 8 minutes
にふん（かん）	(for) 2 minutes	はちふん（かん）	〃
さんぷん（かん）	(for) 3 minutes	きゅうふん（かん）	(for) 9 minutes
よんぷん（かん）	(for) 4 minutes	じゅっぷん（かん）	(for) 10 minutes
ごふん（かん）	(for) 5 minutes	じゅういっぷん（かん）	(for) 11 minutes
ろっぷん（かん）	(for) 6 minutes	じゅうにふん（かん）	(for) 12 minutes
ななふん（かん）	(for) 7 minutes		

なんぷん（かん）　how many minutes

Hours: 〜じかん

いちじかん	(for) 1 hour	はちじかん	(for) 8 hours
にじかん	(for) 2 hours	くじかん	(for) 9 hours
さんじかん	(for) 3 hours	じゅうじかん	(for) 10 hours
よじかん	(for) 4 hours	じゅういちじかん	(for) 11 hours
ごじかん	(for) 5 hours	じゅうにじかん	(for) 12 hours
ろくじかん	(for) 6 hours		
ななじかん	(for) 7 hours		
しちじかん	〃		

なんじかん　how many hours

Days: 〜にち（かん）

いちにち	(for) 1 day	なのか（かん）	(for) 7 days
ふつか（かん）	(for) 2 days	ようか（かん）	(for) 8 days
みっか（かん）	(for) 3 days	ここのか（かん）	(for) 9 days
よっか（かん）	(for) 4 days	とおか（かん）	(for) 10 days
いつか（かん）	(for) 5 days	じゅういちにち（かん）	(for) 11 days
むいか（かん）	(for) 6 days	じゅうににち（かん）	(for) 12 days

なんにち（かん）　how many days

Weeks: 〜しゅうかん

いっしゅうかん	(for) 1 week	ななしゅうかん	(for) 7 weeks
にしゅうかん	(for) 2 weeks	はっしゅうかん	(for) 8 weeks
さんしゅうかん	(for) 3 weeks	きゅうしゅうかん	(for) 9 weeks
よんしゅうかん	(for) 4 weeks	じゅっしゅうかん	(for) 10 weeks
ごしゅうかん	(for) 5 weeks	じゅういっしゅうかん	(for) 11 weeks
ろくしゅうかん	(for) 6 weeks	じゅうにしゅうかん	(for) 12 weeks

なんしゅうかん　how many weeks

Months: ～かげつ（かん）

いっかげつ（かん）	(for) 1 month	はちかげつ（かん）	(for) 8 months
にかげつ（かん）	(for) 2 months	はっかげつ（かん）	〃
さんかげつ（かん）	(for) 3 months	きゅうかげつ（かん）	(for) 9 months
よんかげつ（かん）	(for) 4 months	じゅっかげつ（かん）	(for) 10 months
ごかげつ（かん）	(for) 5 months	じゅういっかげつ（かん）	(for) 11 months
ろっかげつ（かん）	(for) 6 months	じゅうにかげつ（かん）	(for) 12 months
ななかげつ（かん）	(for) 7 months		

なんかげつ（かん）　how many months

Years: ～ねん（かん）

いちねん（かん）	(for) 1 year	はちねん（かん）	(for) 8 years
にねん（かん）	(for) 2 years	きゅうねん（かん）	(for) 9 years
さんねん（かん）	(for) 3 years	じゅうねん（かん）	(for) 10 years
よねん（かん）	(for) 4 years	じゅういちねん（かん）	(for) 11 years
ごねん（かん）	(for) 5 years	じゅうにねん（かん）	(for) 12 years
ろくねん（かん）	(for) 6 years		
ななねん（かん）	(for) 7 years		
しちねん（かん）	〃		

なんねん（かん）　how many years

NOTE: Except for with じかん and しゅうかん , the suffix かん may be considered optional and need be added only when specificity is called for.

Seasons

はる	spring	あき	autumn
なつ	summer	ふゆ	winter

H. Counters

The abstract numbers (いち , に , さん) are given on p. 11 (0-9), p. 22 (10-30; 40, 50, ...), and p. 31 (100, 200, ...). For an explanation of very large numbers, see PLUS ONE on p. 31.

ひとつ、ふたつ、みっつ system

ひとつ	one	いつつ	five	ここのつ	nine
ふたつ	two	むっつ	six	とお	ten
みっつ	three	ななつ	seven	じゅういち	eleven
よっつ	four	やっつ	eight	じゅうに	twelve

いくつ　how many

Thin, flat objects: ～まい

いちまい	one	ごまい	five	きゅうまい	nine
にまい	two	ろくまい	six	じゅうまい	ten
さんまい	three	ななまい	seven	じゅういちまい	eleven
よんまい	four	はちまい	eight	じゅうにまい	twelve

なんまい　how many

Long, slender objects: ～ほん／ぽん／ぼん

いっぽん	one	ごほん	five	きゅうほん	nine
にほん	two	ろっぽん	six	じゅっぽん	ten
さんぼん	three	ななほん	seven	じゅういっぽん	eleven
よんほん	four	はっぽん	eight	じゅうにほん	twelve

なんぼん　how many

People: ～にん

ひとり	1 person	ろくにん	6 people	きゅうにん	9 people
ふたり	2 people	ななにん	7 people	くにん	〃
さんにん	3 people	しちにん	〃	じゅうにん	10 people
よにん	4 people	はちにん	8 people	じゅういちにん	11 people
ごにん	5 people			じゅうににん	12 people

なんにん　how many people

Floors of a house or building: ～かい / がい

いっかい	1st floor	ごかい	5th floor	じゅっかい	10th floor
にかい	2nd floor	ろっかい	6th floor	じゅういっかい	11th floor
さんがい	3rd floor	ななかい	7th floor	じゅうにかい	12th floor
さんかい	〃	はちかい	8th floor		
よんかい	4th floor	きゅうかい	9th floor		

なんがい／なんかい　how many floors, which floor

Also: ちか　いっかい, 1st floor basement, ちか　にかい, 2nd floor basement, etc.

I. Extent, frequency, quantity

Extent

とても	very
あまり…～ないです／～ません	not very
ぜんぜん…～ないです／～ません	not at all

e.g. この　ケーキは　とても　おいしいです。　This cake is very good.
　　 この　ケーキは　あまり　おいしくないです。　This cake is not very good.
　　 この　ケーキは　ぜんぜん　おいしくないです。　This cake is not good at all.

Frequency

いつも	always
よく	often
ときどき	sometimes
たまに	occasionally
あまり…～ません	not often
ぜんぜん…～ません	not at all

e.g. いつも　りょうりを　します。　(I) always cook.
　　 よく　りょうりを　します。　(I) often cook.
　　 ときどき　りょうりを　します。　(I) sometimes cook.
　　 たまに　りょうりを　します。　(I) occasionally cook.
　　 あまり　りょうりを　しません。　(I) don't often cook.
　　 ぜんぜん　りょうりを　しません。　(I) don't cook at all.

Quantity

たくさん	many, much
すこし	a few, a little
あまり…～ません	not many, not much
ぜんぜん…～ません	not at all

e.g. うちの　ちかくに　みせが　たくさん　あります。　There are many stores near my house.
　　 うちの　ちかくに　みせが　すこし　あります。　There are a few stores near my house.
　　 うちの　ちかくに　みせが　あまり　ありません。　There aren't many stores near my house.
　　 うちの　ちかくに　みせが　ぜんぜん　ありません。　There are no stores near my house.

Target Dialogues (with kanji and kana)

LESSON 1
スミス：すみません。のぞみデパートの田中さんですか。
田中　：はい、そうです。
スミス：はじめまして。ABC フーズのスミスです。よろしくお願いします。
田中　：はじめまして。田中です。こちらこそ、よろしくお願いします。

LESSON 2
中村　：これはだれのペンですか。
鈴木　：さあ、わかりません。スミスさんのですか。
スミス：いいえ、私のじゃありません。
中村　：田中さん、これは田中さんのペンですか。
田中　：はい、私のです。ありがとうございます。

LESSON 3
店の人：すしよしです。
スミス：すみません。ランチタイムは何時からですか。
店の人：11 時半からです。
スミス：何時までですか。
店の人：2 時半までです。
スミス：ラストオーダーは何時ですか。
店の人：2 時です。
スミス：ありがとうございます。
■ランチタイムは 11 時半から 2 時半までです。

LESSON 4
店の人：いらっしゃいませ。
スミス：それを見せてください。
店の人：はい、どうぞ。
スミス：ありがとう。これはいくらですか。
店の人：3,000 円です。
スミス：あれはいくらですか。
店の人：あれも 3,000 円です。
スミス：じゃ、これをください。
店の人：はい、ありがとうございます。

LESSON 5
スミス　　　　　　　　　：すみません。ワインショップはどこですか。
インフォメーションの人：地下 1 階です。
スミス　　　　　　　　　：どうもありがとう。
スミス　　　　　　　　　：すみません。そのワインはどこのですか。
店の人　　　　　　　　：フランスのです。
スミス　　　　　　　　　：いくらですか。
店の人　　　　　　　　：2,600 円です。
スミス　　　　　　　　　：じゃ、それを 2 本ください。袋も 2 枚ください。

LESSON 6
チャン：はい、チャンです。
スミス：東京支社のスミスです。おはようございます。
チャン：おはようございます。
スミス：あしたそちらに行きます。会議は 1 時からですね。
チャン：はい、1 時からです。一人で来ますか。
スミス：いいえ、加藤さんと行きます。
チャン：そうですか。では、あした。
スミス：失礼します。
チャン：失礼します。
■スミスさんはあした加藤さんと大阪支社に行きます。

LESSON 7
中村　　：あ、スミスさん、出張ですか。
スミス：ええ、加藤さんと大阪支社に行きます。金曜日に東京に帰ります。
中村　　：飛行機で行きますか。
スミス：いいえ、新幹線で行きます。
中村　　：そうですか。いってらっしゃい。
■スミスさんは加藤さんと新幹線で大阪に行きます。金曜日に東京に帰ります。

LESSON 8
佐々木：週末に何をしますか。
スミス：土曜日に銀座で鈴木さんと天ぷらを食べます。
佐々木：そうですか。いいですね。
スミス：佐々木さんは？
佐々木：日曜日に友達と歌舞伎を見ます。
スミス：いいですね。
■スミスさんは土曜日に銀座で鈴木さんと天ぷらを食べます。佐々木さんは日曜日に友達と歌舞伎を見ます。

LESSON 9
店の人　　　：いらっしゃいませ。
鈴木　　　　：鈴木です。
店の人　　　：鈴木様ですね。どうぞこちらへ。
スミス　　　：いい店ですね。鈴木さんはよくこの店に来ますか。
鈴木　　　　：ええ、時々来ます。先週はここでグリーンさんに会いました。
スミス　　　：え、本当ですか。
スミス・鈴木：あ、グリーンさん！
■スミスさんと鈴木さんは銀座の天ぷら屋でグリーンさんに会いました。

LESSON 10
佐々木：お茶をどうぞ。
エマ　：ありがとうございます。
佐々木：お菓子はいかがですか。
エマ　：はい、いただきます。きれいなお菓子ですね。日本のお菓子ですか。
佐々木：ええ、そうです。京都のお菓子です。
エマ　：とてもおいしいです。
■エマさんは佐々木さんのうちできれいな日本のお菓子を食べました。

LESSON 11
エマ　：先週富士山に登りました。
佐々木：どうでしたか。
エマ　：とてもきれいでした。
佐々木：写真を撮りましたか。
エマ　：ええ、これです。
佐々木：本当にきれいですね。どのくらい歩きましたか。
エマ　：8時間ぐらい歩きました。大変でしたが、楽しかったです。
■エマさんは佐々木さんと佐々木さんのご主人に写真を見せました。

LESSON 12
中村　：土曜日にエマさんと日光に行きます。
ラジャ：そうですか。日光に何がありますか。
中村　：大きいお寺や神社があります。温泉もあります。
ラジャ：温泉って何ですか。
中村　：これです。日本のスパですよ。
ラジャ：いいですね。
■中村さんは土曜日にエマさんと日光に行きます。日光に大きいお寺や神社があります。

LESSON 13
中村　：すみません。この近くにおいしいおそば屋さんがありますか。
店の人：ええ。そばいちがおいしいですよ。
エマ　：どこにありますか。

店の人：あそこにお寺がありますね。そばいちはあのお寺の前です。
エマ　：そうですか。それから、この滝はここから近いですか。
店の人：いいえ、ちょっと遠いです。バスで15分ぐらいです。
エマ　：そうですか。どうもありがとうございます。
▪そばいちはお寺の前にあります。

LESSON 14
エマ：ちょっと寒いですね。
中村：あ、スカーフがありますよ。これ、どうぞ。
エマ：え、いいんですか。
中村：ええ、私は寒くないですから。
エマ：ありがとうございます。すてきなスカーフですね。
中村：ええ、誕生日に友達にもらいました。
▪中村さんはエマさんにスカーフを貸しました。

LESSON 15
スミス　　　　：いとこのポールです。
ポール　　　　：はじめまして。ポールです。よろしくお願いします。私は日本のアニメが好きです。
鈴木　　　　　：どんなアニメが好きですか。
ポール　　　　：ロボットのアニメが好きです。
鈴木　　　　　：あ、私もです。描くのも好きです。
スミス・ポール：わあ！　すごい！　上手ですね。
▪ポールさんと鈴木さんはロボットのアニメが好きです。

LESSON 16
鈴木　：次の日曜日に秋葉原でアニメのイベントがあります。おもしろいイベントですから、いっしょに
　　　　行きませんか。
ポール：いいですね。ぜひ。イベントは何時からですか。
鈴木　：1時からです。昼ご飯もいっしょに食べましょう。スミスさんもいっしょにどうですか。
スミス：すみません。アニメはちょっと…。
鈴木　：そうですか。
▪鈴木さんとポールさんは次の日曜日にアニメのイベントに行きます。

LESSON 17
ポール：弟もアニメが好きですから、秋葉原でお土産を買いたいです。
鈴木　：そうですか。じゃ、昼ご飯の前に、買い物をしましょう。
ポール：ありがとうございます。
鈴木　：ポールさん、ホテルはどこですか。
ポール：新宿ののぞみホテルです。
鈴木　：じゃ、10時にホテルのロビーで会いましょう。
ポール：10時ですね。わかりました。
▪鈴木さんとポールさんは昼ご飯を食べる前に買い物をします。

LESSON 18
エマ：加藤さん、ちょっとよろしいですか。
加藤：はい。
エマ：あした大阪に行きます。
加藤：あ、パッケージフェアですね。
エマ：ええ。フェアの後、支社に行って、チャンさんに会います。あさって工場を見て、4時の飛行機で東
　　　京に帰ります。
加藤：わかりました。気をつけて。
▪エマさんはあした大阪に行きます。あさって工場を見て、東京に帰ります。

LESSON 19
加藤：フェアはどうでしたか。
エマ：おもしろいパッケージがたくさんありました。いろいろなサンプルをもらいましたから、宅配便で送
　　　りました。
加藤：そうですか。じゃ、月曜日の会議で報告してください。
エマ：はい、わかりました。

加藤　：今から大阪支社ですか。
エマ　：はい、そうです。
加藤　：チャンさんによろしく伝えてください。
エマ　：はい、伝えます。
■エマさんは月曜日の会議でパッケージフェアについて報告します。

LESSON 20
鈴木　　：スミスさん、すみません。寝坊しました。今うちを出ました。
スミス　：ここまでどのくらいかかりますか。
鈴木　　：30分ぐらいかかります。
スミス　：そうですか。じゃ、1階のカフェにいます。
鈴木　　：すみません。
■鈴木さんのうちから博物館まで30分ぐらいかかります。

LESSON 21
スミス　　：これは昔のお金ですか。
鈴木　　　：ええ、そうです。あ、ここに英語のパンフレットがありますよ。
スミス　　：そうですね。すみません。このパンフレットをもらってもいいですか。
博物館の人：はい、どうぞ。
鈴木　　　：疲れましたね。
スミス　　：そうですね。脚が痛いです。すみません。ここに座ってもいいですか。
博物館の人：はい、どうぞ。
■スミスさんは博物館で英語のパンフレットをもらいました。

LESSON 22
スミス　　：きれいな着物ですね。
鈴木　　　：本当にきれいですね。これは300年ぐらい前の着物です。
スミス　　：そうですか。妹に見せたいです。
博物館の人：すみません。ここで写真を撮らないでください。
スミス　　：わかりました。すみません。
鈴木　　　：スミスさん、あそこにもきれいな着物がありますよ。
スミス　　：あ、そうですね。行きましょう。

LESSON 23
加藤　：もう会議の準備はできましたか。
スミス：すみません。まだです。会議室は予約しましたが、資料は今、作っています。
加藤　：そうですか。3時までに終わりますか。
スミス：はい、もうすぐできます。
スミス：加藤さん、資料ができました。チェックをお願いします。
加藤　：はい。

LESSON 24
鈴木　：スミスさん、妹さんは日本語がわかりますか。
スミス：はい、少しわかりますよ。
鈴木　：リサさん、お仕事は？
リサ　：デザイナーです。ニューヨークのアパレルメーカーに勤めています。
鈴木　：お仕事は楽しいですか。
リサ　：ええ、とても楽しいです。私の夢は自分のブランドをつくることです。
鈴木　：そうですか。がんばってください。
リサ　：はい、ありがとうございます。
■リサさんはニューヨークのアパレルメーカーに勤めています。夢は自分のブランドをつくることです。

GLOSSARY

Japanese-English Glossary

あ

あ ah, oh 61
アイスクリーム ice cream 76
あいます meet 84
あおい blue 39
あかい red 40
あかさか Akasaka (district in Tokyo) 194
あかワイン red wine 45
あきはばら Akihabara (district in Tokyo) 151
あけます（R2）open 201
あげます（R2）give 132
あさ morning 26
あさくさ Asakusa (district in Tokyo) 102
あさごはん breakfast 26
あさって day after tomorrow 54
あし foot, leg 199
あした tomorrow 21
アジャルト・スクール AJALT School (fictitious school name) 165
あずかります keep, take care of 187
あそこ over there 123
あたたかい warm 98
あたま head 200
あたらしい new, fresh 97
あちら over there 47
あつい hot 98
アップルパイ apple pie 47
あと→〜のあと after 172
あとで later 226
あなた you 6
あに (my) older brother 230
アニメ anime, animation 142
あね (my) older sister 230
あの that (over there) 39
あの that one over there 28
アパレル apparel 228
アパレルメーカー apparel maker 228
あぶない dangerous 212
アプリ application 101
あまり…〜ません not often, not very 85
アメリカ United States 4
アメリカじん American (person) 3
あらいます wash 163
ありがとうございます。Thank you. 9
あります be, exist 114
あります have 131
あります there is, take place 151
あるいて on foot, walking 67
あるきます walk 105
あれ that one over there 28
アレン Allen (surname) 57
アンティーク antiques 165
アンティークとうきょう Antique Tokyo (fictitious shop name) 165
あんどう Ando (surname) 232

い

いい nice, good 84
いいえ no 6
いいですね。That's good. 74
いいます say 181
いいんですか。Are you sure? 131
いかがですか。How about...? 96
いきたいんですが I'd like to go 198
いきました went 51
いきましょう let's go 152
いきます go 50
いきませんか shall we go? 151
イギリス United Kingdom 4
いくつ how many 126
いくら how much 28
いけばな flower arrangement 163
いしゃ medical doctor 207
いす chair 116
いそがしい busy 107
いたい hurt, sore, painful 199
いたい！ Ouch! 139
いただきます 96
いただきます。[said before eating] 168
イタリア Italy 43
イタリアりょうり Italian cuisine 148
いち one 11
いちおく one hundred million 31
いちがつ January 63
いちど one time 18
いちまん ten thousand 31
いつ when 25
いつか fifth (of the month) 63
1かい first floor 38
1しゅうかん one week 191
いっしょに together 151
いっちょう one trillion 31
いつつ five 40
いって go (て-form of いきます) 172
いってらっしゃい。Have a good trip., Have a good day. 61
いつも always 87
いとう Ito (surname) 233
いとこ cousin 142
イベント event 151
いま now 21
います（R2）be, exist 115
います（R2）stay, be 191
いもうと (my) younger sister 209
いもうとさん (another person's) younger sister 228
イヤリング earrings 133
いらっしゃいませ。May I help you?, Welcome. 28
いりぐち entrance 213
いれないでください please don't add/ put in 210
いれます（R2）put in, add 210
いろいろ（な）various 180
インターン intern 59
インド India 4
インフォメーション information desk 38

う

ウイスキー whiskey 146
うえ on, above 115
うけつけ reception desk, receptionist 8
うしろ behind 117
うた song 146
うたいます sing 145
うち house, home 53
うちあわせを　します have a preparatory meeting 178

うみ ocean 101
うんてんしゅ driver 60
うんどうを　します do exercise 227

え

え 72
え painting, picture 101
エアコン air conditioner 30
ABCフーズ ABC Foods (fictitious company name) 2
えいが movie 78
えいご English 199
ええ yes (a softer way of saying はい) 61
えき station 53
えきいん station employee 198
えびす Ebisu (district in Tokyo) 186
えびすえき Ebisu Station 186
〜えん …yen 28
エンジニア engineer 233
えんぴつ pencil 125

お

お〜 (honorific prefix) 8
お〜 (polite prefix) 18
おいしい delicious, tasty 96
おおきい big, large 40
おおさか Osaka (city in western Japan) 50
おおさかししゃ Osaka branch 50
オーストラリア Australia 4
おおてまち Otemachi (district in Tokyo) 194
おかあさん (another person's) mother 86
おかいけい→かいけい bill, check 93
おかけください。Please have a seat. 71
おかし→かし sweets 18
おかね→かね money 133
おきなわ Okinawa (islands in southern Japan) 101
おきます put, place 201
おきゃくさん guest, customer 124
おくさん (another person's) wife 86
おくに your country 8
おくります send 86
おこさん (another person's) child 230
おさけ→さけ alcoholic drink, sake 216
おさら→さら dish, plate 40
おしえてください→〜を　おしえてください please tell me 16
おしえます（R2）tell, teach 85
おしごと your work 228
おじゃまします。May I come in? 104
おじょうさん (another person's) daughter 230
おすし→すし sushi 76
おすすめ recommendation 93
おそばやさん soba shop 123
おだいば Odaiba (district in Tokyo) 102
おちゃ green tea 76
おっと (my) husband 86
おてあらい restroom 47
おてら →てら temple 114
おでんわばんごう your phone number 83
おとうさん (another person's) father 86

255

おとうと (my) younger brother 161
おとうとさん (another person's) younger brother 230
おとこ male, man 118
おとこの こ boy 126
おとこの ひと man 118
おととい day before yesterday 54
おなか stomach, belly 201
おなかが すきました。I'm hungry. 153
おなまえ your name 83
おにいさん (another person's) older brother 230
おねえさん (another person's) older sister 230
おねがいします please (lit. "I request you") 18
おねがいできますか。May I ask [you to do this]? 187
おのみもの→のみもの beverage 93
おはなみを します→はなみを します view cherry blossoms 165
おはようございます。Good morning. 50
おべんとう→べんとう box lunch, bento 100
おまつり→まつり festival 64
おみやげ →みやげ souvenir 112
おもしろい interesting 97
およぎます swim 145
おります (R2) get off 191
オレンジジュース orange juice 35
おわります finish 218
おんがく music 78
おんせん hot spring 114
おんな female, woman 115
おんなの こ girl 126
おんなの ひと woman 115
オンラインかいぎを します have an online meeting 221

か

か (particle) 2
が (particle) 60
が but (particle) 105
が (particle) 114
～か (かん) ...days 192
カーテン curtain 202
カード credit cart 37
～かい／がい ...floor 40
かいぎ meeting 21
かいぎしつ meeting room 116
かいぎを します have a meeting 178
かいけい bill, check 93
かいしゃ company 11
かいしゃいん company employee 233
かいしゃの なまえ company name 11
かいたいです want to buy 161
かいます buy 76
かいものを します shop 76
かえります return, come back 61
かかります take [time] 190
かぎ key 11
かきます draw 142
かきます write 163
かく draw 142
かぐ furniture 165
がくせい student 53
～かげつ (かん) ...months 192
かさ umbrella 11
かし sweets 18
かします lend, loan 131

カシューナッツ cashew nuts 122
かぞく family 53
かた shoulder 201
カタログ catalog 183
～がつ month 63
がっこう school 88
かど corner 182
かない (my) wife 86
かね money 133
かばん bag 11
かびん vase 212
カフェ café 190
かぶき kabuki 74
かまくら Kamakura (historic area south of Tokyo) 121
カメラ camera 43
かようび Tuesday 63
から from (particle) 20
から from (particle) 51
から because (particle) 131
から because, so (particle) 151
からて karate 163
かります (R2) borrow 133
カレー curry 29
かんこく South Korea, ROK 54
かんこくご Korean 234
かんじ kanji 224
かんたん(な) simple, easy 107
がんばってください。I hope it works out. 228
がんばります do one's best 228

き

ききます listen to 76
ききます ask 86
きた north 153
ギター guitar 220
きたぐち north exit 153
きてください please come 111
きに しないでください。Please don't worry about it. 216
きに します worry about 216
きねんび anniversary 138
きのう yesterday 51
ギブソン Gibson (surname) 66
きぶん feeling 201
きぶんが わるい feel sick, unwell 201
きました came 51
きます come 50
きもの kimono 209
キャビネット cabinet 125
きゅう nine 11
きゅうじゅう ninety 22
ぎゅうにく beef 43
きょう today 22
きょうかい church 122
きょうと Kyoto 54
きょねん last year 51
きれい(な) pretty, beautiful, clean 96
きれいでした it was beautiful 105
きを つけて。Take care. 172
きんえん no smoking 211
ぎんこう bank 4
ぎんざ Ginza (district in Tokyo) 55
ぎんざどおり Ginza Street 184
きんようび Friday 61

く

く nine 11
くうこう airport 53
くがつ September 63
9じ (くじ) 9:00, nine o'clock 21
ください please give me 28

くだもの fruit 147
くつ shoes 43
くに country 8
くまのじんじゃ Kumano Shrine 129
～ぐらい about (amount) 105
クラス class 107
グラス glass, wine glass 91
クラブ club 165
クリアファイル clear file 125
クリスマス Christmas 136
クリップ paper clip 126
くるま car 64
くろい black 40

け

けいたい mobile phone 234
ケーキ cake 101
けしゴム eraser 125
けします turn off 201
ケチャップ ketchup 215
けっこん wedding, marriage 138
けっこんきねんび wedding anniversary 138
げつようび Monday 63

こ

こ child 126
ご five 11
ご～ (honorific prefix) 86
～ご language 88
ゴア Goa (state in India) 122
こうえん park 53
こうさてん intersection 182
こうじょう factory 172
こうちゃ (black) tea 30
こうばん police box 125
こうべ Kobe (city near Osaka) 178
こうベビーフ Kobe Beef (famous, high-quality beef) 179
コーヒー coffee 30
コーヒーカップ coffee cup 45
5かい fifth floor 39
ごかぞく (another person's) family 86
ごがつ May 63
ここ here 84
ごご P.M., in the afternoon 22
ここのか ninth (of the month) 63
ここのつ nine 40
こし lower back 201
5じ 5:00, five o'clock 21
こじま Kojima (surname) 233
ごじゅう fifty 22
ごじゅうしょ your address 185
ごしゅじん (another person's) husband 86
ごぜん A.M., in the morning 22
こちら this one (polite for "this person") 3
こちら (polite word for これ) 93
こちらこそ same here 2
コップ glass 40
こと (nominalizer) 228
ことし this year 53
こども child 230
この this 39
この ちかく vicinity, near here 123
こばやし Kobayashi (surname) 233
ごはん meal, cooked rice 26
5ばんせん Platform 5 198
コピーします make a copy 203
コピーを します make a copy 221
ごみばこ trash basket 116
ゴルフ golf 146

256

English-Japanese Glossary

Note: Idiomatic expressions have been omitted, as have words that do not translate into English. Counters and particles are listed in the Appendixes of this book.

あ	a	い	i	う	u	え	e	お	o
か	ka	き	ki	く	ku	け	ke	こ	ko
さ	sa	し	shi	す	su	せ	se	そ	so
た	ta	ち	chi	つ	tsu	て	te	と	to
な	na	に	ni	ぬ	nu	ね	ne	の	no
は	ha	ひ	hi	ふ	fu	へ	he	ほ	ho
ま	ma	み	mi	む	mu	め	me	も	mo
や	ya			ゆ	yu			よ	yo
ら	ra	り	ri	る	ru	れ	re	ろ	ro
わ	wa							を	o
ん	n								

きゃ	kya	きゅ	kyu	きょ	kyo
しゃ	sha	しゅ	shu	しょ	sho
ちゃ	cha	ちゅ	chu	ちょ	cho
にゃ	nya	にゅ	nyu	にょ	nyo
ひゃ	hya	ひゅ	hyu	ひょ	hyo
みゃ	mya	みゅ	myu	みょ	myo

りゃ	rya	りゅ	ryu	りょ	ryo

が	ga	ぎ	gi	ぐ	gu	げ	ge	ご	go
ざ	za	じ	ji	ず	zu	ぜ	ze	ぞ	zo
だ	da	ぢ	ji	づ	zu	で	de	ど	do
ば	ba	び	bi	ぶ	bu	べ	be	ぼ	bo
ぱ	pa	ぴ	pi	ぷ	pu	ぺ	pe	ぽ	po

ぎゃ	gya	ぎゅ	gyu	ぎょ	gyo
じゃ	ja	じゅ	ju	じょ	jo

びゃ	bya	びゅ	byu	びょ	byo
ぴゃ	pya	ぴゅ	pyu	ぴょ	pyo

ア	a	イ	i	ウ	u	エ	e	オ	o
カ	ka	キ	ki	ク	ku	ケ	ke	コ	ko
サ	sa	シ	shi	ス	su	セ	se	ソ	so
タ	ta	チ	chi	ツ	tsu	テ	te	ト	to
ナ	na	ニ	ni	ヌ	nu	ネ	ne	ノ	no
ハ	ha	ヒ	hi	フ	fu	ヘ	he	ホ	ho
マ	ma	ミ	mi	ム	mu	メ	me	モ	mo
ヤ	ya			ユ	yu			ヨ	yo
ラ	ra	リ	ri	ル	ru	レ	re	ロ	ro
ワ	wa							ヲ	o
ン	n								

キャ	kya	キュ	kyu	キョ	kyo
シャ	sha	シュ	shu	ショ	sho
チャ	cha	チュ	chu	チョ	cho
ニャ	nya	ニュ	nyu	ニョ	nyo
ヒャ	hya	ヒュ	hyu	ヒョ	hyo
ミャ	mya	ミュ	myu	ミョ	myo

リャ	rya	リュ	ryu	リョ	ryo

ガ	ga	ギ	gi	グ	gu	ゲ	ge	ゴ	go
ザ	za	ジ	ji	ズ	zu	ゼ	ze	ゾ	zo
ダ	da	ヂ	ji	ヅ	zu	デ	de	ド	do
バ	ba	ビ	bi	ブ	bu	ベ	be	ボ	bo
パ	pa	ピ	pi	プ	pu	ペ	pe	ポ	po

ギャ	gya	ギュ	gyu	ギョ	gyo
ジャ	ja	ジュ	ju	ジョ	jo

ビャ	bya	ビュ	byu	ビョ	byo
ピャ	pya	ピュ	pyu	ピョ	pyo

Newly revised edition of the all-time best-selling textbook

JAPANESE FOR BUSY PEOPLE:
Revised 4th Edition

Association for Japanese-Language Teaching (AJALT)

The leading textbook series for conversational Japanese has been redesigned, updated, and consolidated to meet the needs of today's students and businesspeople.

- Free downloadable audio with each text and workbook
- Edited for smoother transition between levels
- Hundreds of charming illustrations make learning Japanese easy
- Clear explanations of fundamental grammar

VOLUME 1 Teaches survival Japanese, providing a comprehensive introduction to the three-volume series of *Japanese for Busy People*.

- **Japanese for Busy People I: Revised 4th Edition, Romanized Version**
  Paperback, ISBN: 978-1-56836-619-7, Spring 2022

- **Japanese for Busy People I: Revised 4th Edition, Kana Version**
  Paperback, ISBN: 978-1-56836-620-3, Spring 2022

- **Japanese for Busy People I: The Workbook for the Revised 4th Edition**
  Paperback, ISBN: 978-1-56836-621-0, Spring 2022

- **Japanese for Busy People: Kana Workbook for the Revised 4th Edition**
  Paperback, ISBN: 978-1-56836-622-7, Spring 2022

- **Japanese for Busy People I—App**
  Skill Practice on the Go app based on Volume I for iPhone, iPad, iPod and Android

VOLUME 2 Brings learners to the intermediate* level, enabling them to carry on basic conversations in everyday situations. (*upper beginners in Japan)

- **Japanese for Busy People II: Revised 4th Edition**
  Paperback, ISBN: 978-1-56836-627-2, Fall 2022

- **Japanese for Busy People II: The Workbook for the Revised 4th Edition**
  Paperback, ISBN: 978-1-56836-628-9, Fall 2022

VOLUME 3 Covers intermediate-level** Japanese. (**pre-intermediate in Japan)

- **Japanese for Busy People III: Revised 4th Edition**
  Paperback, ISBN: 978-1-56836-630-2, Spring 2023

- **Japanese for Busy People III: The Workbook for the Revised 4th Edition**
  Paperback, ISBN: 978-1-56836-631-9, Spring 2023

TEACHER'S MANUAL

Now available in eBook format (all in Japanese):

- **Japanese for Busy People I:**   ISBN: 978-1-56836-623-4, Spring 2022
- **Japanese for Busy People II:**   ISBN: 978-1-56836-629-6, Fall 2022
- **Japanese for Busy People III:**   ISBN: 978-1-56836-632-6, Spring 2023

JAPANESE LANGUAGE GUIDES

Easy-to-use Guides to Essential Language Skills

JAPANESE FOR PROFESSIONALS   *AJALT*
Revised Edition
A comprehensive course for students who need to use Japanese in a real-life business environment. Eight lessons introduce common business situations—first-time meetings, directing subordinates, client negotiations—with key sentences and a dialogue to illustrate how Japanese is used in a business context. Free audio recordings are available for download.

Paperback, 216 pages, ISBN 978-1-56836-599-2

JAPANESE SENTENCE PATTERNS FOR EFFECTIVE COMMUNICATION
A Self-Study Course and Reference   *Taeko Kamiya*
Presents 142 essential sentence patterns for daily conversation—all the ones an intermediate student should know, and all the ones a beginner should study to become minimally proficient in speaking. All in a handy, step-by-step format with pattern practice every few pages.

Paperback, 368 pages, ISBN 978-1-56836-420-9

THE HANDBOOK OF JAPANESE VERBS   *Taeko Kamiya*
An indispensable reference and guide to Japanese verbs, aimed at beginning and intermediate students. Precisely the book that verb-challenged students have been looking for.
- Verbs are grouped, conjugated, and combined with auxiliaries
- Different forms are used in sentences
- Each form is followed by reinforcing examples and exercises

Paperback, 256 pages, ISBN 978-1-56836-484-1

THE HANDBOOK OF JAPANESE ADJECTIVES AND ADVERBS   *Taeko Kamiya*
The ultimate reference manual for those seeking a deeper understanding of Japanese adjectives and adverbs and how they are used in sentences. Ideal, too, for those simply wishing to expand their vocabulary or speak livelier Japanese.

Paperback, 336 pages, ISBN 978-1-56836-416-2

MAKING SENSE OF JAPANESE   *Jay Rubin*
What the Textbooks Don't Tell You
"Brief, wittily written essays that gamely attempt to explain some of the more frustrating hurdles [of Japanese]… They can be read and enjoyed by students at any level."
—*Asahi Evening News*

Paperback, 144 pages, ISBN 978-1-56836-492-6

JAPANESE LANGUAGE GUIDES

Easy-to-use Guides to Essential Language Skills

BREAKING INTO JAPANESE LITERATURE   *Giles Murray*
Seven Modern Classics in Parallel Text
Read classics of modern Japanese fiction in the original with the aid of a built-in, customized dictionary, free MP3 sound files of professional Japanese narrators reading the stories, and literal English translations. Features Ryunosuke Akutagawa's "Rashomon" and other stories.

Paperback, 240 pages, ISBN 978-1-56836-589-3

EXPLORING JAPANESE LITERATURE   *Giles Murray*
Read Mishima, Tanizaki and Kawabata in the Original
Provides all the backup you need to enjoy three works of modern Japanese fiction in the original language: Yukio Mishima's "Patriotism," Jun'ichiro Tanizaki's "The Secret," and Yasunari Kawabata's "Snow Country Miniature."

Paperback, 352 pages, ISBN 978-1-56836-541-1

READ REAL JAPANESE FICTION   *Edited by Michael Emmerich*
Short Stories by Contemporary Writers
Short stories by cutting-edge writers, from Otsuichi to Tawada Yoko. Set in vertical text with translations, notes, and free downloadable audio containing narrations of the works.

Paperback, 256 pages, ISBN 978-1-56836-617-3

READ REAL JAPANESE ESSAYS   *Edited by Janet Ashby*
Contemporary Writings by Popular Authors
Essays by Japan's leading writers. Set in vertical text with translations, notes, and free downloadable audio containing narrations of the works.

Paperback, 240 pages, ISBN 978-1-56836-618-0

BASIC CONNECTIONS   *Kakuko Shoji*
Making Your Japanese Flow
Explains how words and phrases dovetail, how clauses pair up with other clauses, how sentences come together to create harmonious paragraphs. The goal is to enable the student to speak both coherently and smoothly.

Paperback, 160 pages, ISBN 978-1-56836-421-6

ALL ABOUT PARTICLES   *Naoko Chino*
The most common and less common particles brought together and broken down into some 200 usages, with abundant sample sentences.

Paperback, 160 pages, ISBN 978-1-56836-419-3

KODANSHA DICTIONARIES

Easy-to-use Dictionaries Designed for Learners of Japanese

KODANSHA'S FURIGANA JAPANESE DICTIONARY
JAPANESE-ENGLISH / ENGLISH-JAPANESE

Both of Kodansha's popular furigana dictionaries in one portable, affordable volume. A truly comprehensive and practical dictionary for English-speaking learners, and an invaluable guide to using the Japanese language.

- 30,000-word basic vocabulary
- Hundreds of special words, names, and phrases
- Clear explanations of semantic and usage differences
- Special information on grammar and usage

Hardcover, 1318 pages, ISBN 978-1-56836-457-5

KODANSHA'S FURIGANA JAPANESE-ENGLISH DICTIONARY

The essential dictionary for all students of Japanese.

- Furigana readings added to all kanji
- 16,000-word basic vocabulary

Paperback, 592 pages, ISBN 978-1-56836-422-3

KODANSHA'S FURIGANA ENGLISH-JAPANESE DICTIONARY

The companion to the essential dictionary for all students of Japanese.

- Furigana readings added to all kanji
- 14,000-word basic vocabulary

Paperback, 728 pages, ISBN 978-4-7700-2751-1

A DICTIONARY OF JAPANESE PARTICLES   *Sue A. Kawashima*

Treats over 100 particles in alphabetical order, providing sample sentences for each meaning.

- Meets students' needs from beginning to advanced levels
- Treats principal particle meanings as well as variants

Paperback, 368 pages, ISBN 978-4-7700-2352-0

THE KODANSHA KANJI LEARNER'S COURSE   *Andrew Scott Conning*
A Step-by-Step Guide to Mastering 2300 Characters

A complete, logical system for acquiring all the kanji characters needed for genuine literacy

- Includes all 2,136 official Jōyō Kanji plus 164 most useful non-Jōyō characters
- Summarizes kanji meanings in concise, easy-to-memorize keywords
- Mnemonic annotations for each kanji help in remembering its meaning(s)
- Cross-references, character meanings, readings, and sample vocabulary drawn from *The Kodansha Kanji Learner's Dictionary*

Paperback, 720 pages, ISBN 978-1-56836-526-8

KODANSHA DICTIONARIES

Easy-to-use Dictionaries Designed for Learners of Japanese

THE KODANSHA KANJI LEARNER'S DICTIONARY   *Jack Halpern*
Revised and Expanded: 2nd Edition

The perfect kanji tool for beginners to advanced learners.

- Revolutionary SKIP lookup method
- Five lookup methods and three indices
- 3,002 kanji entries and approximately 46,000 senses for 35,000 words, word elements, and illustrative examples
- Includes latest 2020 revision of Education Kanji

"Up-to-date, and easy to use...this beautifully designed dictionary meets the needs of a wide range of Japanese language learners."
      —*Y.-H. Tohsaku, former President, American Association of Teachers of Japanese*

Paperback, 1060 pages (2-color), ISBN 978-1-56836-625-8

THE KODANSHA'S KANJI DICTIONARY   *Jack Halpern*

The most sophisticated kanji dictionary ever developed

- Includes all the current Jōyō and Jinmei Kanji
- 5,458 character entries – all the kanji that advanced learners are likely to encounter
- 6 lookup methods, including the SKIP method; 3 indexes; 13 appendixes
- Features core meanings or concise keywords that convey the dominant sense of each character

Hardcover, 2,112 pages (53 in 2 color), ISBN 978-1-56836-408-7

THE KODANSHA'S KANJI SYNONYMS GUIDE   *Jack Halpern*

A groundbreaking bilingual kanji thesaurus that provides complete, precise guidance on the distinctions between characters of similar meanings

- 1,245 synonym groups, arranged alphabetically by shared concept
- Covers 5,630 synonym members from the Jōyō Kanji, Jinmei Kanji, and non-Jōyō Kanji character sets
- Over 22,000 compounds illustrate the function of kanji as word elements
- Compound words and readings in hiragana
- Two indexes to help locate synonym groups quickly

Paperback,680 pages, ISBN 978-1-56836-585-5

THE KODANSHA'S KANJI USAGE GUIDE   *Jack Halpern*

An A to Z of Kun Homophones

- The first Japanese-English resource devoted exclusively to kun homophones
- Presents detailed usage articles that show the differences and similarities for 675 homophone groups
- Includes thousands of illustrative samples of kanji in context

Paperback,352 pages, ISBN 978-1-56836-559-6